SIN SALIDA

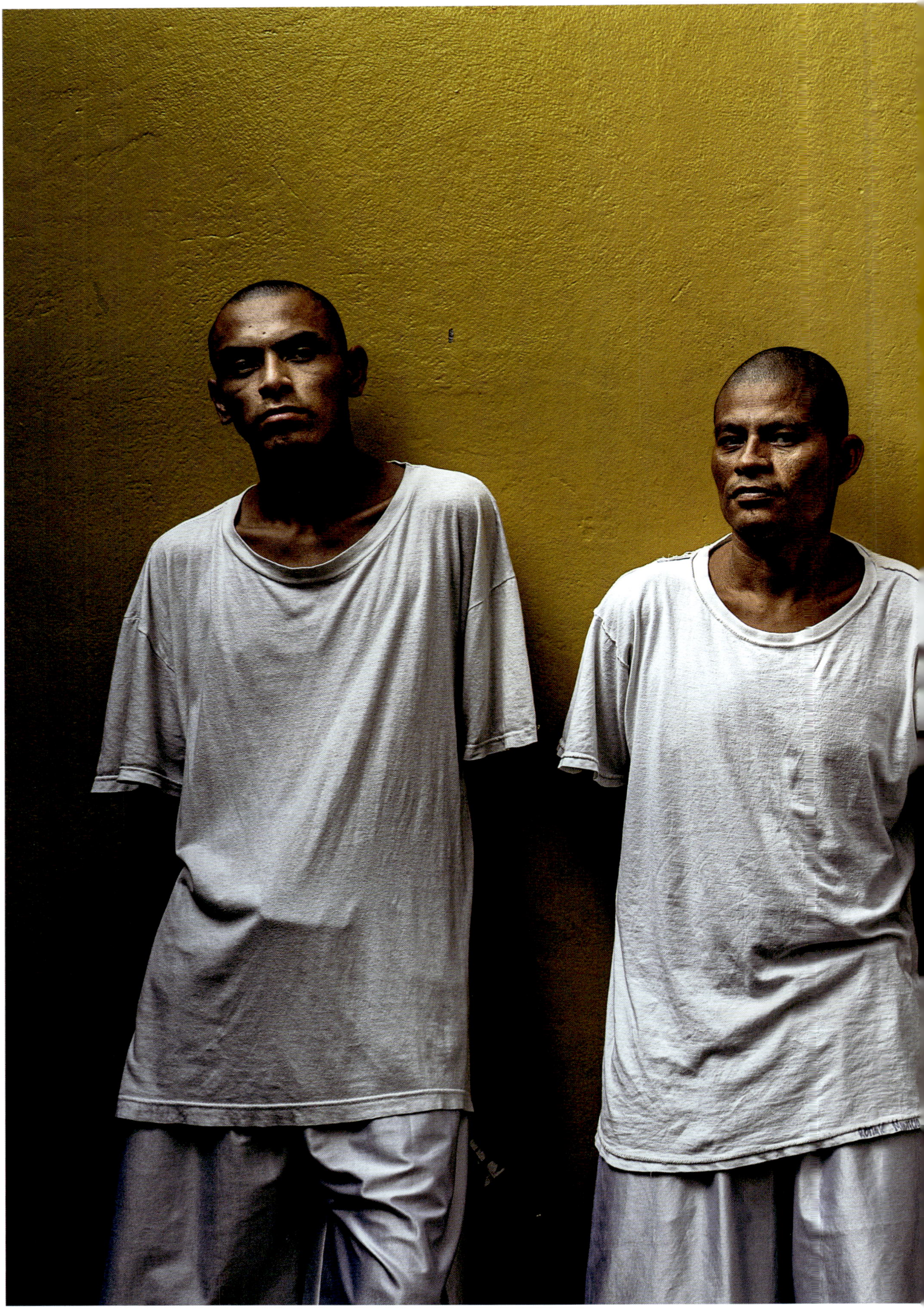

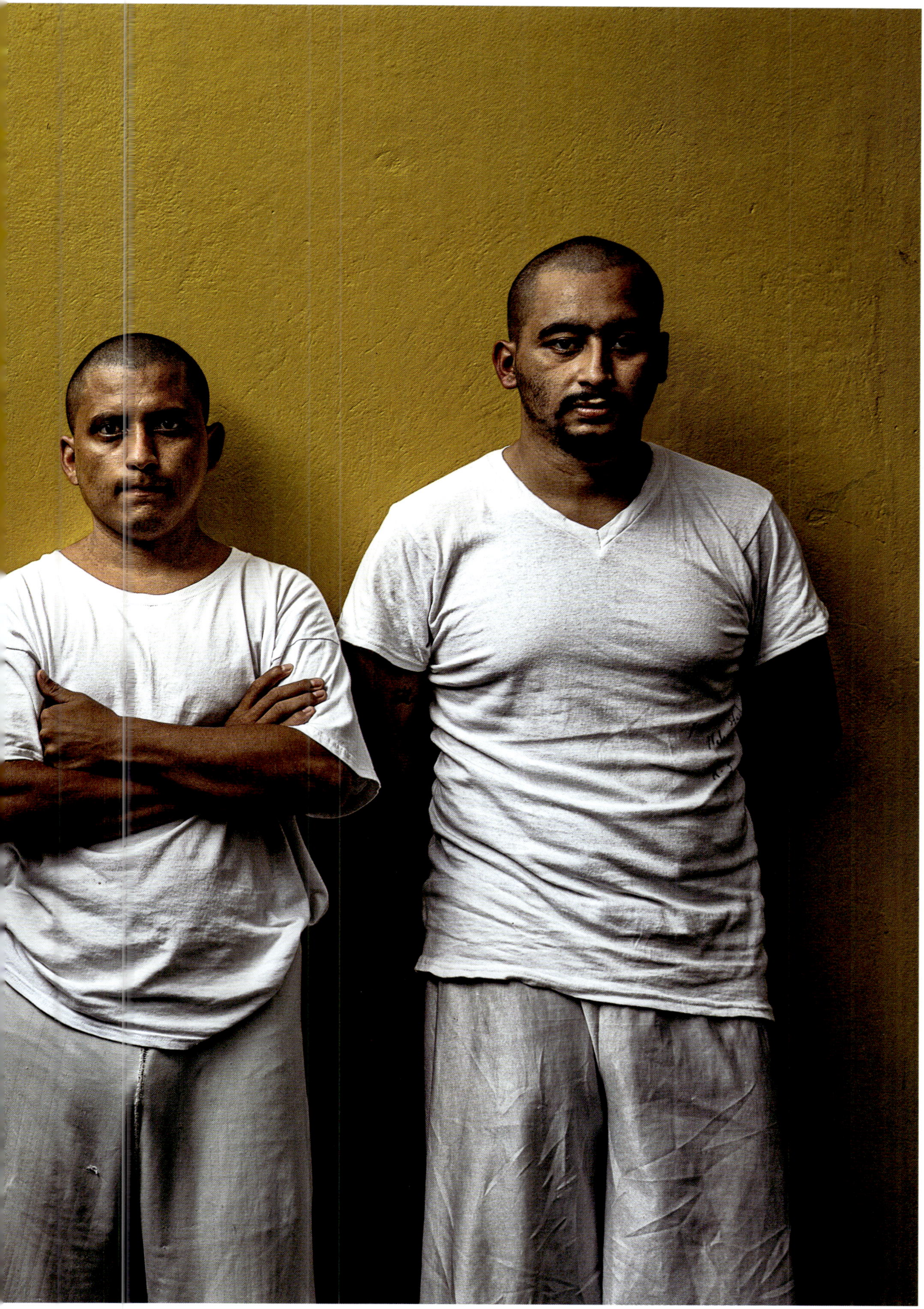

TARIQ ZAIDI

SIN SALIDA

GOST

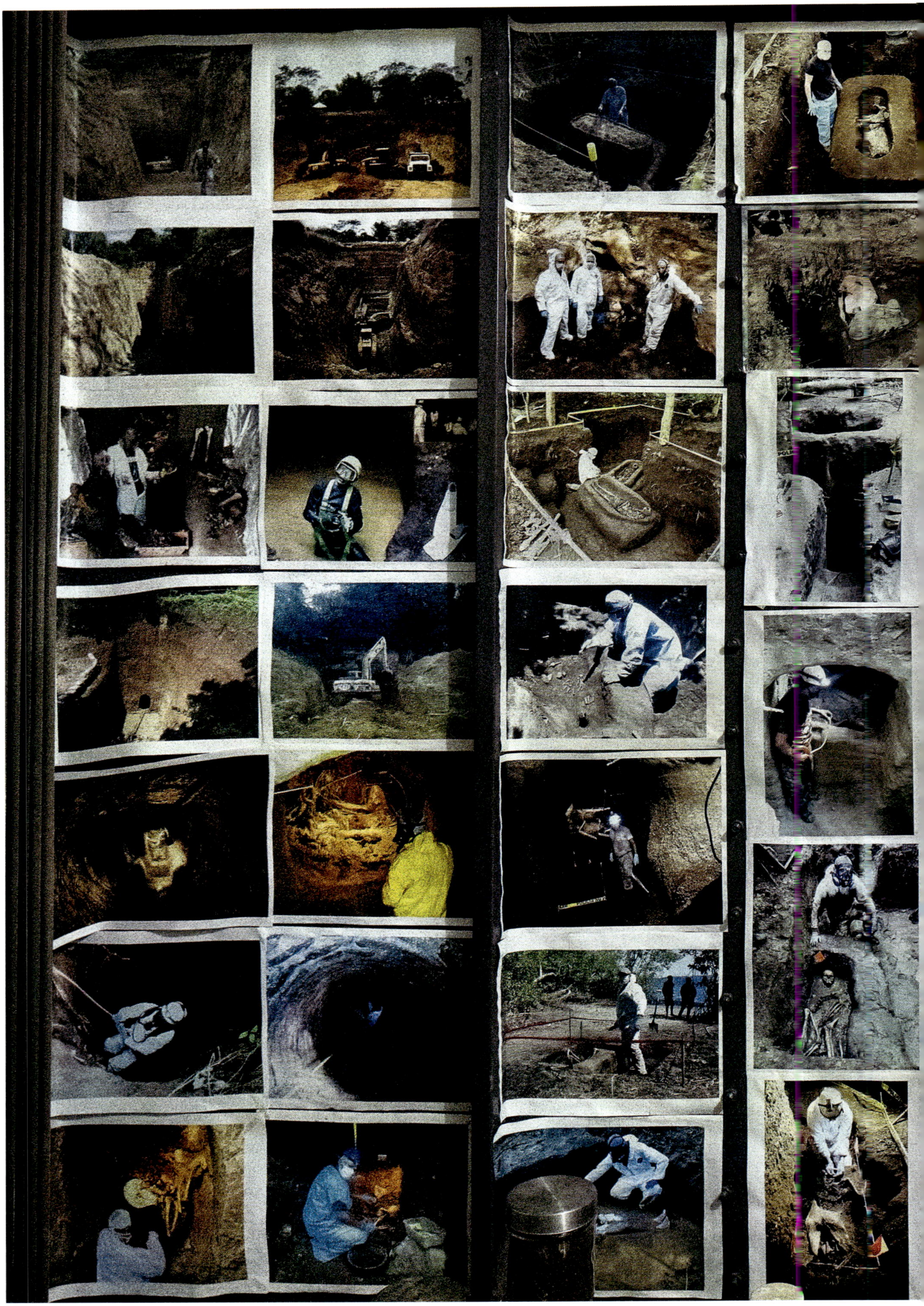

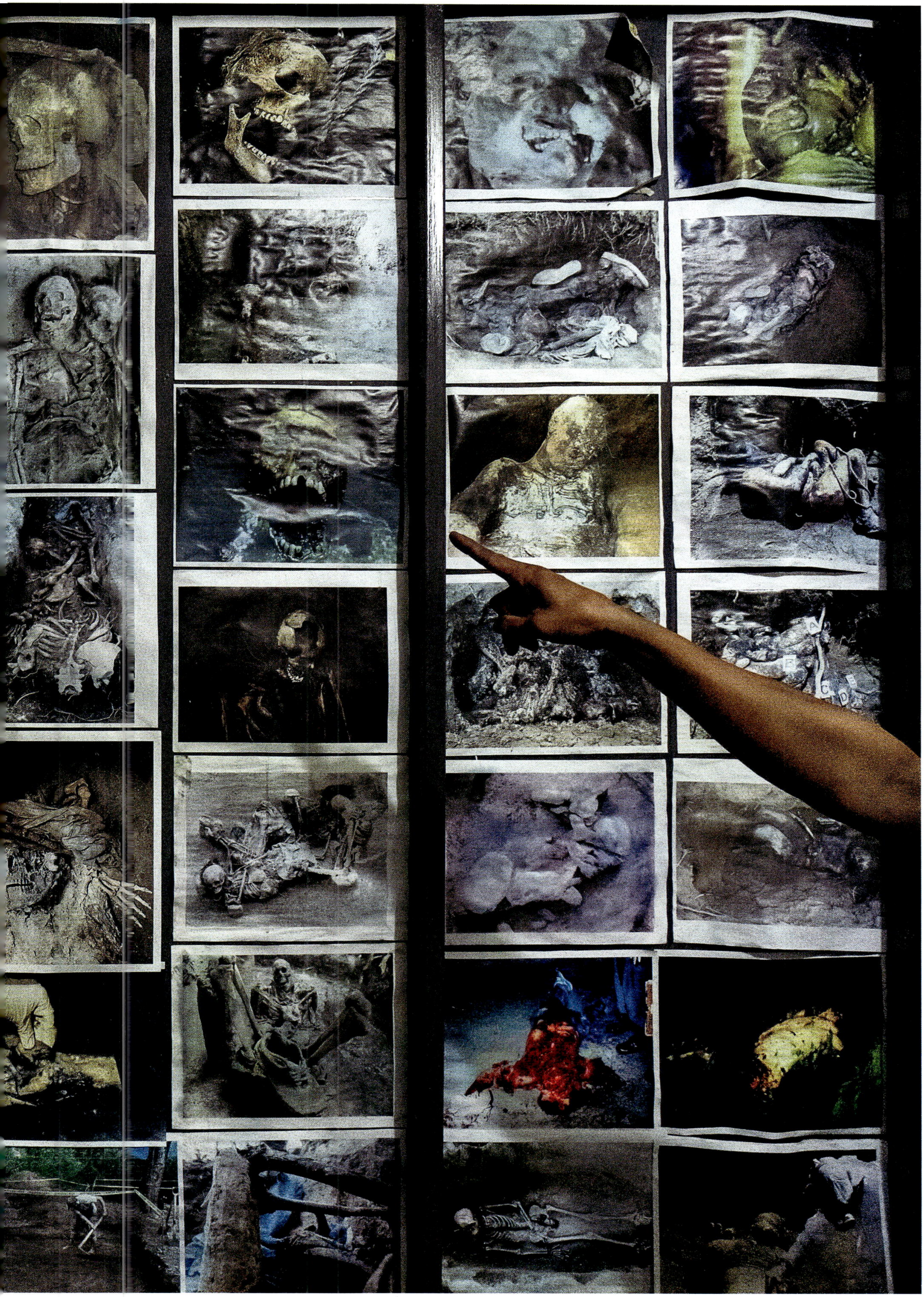

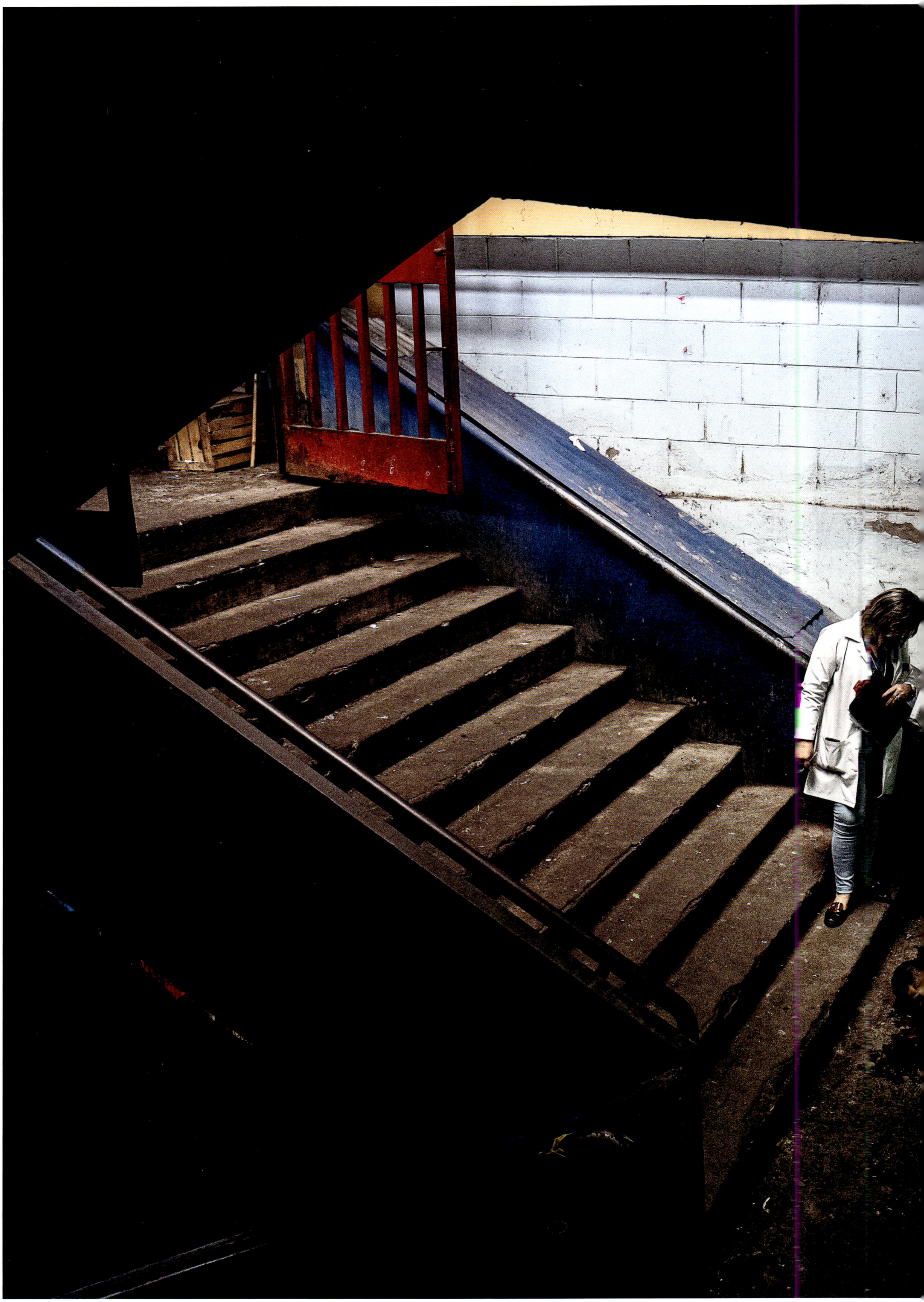

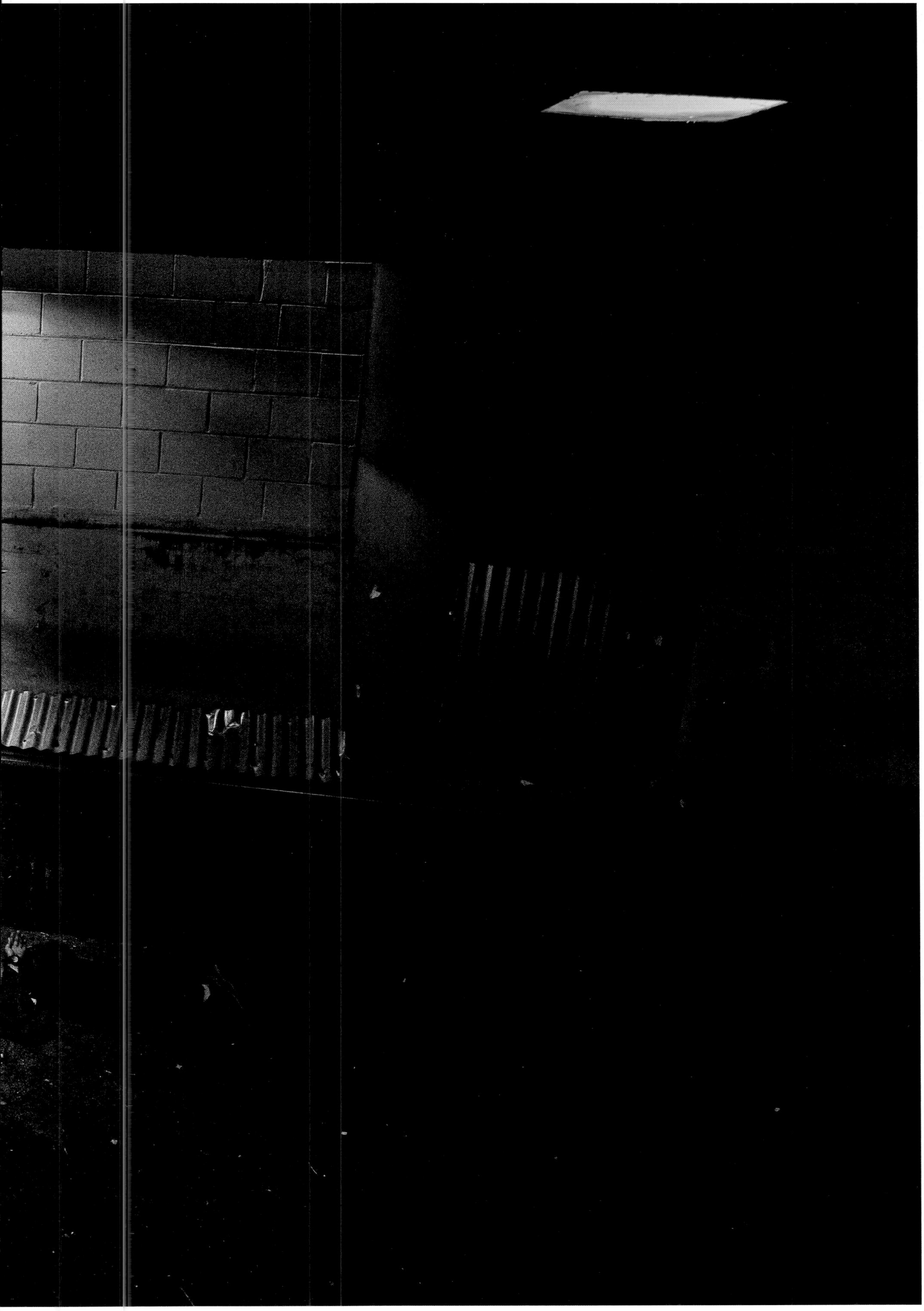

'KILL, RAPE, CONTROL'

is the motto of the notorious Mara Salvatrucha gang (MS-13). The street gang, along with its rival, Barrio 18, has become infamous across Central and North America for its brutal violence and iron grip on communities. Particularly well established in El Salvador, both gangs have developed extensive and sophisticated networks of extortion and domination across the region.

Levels of violence have varied over the years, but the country's murder rate has consistently been among the world's highest. The particularly savage nature of the violence—often with machetes, and with satanic and occult references—has shocked and paralysed the country. The state has responded by cracking down hard on prisons and gang members, and although the state's 'no-tolerance policies' are largely popular within the country, they have been criticised by a number of human rights observers for being too harsh.

President Nayib Bukele—who came to power in 2019—has achieved significant success, bringing murder rates down consistently. However, an explosion of violence in early 2020, when street gangs killed over seventy-six people in just four days, illustrates how volatile the country still is.

In many cities in El Salvador, social norms have disintegrated. In some areas, it is impossible to cross the street due to differing gang territorial control—entirely cordoning off neighbourhoods and roads. When entering an unfamiliar neighbourhood, drivers—fearing violence—take precaution and flash their lights or roll their windows down to indicate allegiance to the gang that controls it. Society is gripped by pervasive fear, violence and intimidation and thousands of Salvadorans flee their homes in search of a safer life—usually north to Mexico or to the United States.

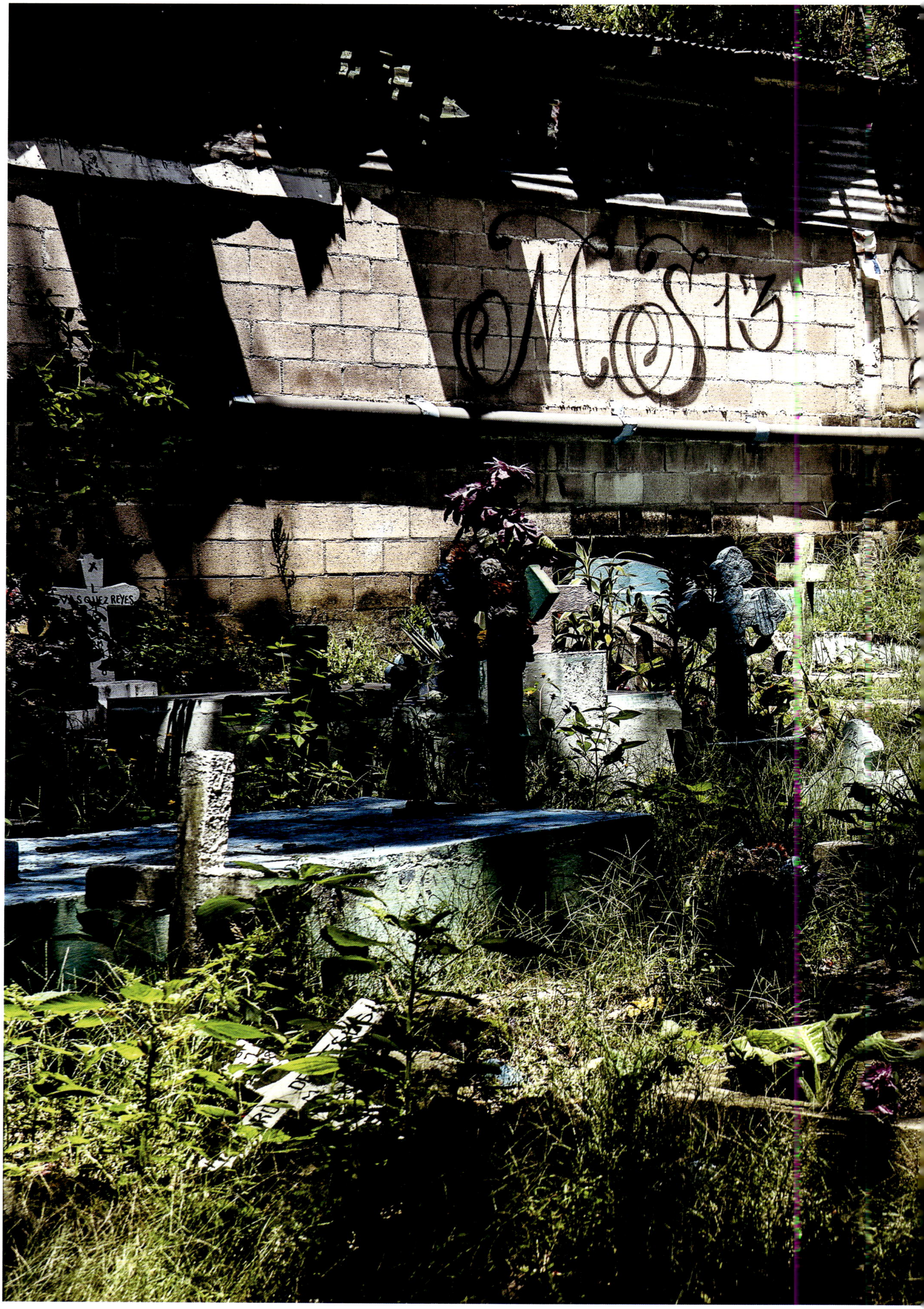
MS13

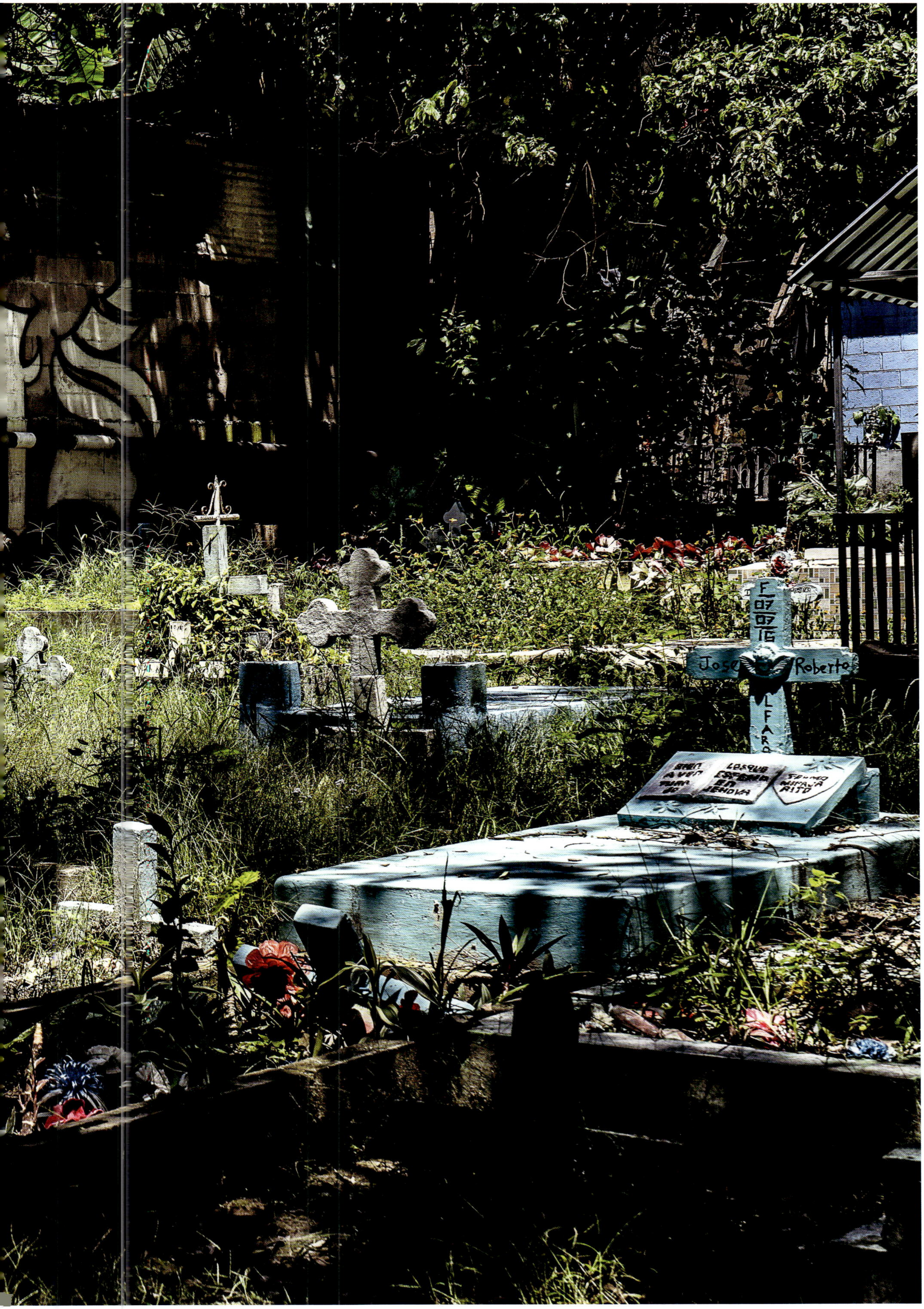
Jose
Roberto

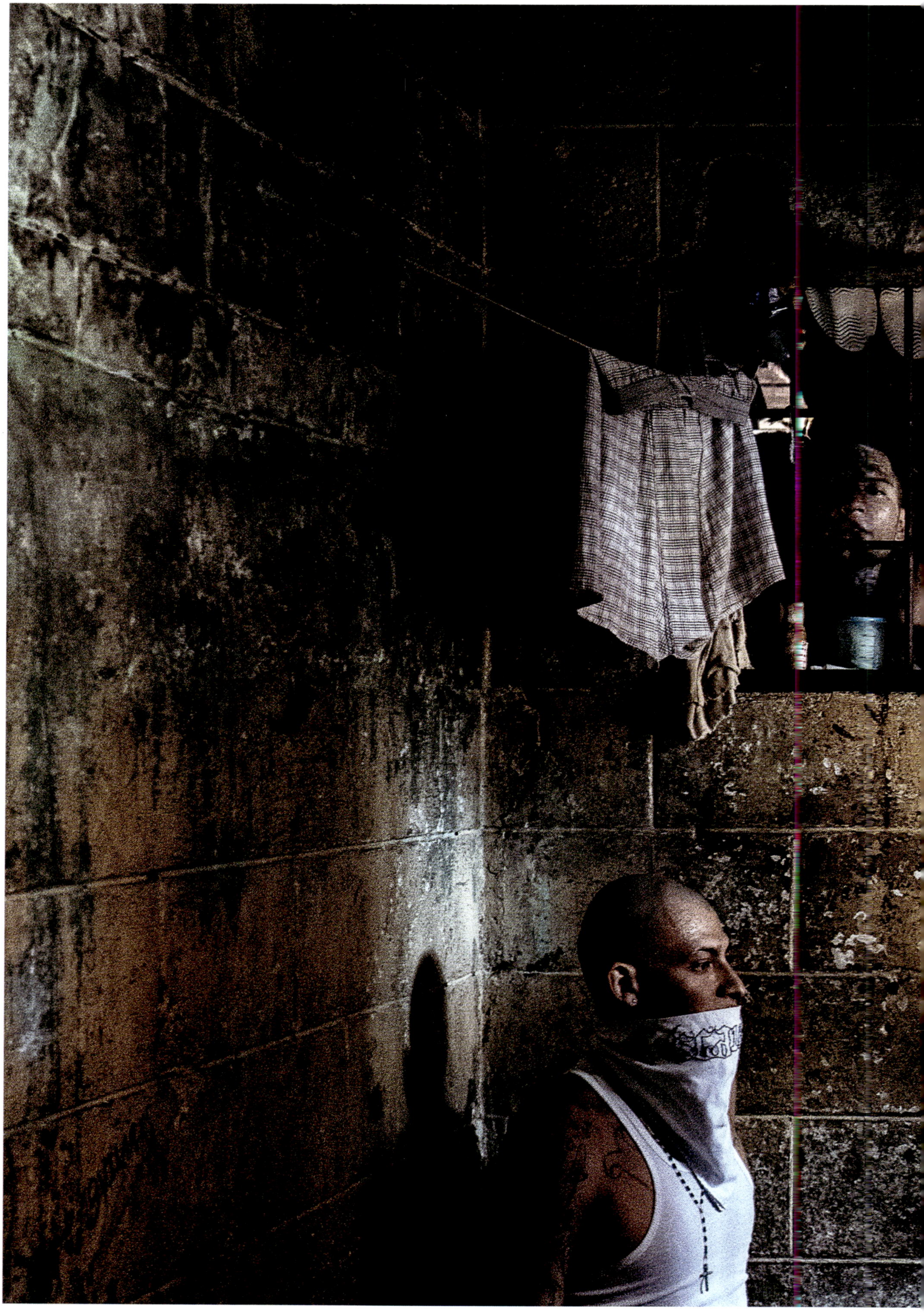

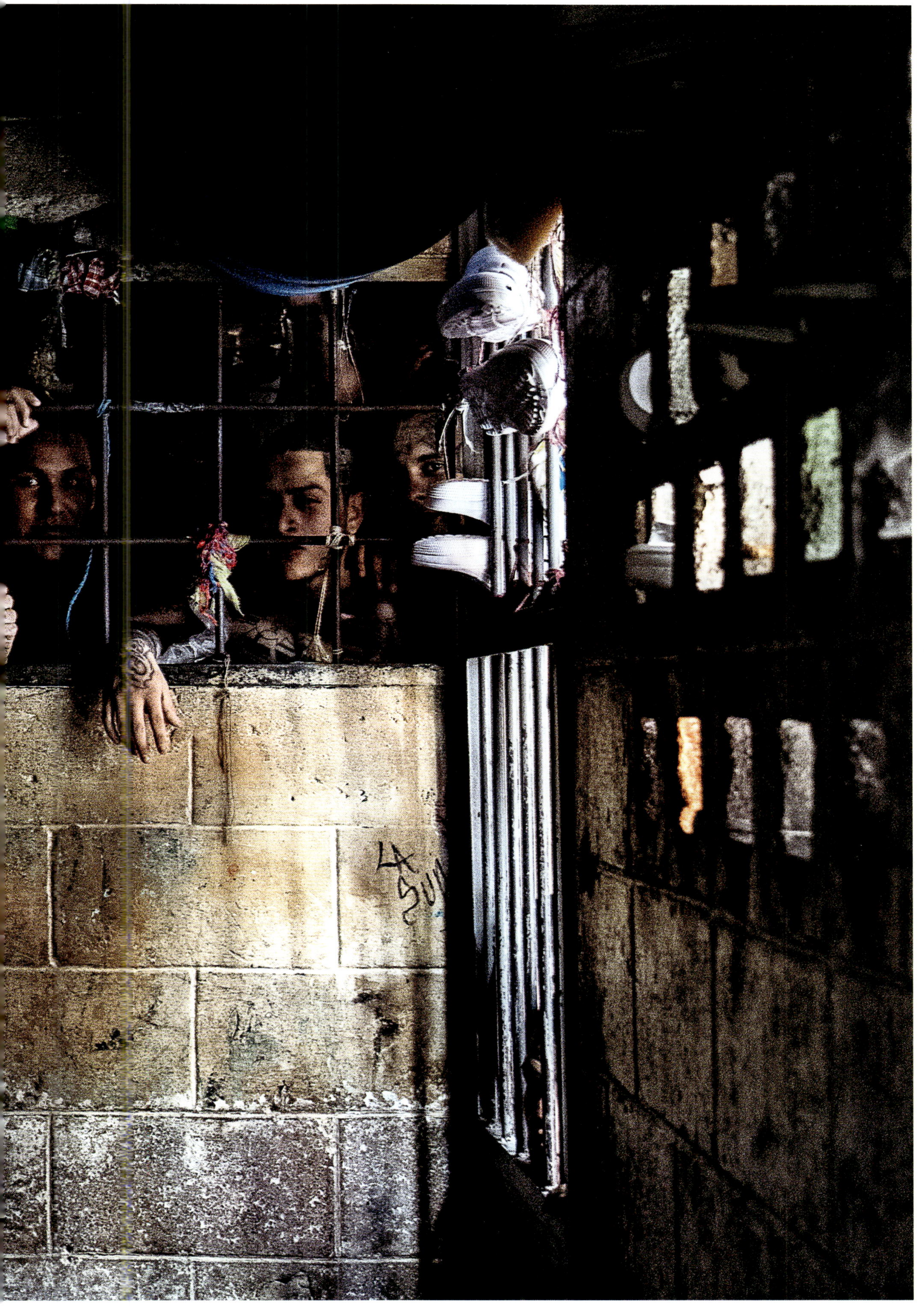

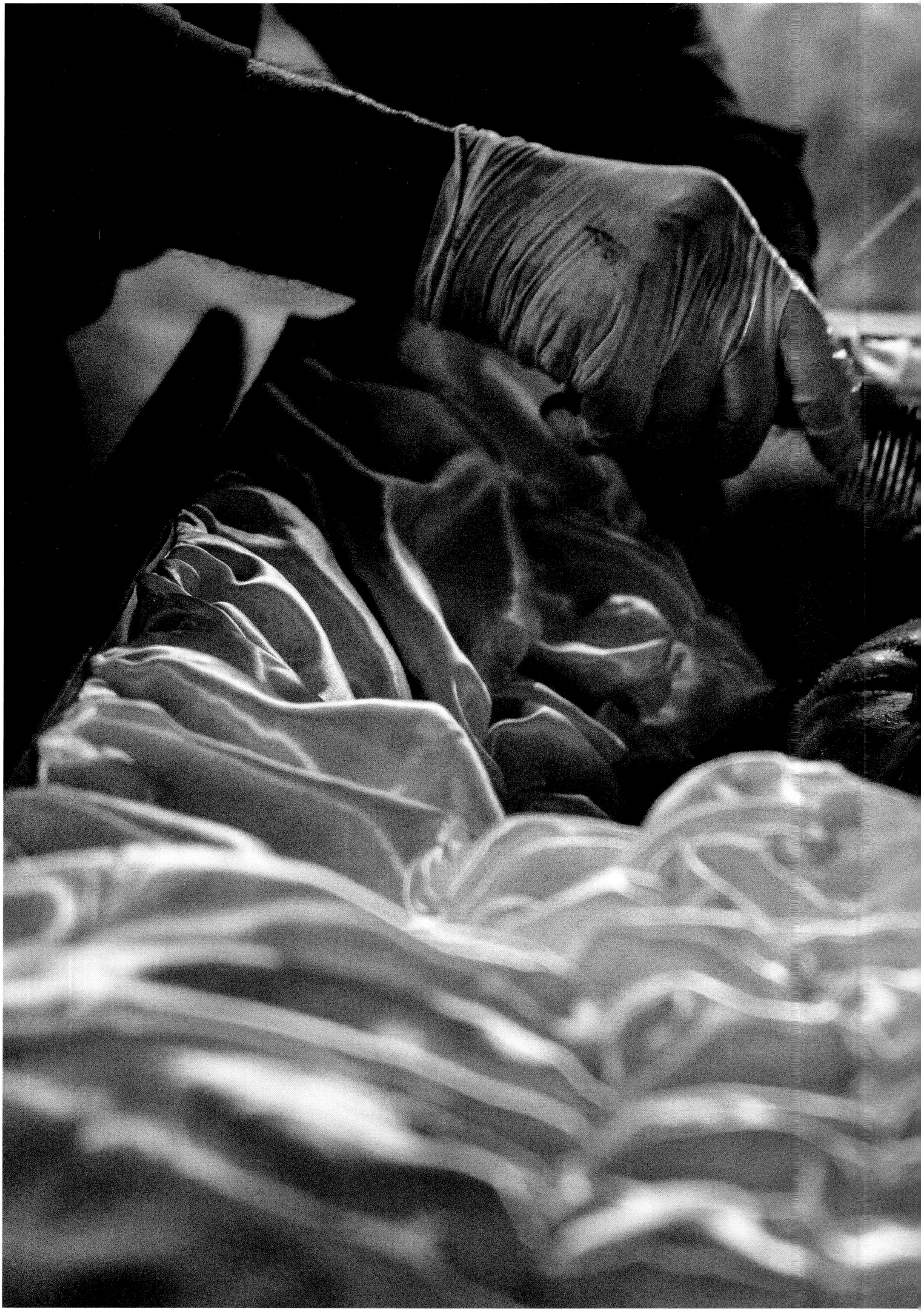

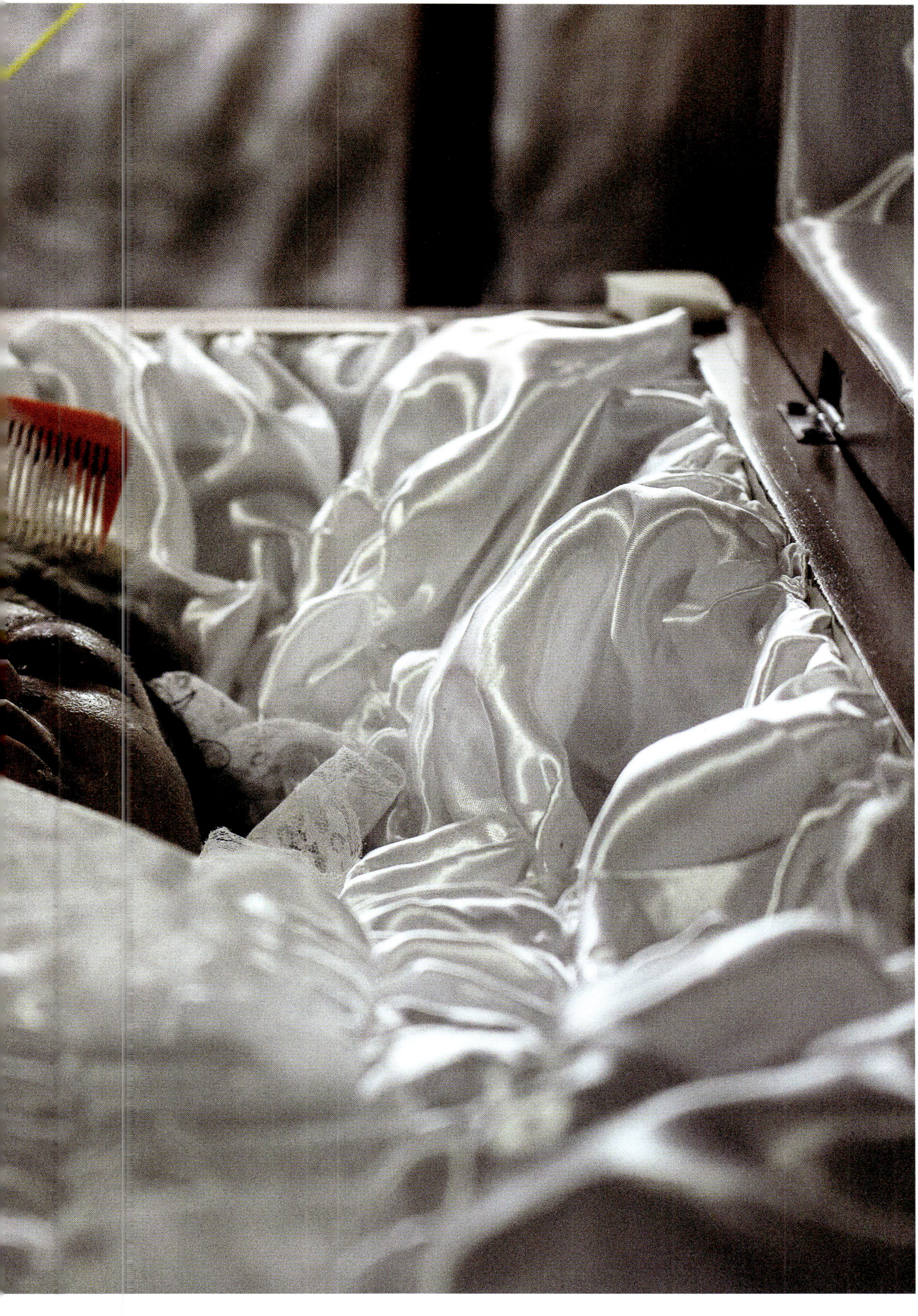

TO UNDERSTAND THE HISTORY OF EL SALVADOR'S GANG WAR,

it is important to understand the civil war which lasted from 1979–92. The war was notorious for its brutal violence and human rights violations, and left at least 75,000 people dead, others were victims of forced disappearance or displaced. These Salvadoran refugees can be traced to the origins of the two main gangs in the country: MS-13—the roots of the name 'Mara Salvatrucha' are still disputed, but 'Mara' is used in El Salvador for 'gang,' and 'Salva' is short for Salvadoran, while 'Trucha' is a slang term for 'clever' or 'sharp'— and Barrio 18 (also known as La 18 or 18th Street gang) which originated near 18th Street and Union Avenue in Los Angeles.

Both gangs were formed in Los Angeles by Salvadoran teenagers attempting to protect themselves against other established gangs in the city. Many of these young people served jail time for nonviolent crimes and upon leaving prison, turned to violence, eventually establishing the methods and networks now associated with MS-13. They also were 'educated' in various extortion techniques, and developed the gang's 'criminal economy,' and collecting dues known as 'la renta' (the rent) took form. In contrast, Barrio 18, was established in the 1960s as the first multi-racial, multi-ethnic gang in Los Angeles, but during the 1980s was mostly comprised of Salvadoran refugees and became associated almost entirely with them.

Both gangs were largely limited to Los Angeles until the end of the civil war in El Salvador in 1992, but this changed after a hardening of US immigration policies in 1997. Many Salvadoran refugees were sent back to El Salvador, and established branches of the gangs, gradually beginning to gain deeper control in the country.

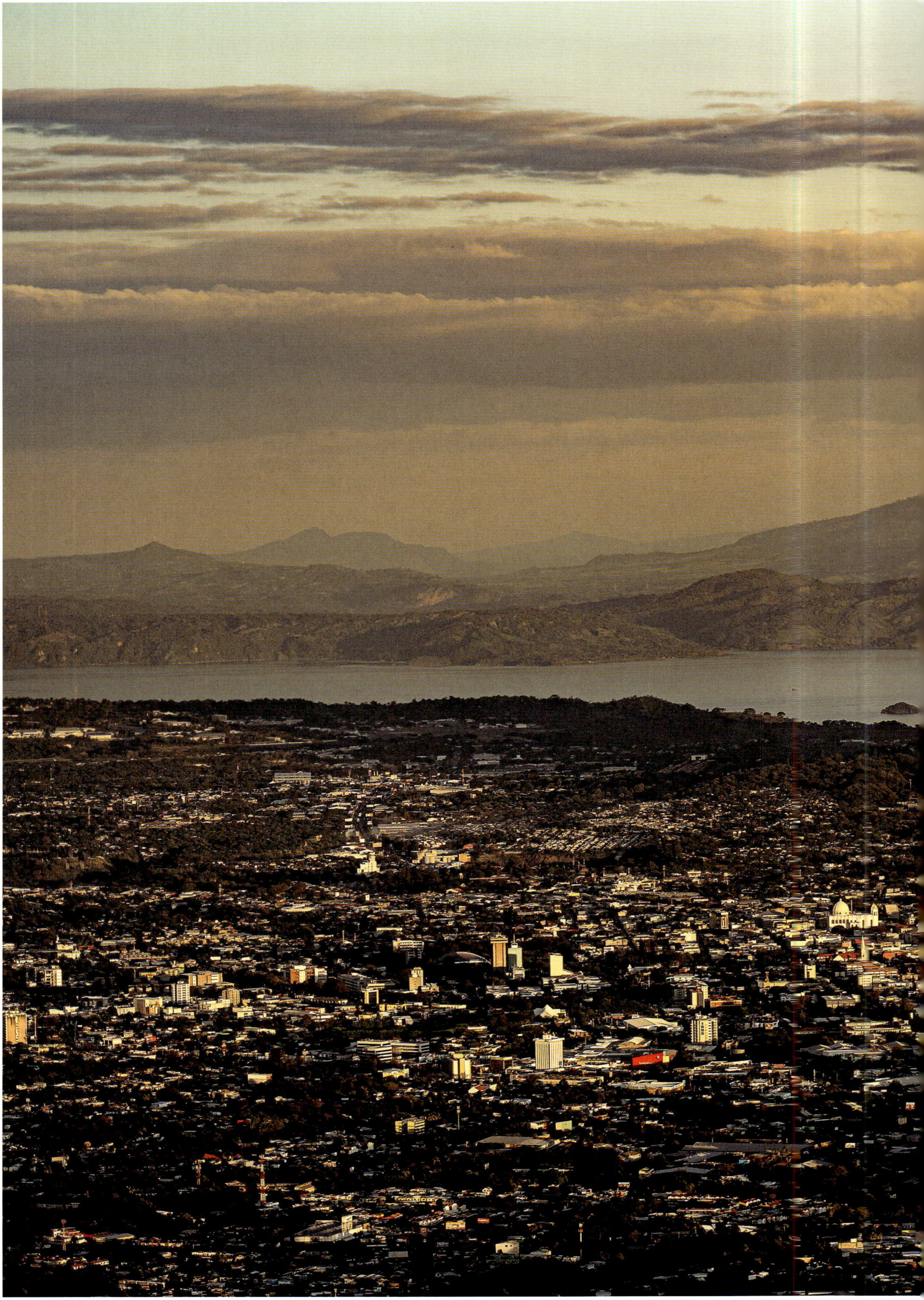

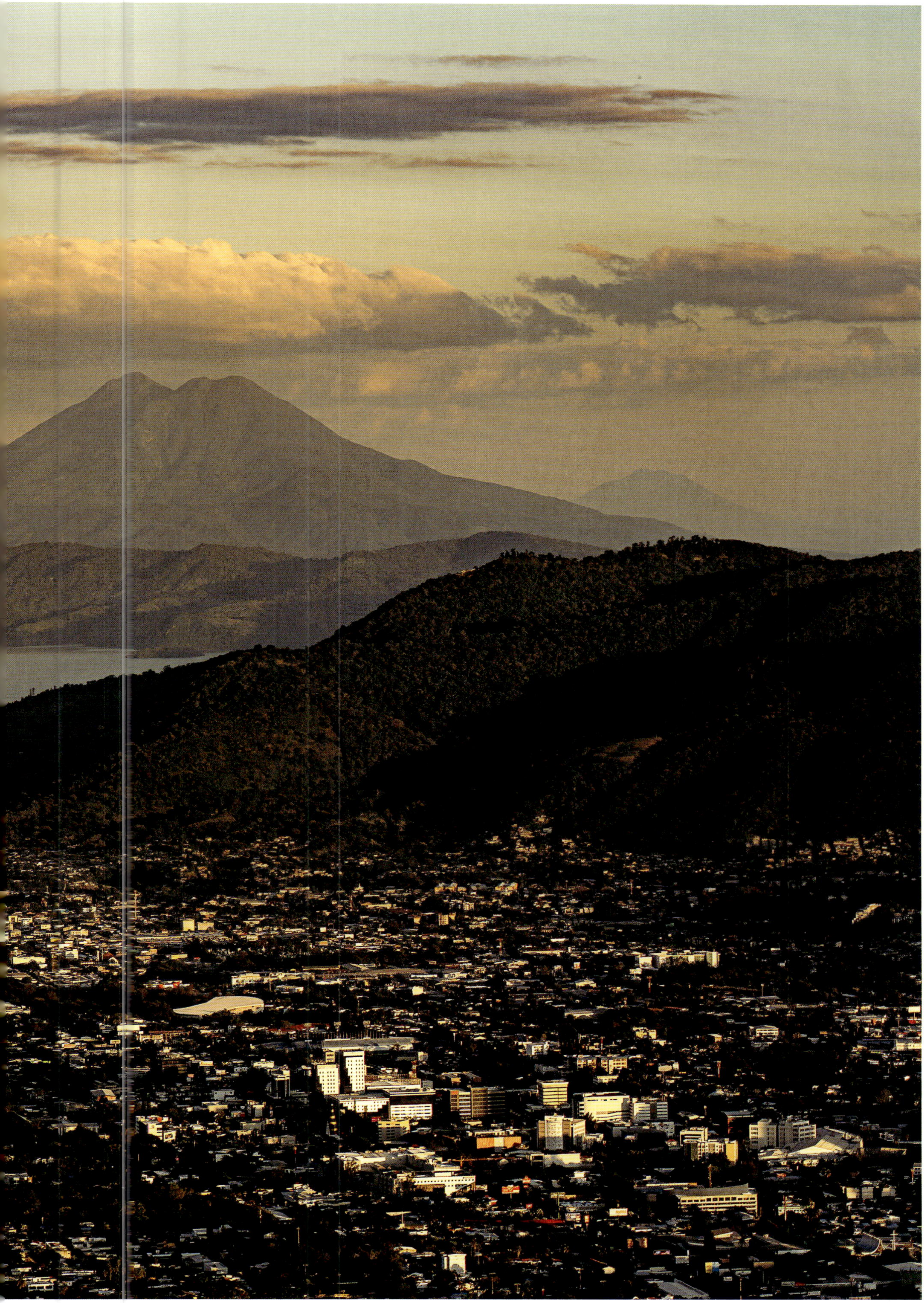

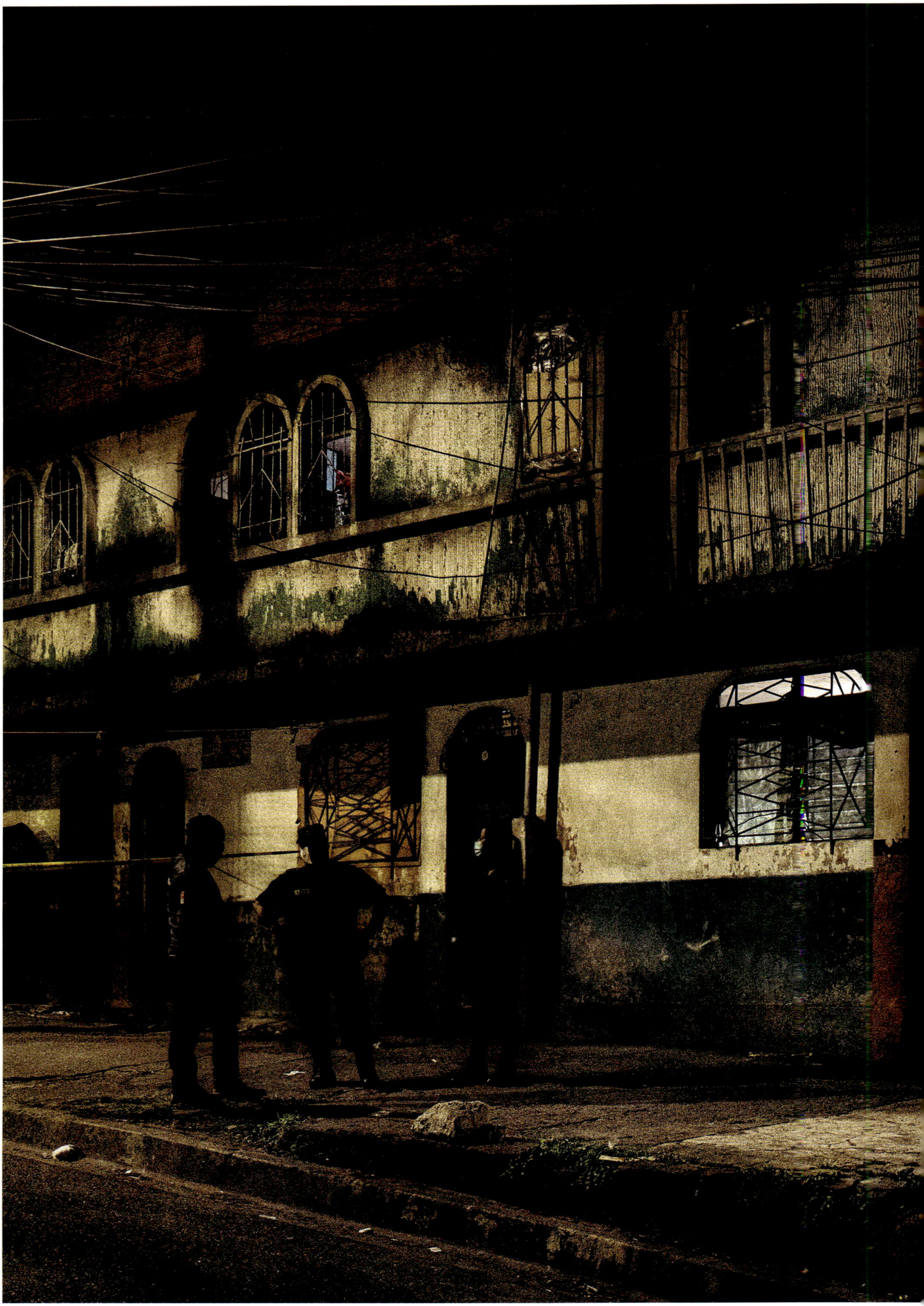

POLICIA NO PASAR
POLICIA NO PASAR
POLICIA NO PASAR
POLICIA NO PASAR
POLICIA NO PASAR

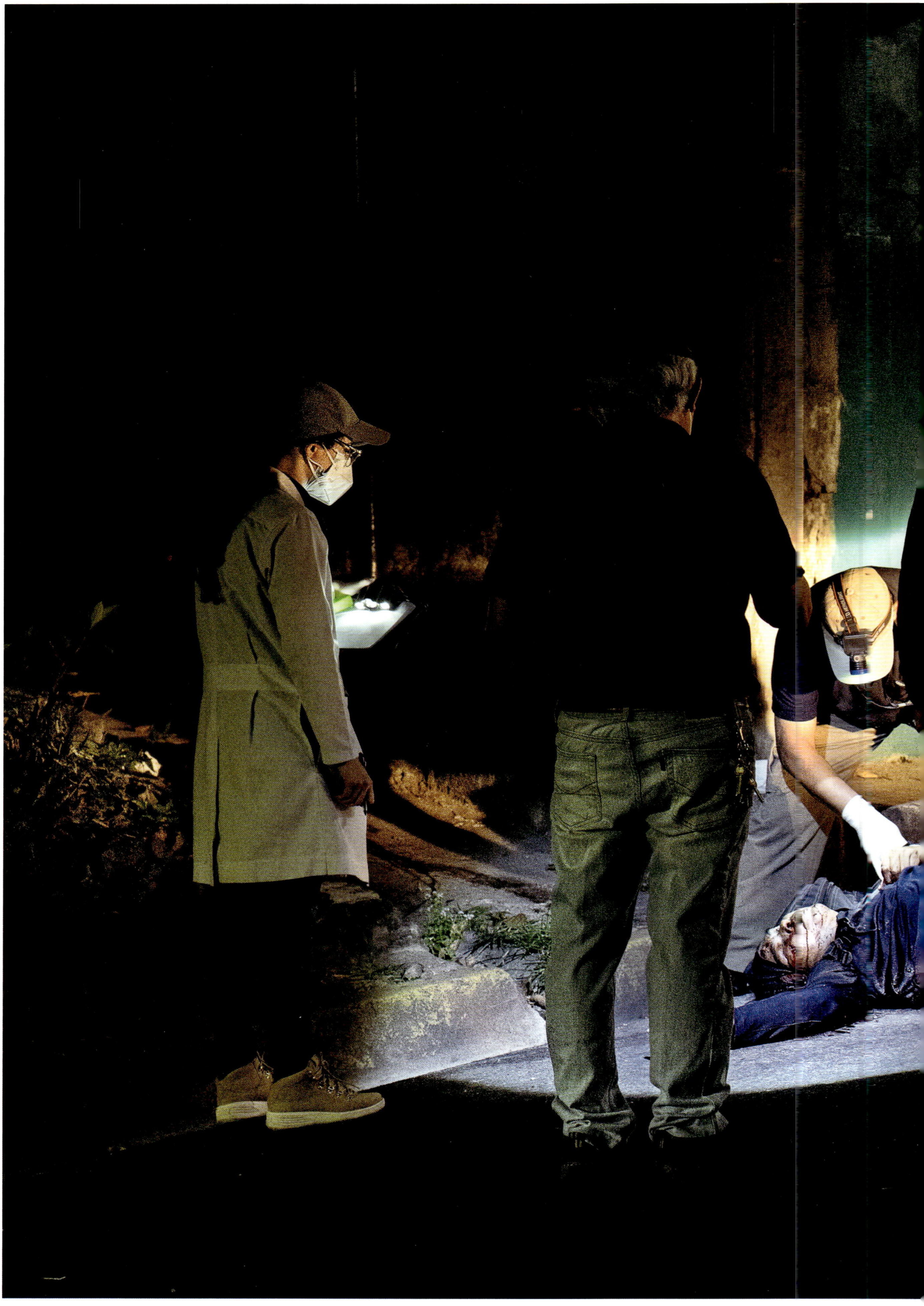

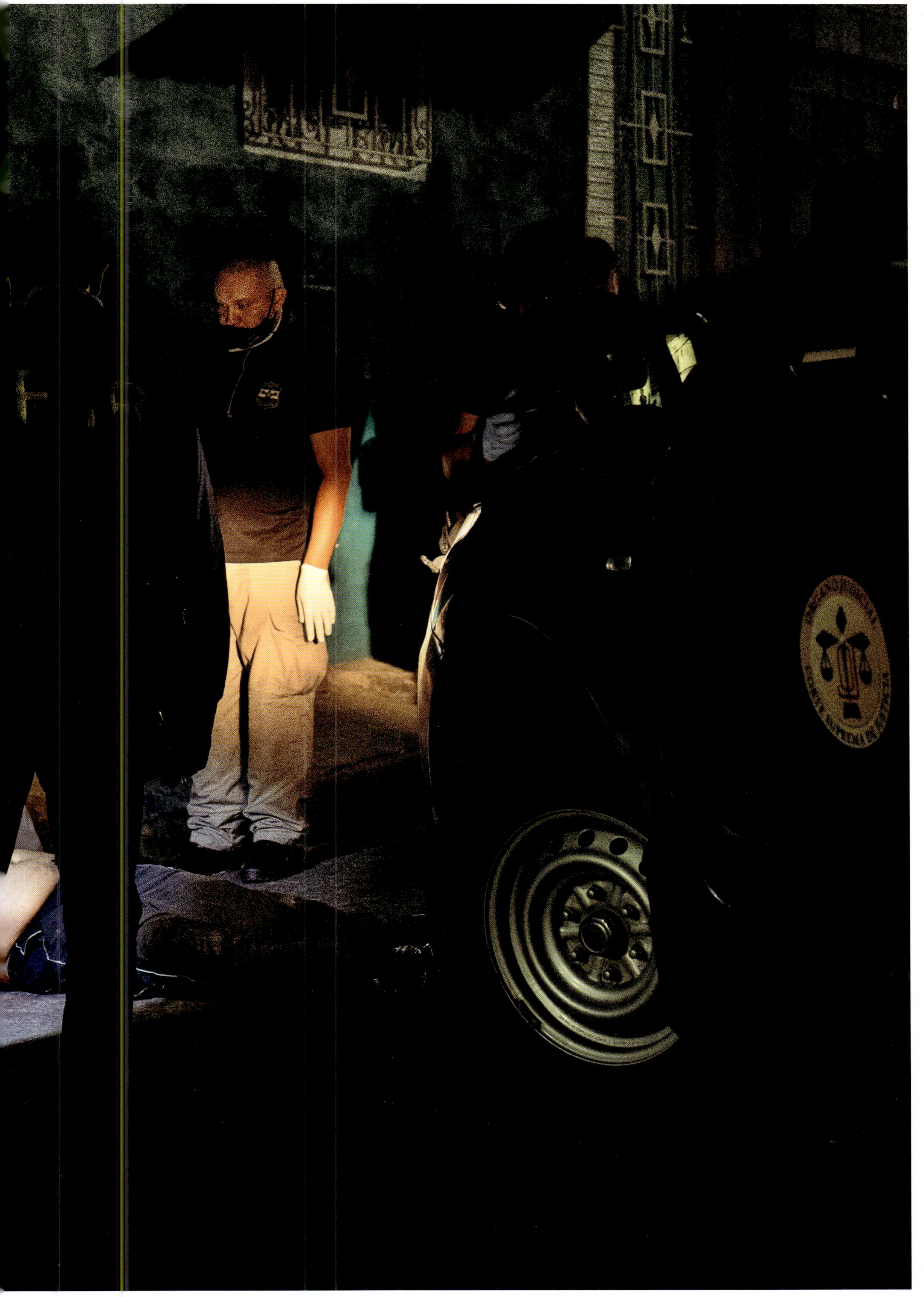

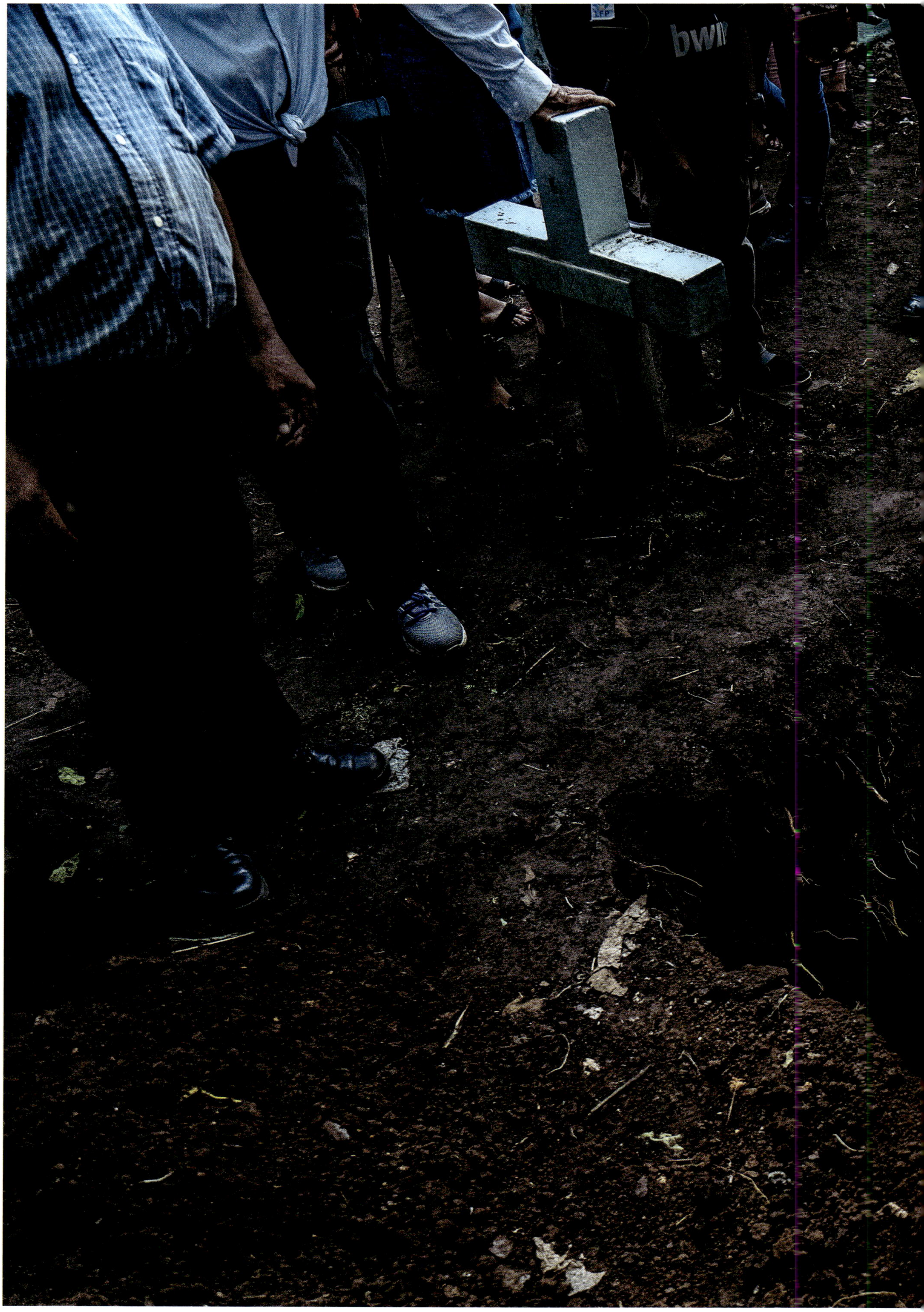

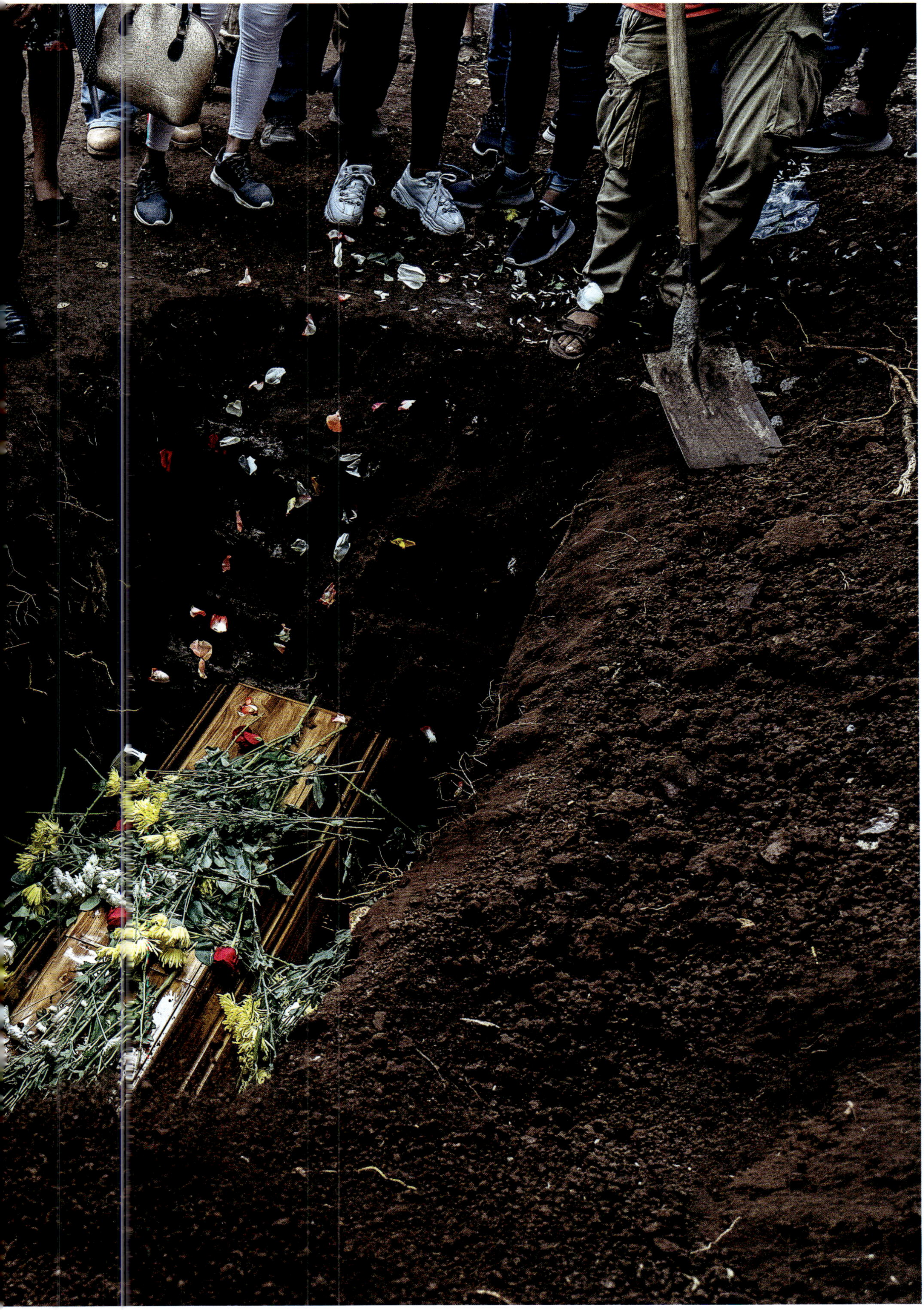

VIOLENCE IN EL SALVADOR IS UNMATCHED IN ITS SCALE, BRUTALITY AND METHODS.

Between 2005 and 2017, the country registered the highest murder rate (except in 2012) for any country not in a war zone. The impact of this violence has paralysed the country's economy and society.

The pervasive control of the gangs in El Salvador reaches down to the neighbourhood level, and often makes travel impossible. Even politicians have admitted having to 'pay to enter' certain neighbourhoods, and families are often separated from each other, unable to visit for fear of crossing gang neighbourhood lines. The main way gangs maintain local control is by extortion and economic blackmail. Estimates suggest that MS-13 alone extorts 70% of all Salvadoran businesses, amounting to $31.2 million in revenue. Indeed, the massive scale of revenue generated by both gangs means they now resemble multinational companies. They have begun investing in property, small businesses, the stealing and reselling of cars, and drug trafficking.

Gang presence at almost all levels of daily life presents major challenges for law enforcement. Most police officers wear balaclavas to protect their identities and families, and often work together with the country's military and paramilitary forces. Nevertheless, police officers are among those most targeted by gangs, and many have been forced to flee the country.

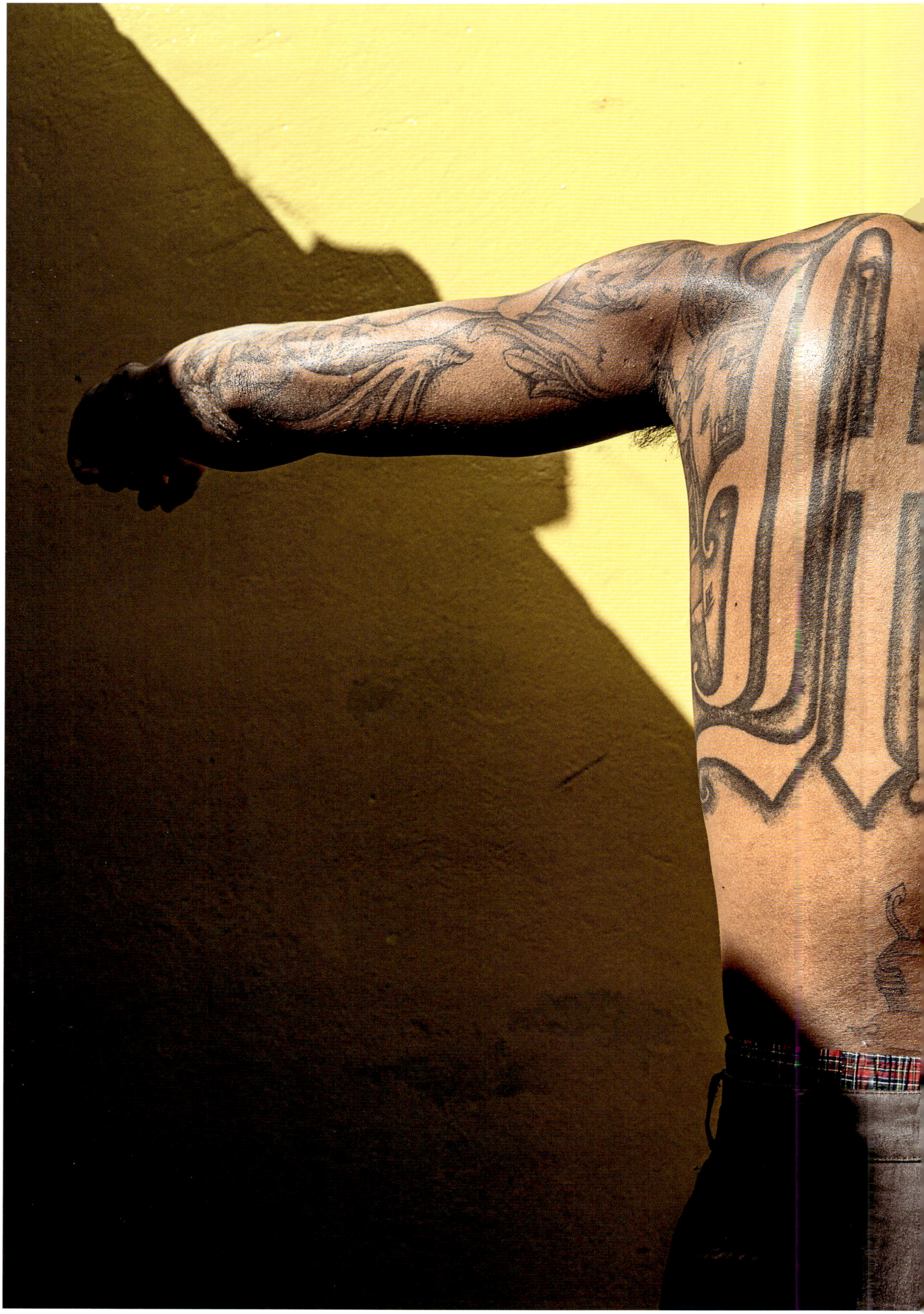

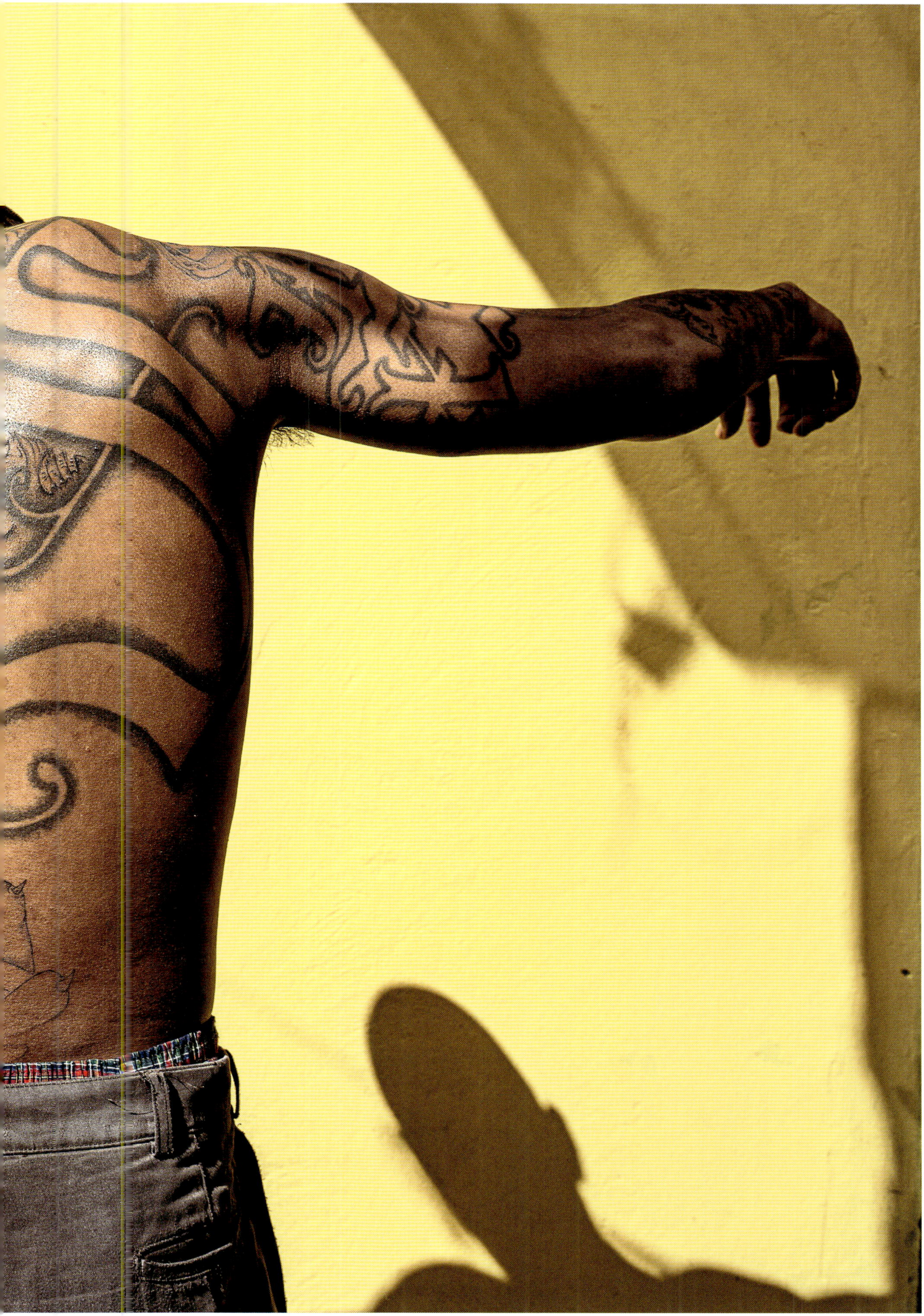

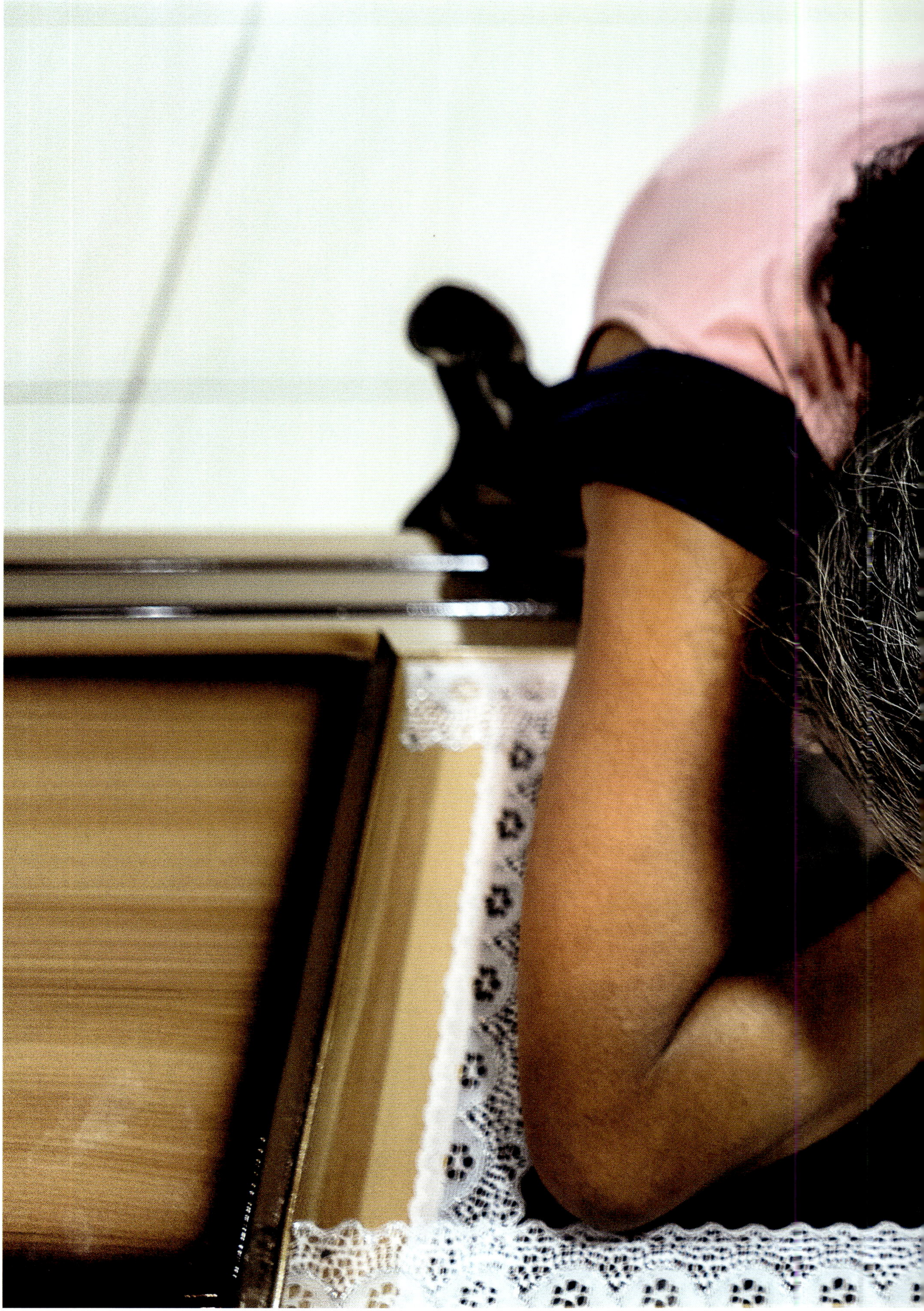

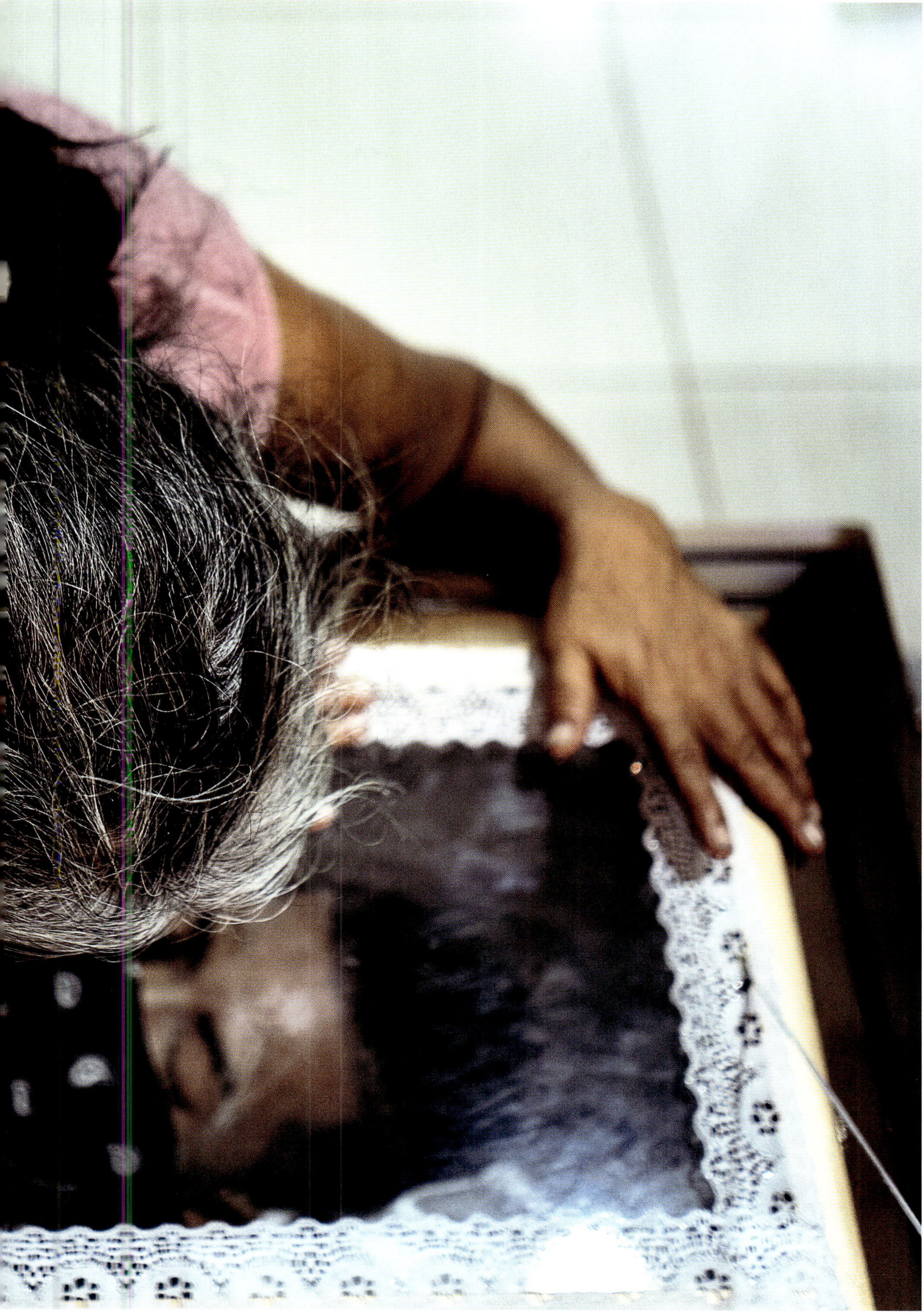

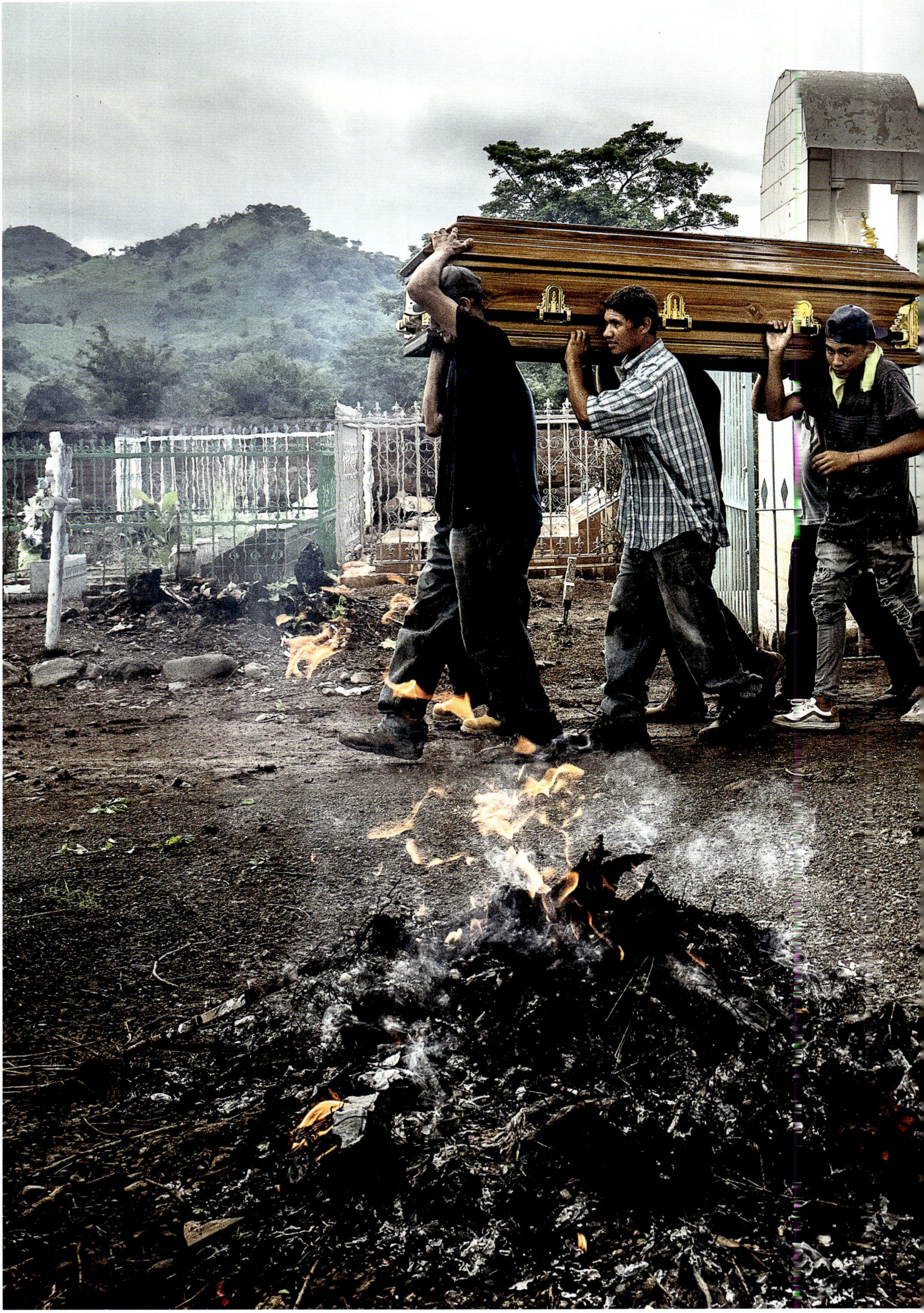

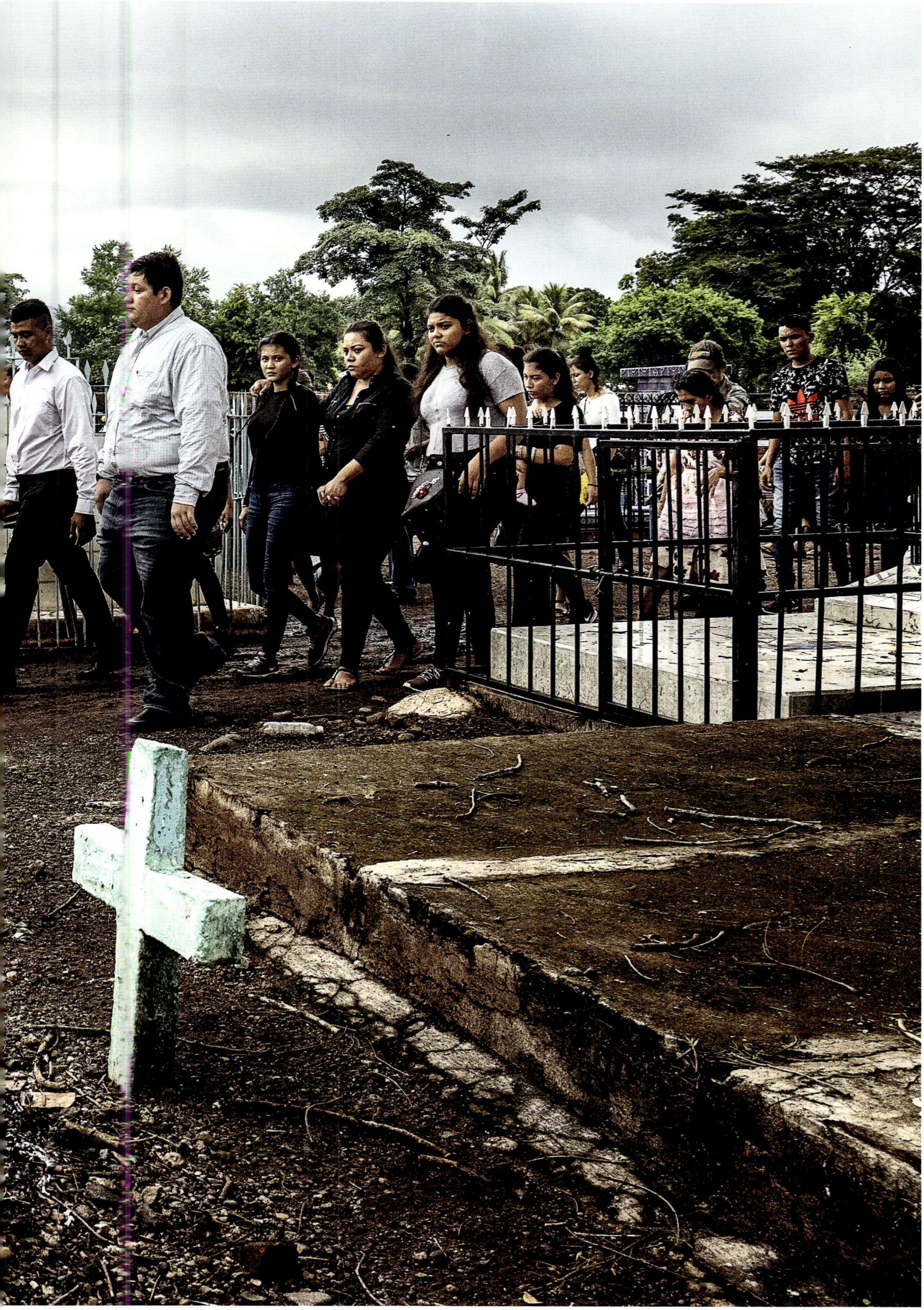

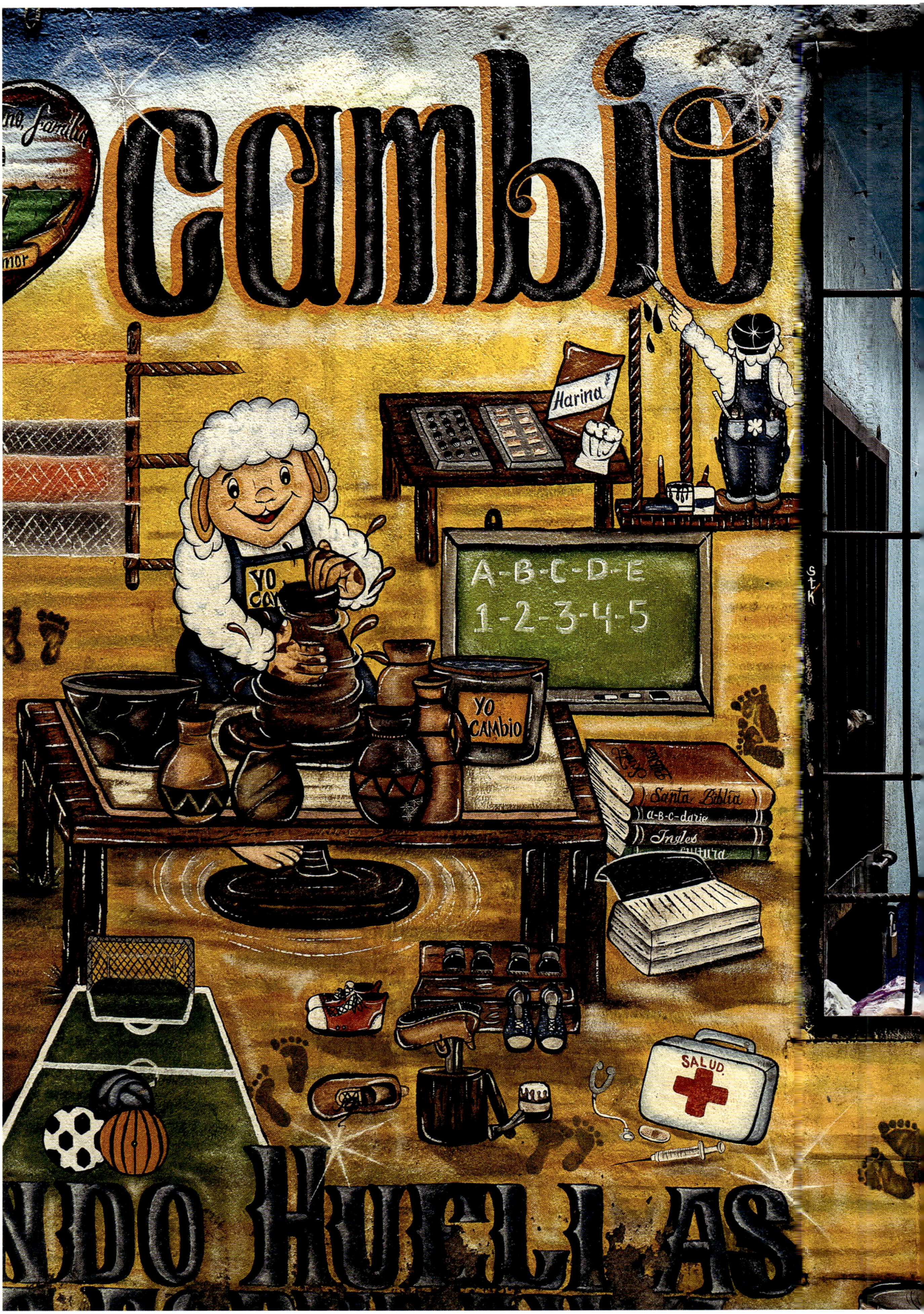
cambio
Harina
YO CAMBIO
A-B-C-D-E
1-2-3-4-5
Santa Biblia
a-b-c-darie
Ingles
SALUD
NDO HUELLAS

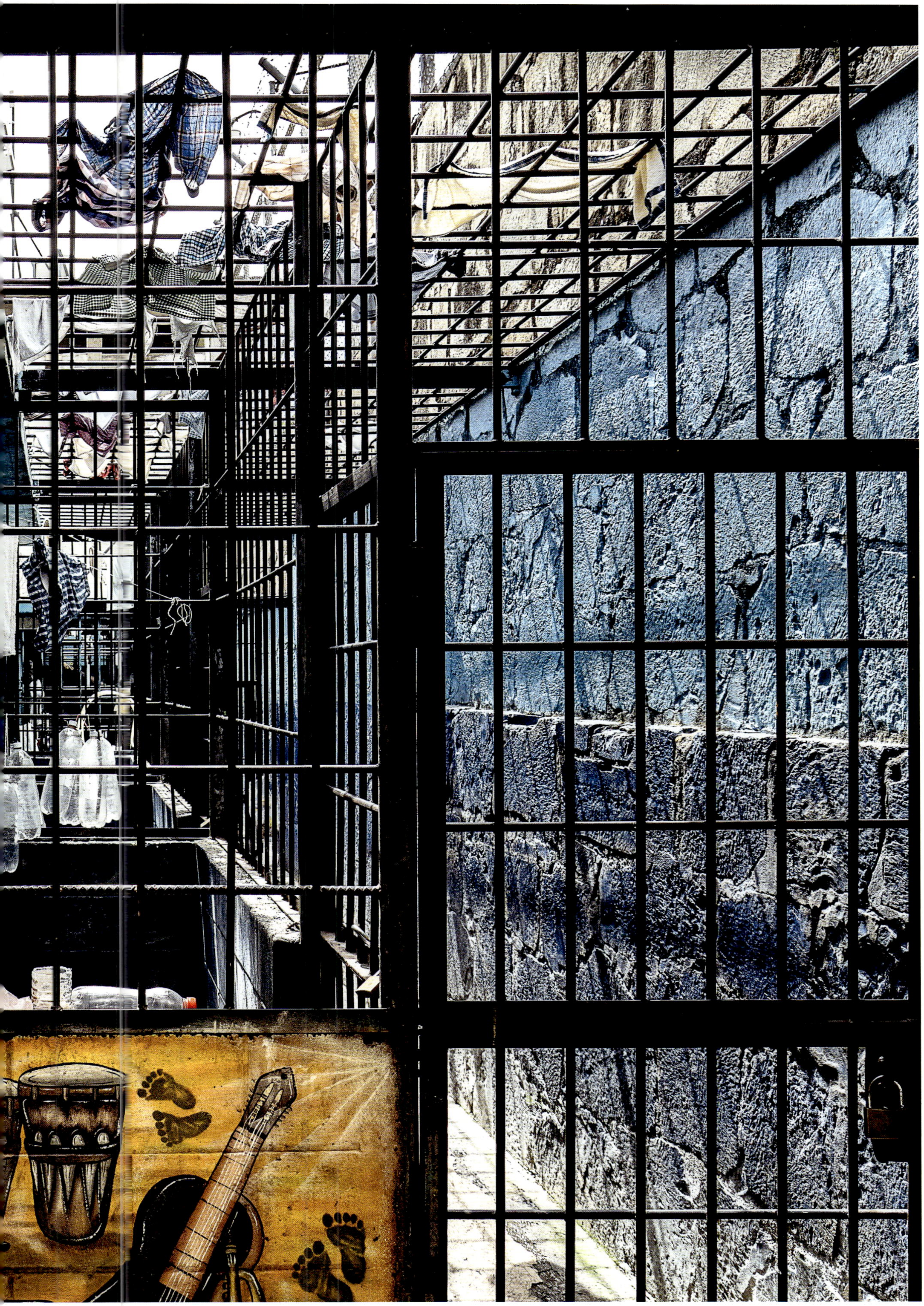

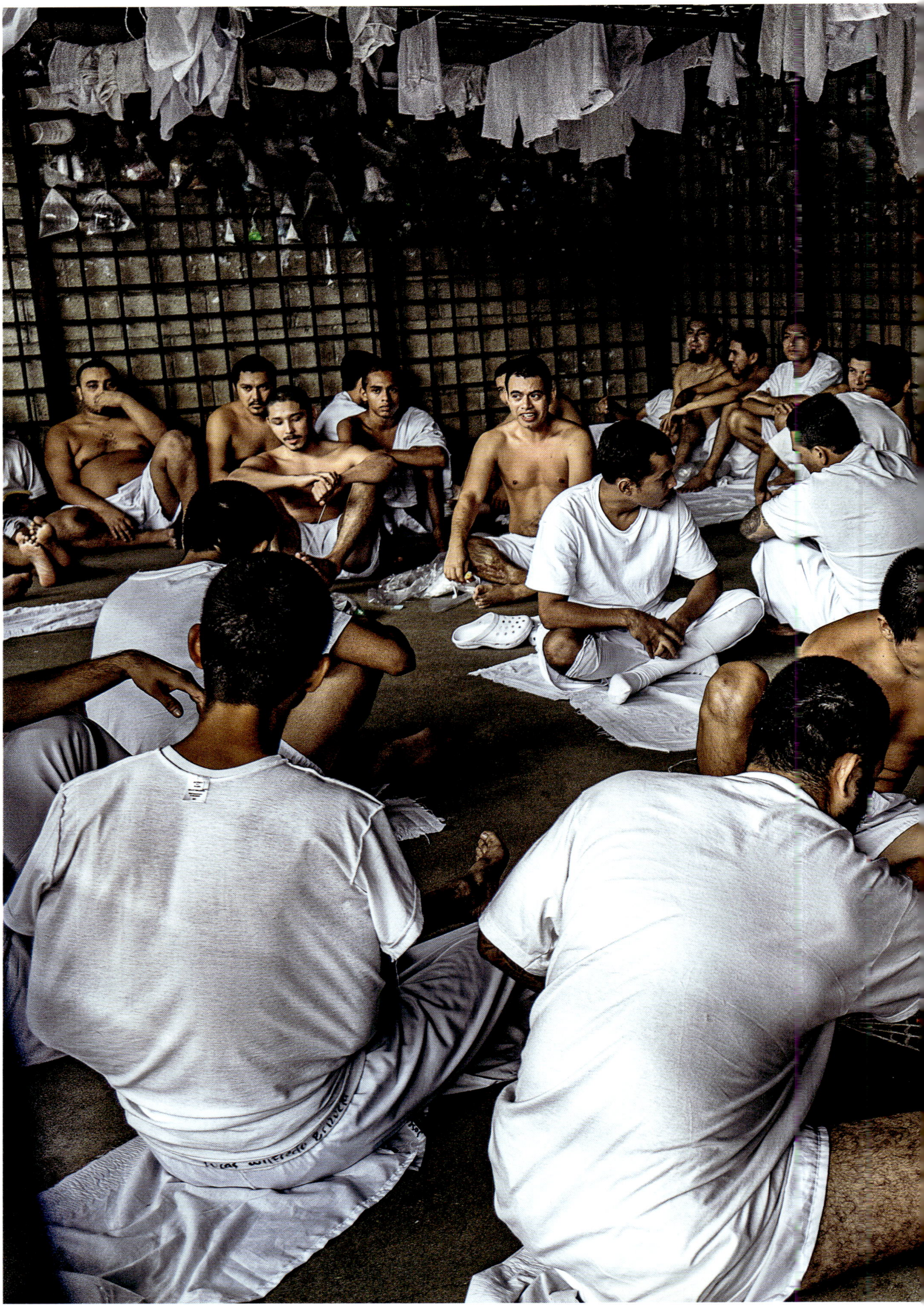

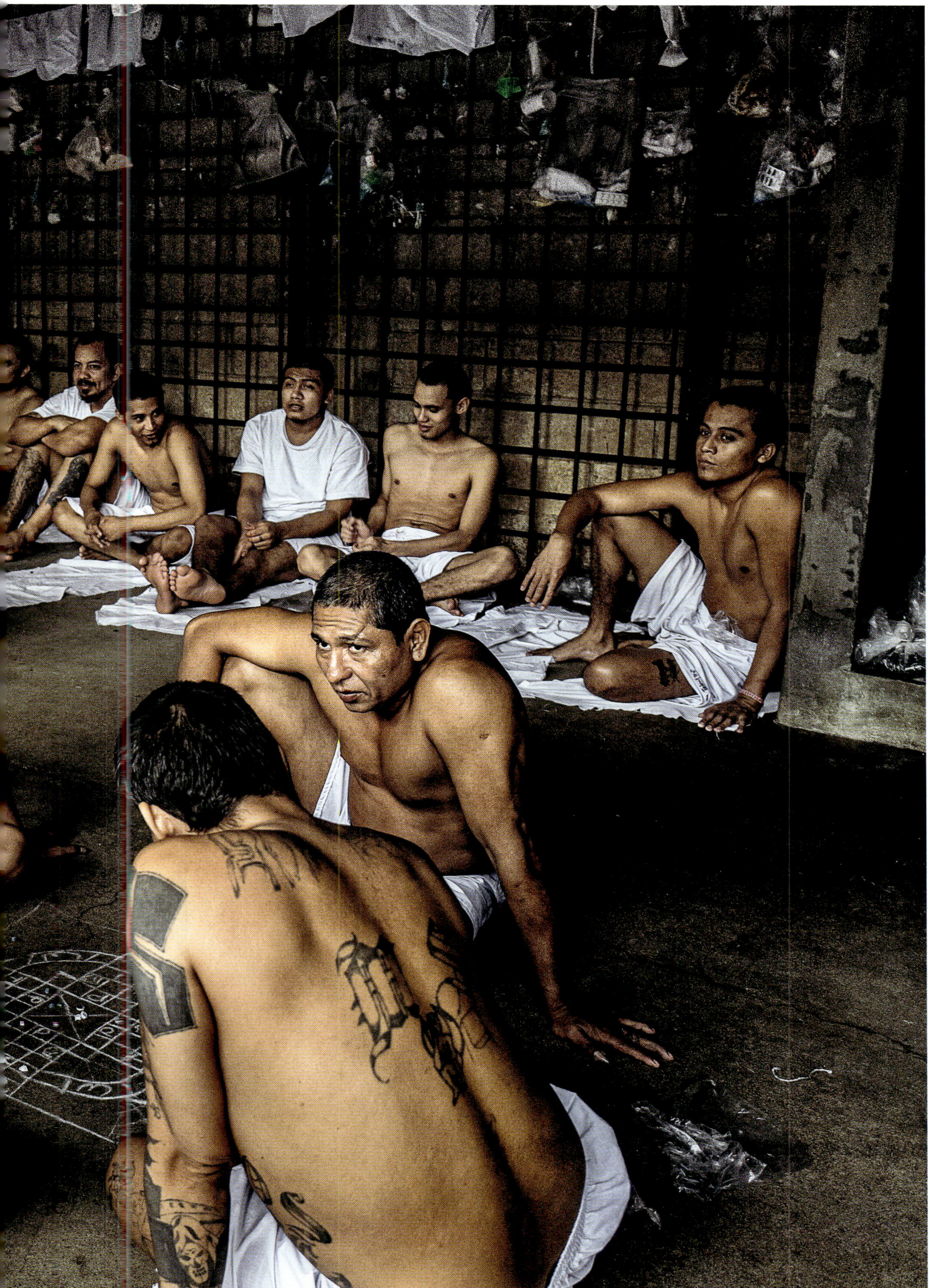

ECONOMIC PARALYSIS HAS CONTRIBUTED TO THE DESPAIR FELT BY THE COUNTRY'S YOUTH:

young people grow up in what are effectively hostage-like conditions and can be socialised into a gang as young as eight or nine-years-old. Physical, emotional and mental trauma is widespread amongst Salvadoran youth and contributes to the normalisation of violence in gang life. Gangs develop their own cultures and often include references to the occult and satanism, developing an ideological and cult identity. Gang members often refer to killings as 'sacrifices,' and initiate new recruits as 'true believers.'

MS-13 recruits are initiated with a 13 second beating, and female recruits can be gang-raped or beat as their initiation. Women are both vulnerable to violence in El Salvador (in 2015 the country held the third highest femicide rate in the world) and partakers in it.

The kind of violence MS-13 and Barrio 18 partake in is brutal and terrifying. It is common for the members to use machetes to hack off limbs and document their killings on their phones, clips of which are widely shared among the gangs. There is a method to the madness, however—the body parts are buried in clandestine graves, so that no 'complete' body is ever found, and the murder is not recorded. The victim remains 'disappeared' rather than another murder statistic, thus reducing the chances of a government crackdown against gangs.

It is nearly impossible to leave the gang once initiated. Anything but total loyalty arouses suspicion and from the gang's perspective, it is easier to kill those who express a desire to leave than run the risk of them becoming an informant.

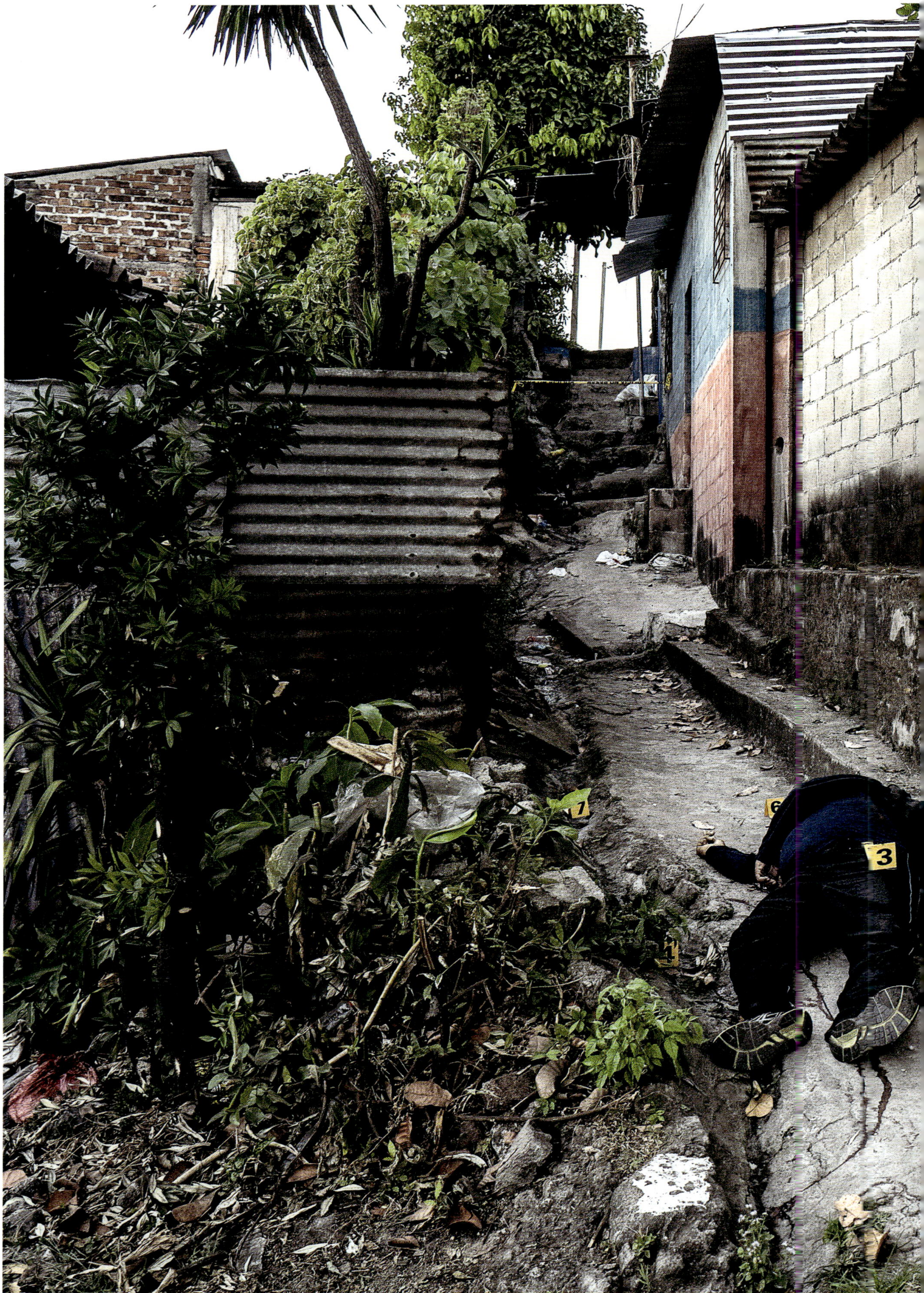

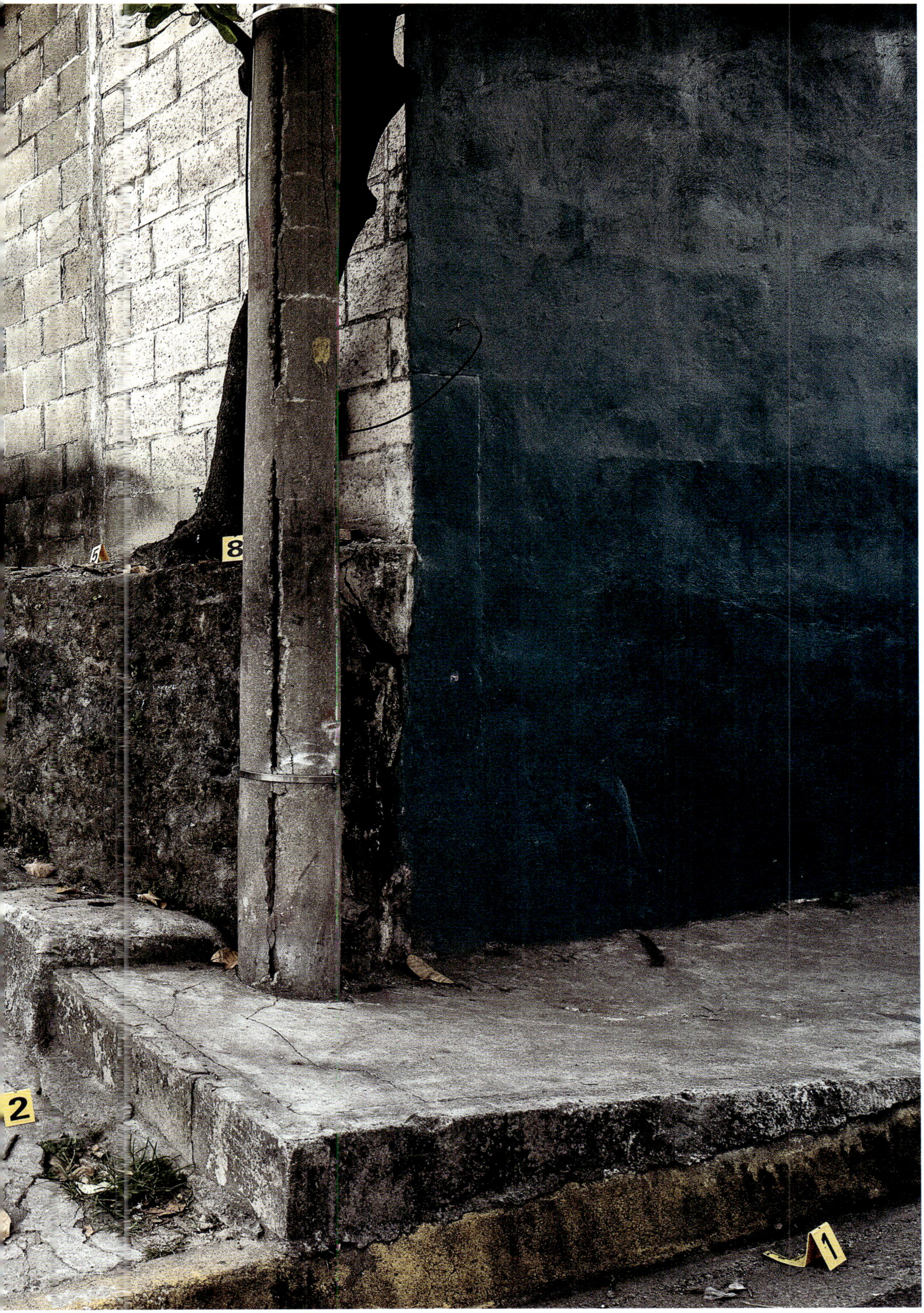
5
8
2
1

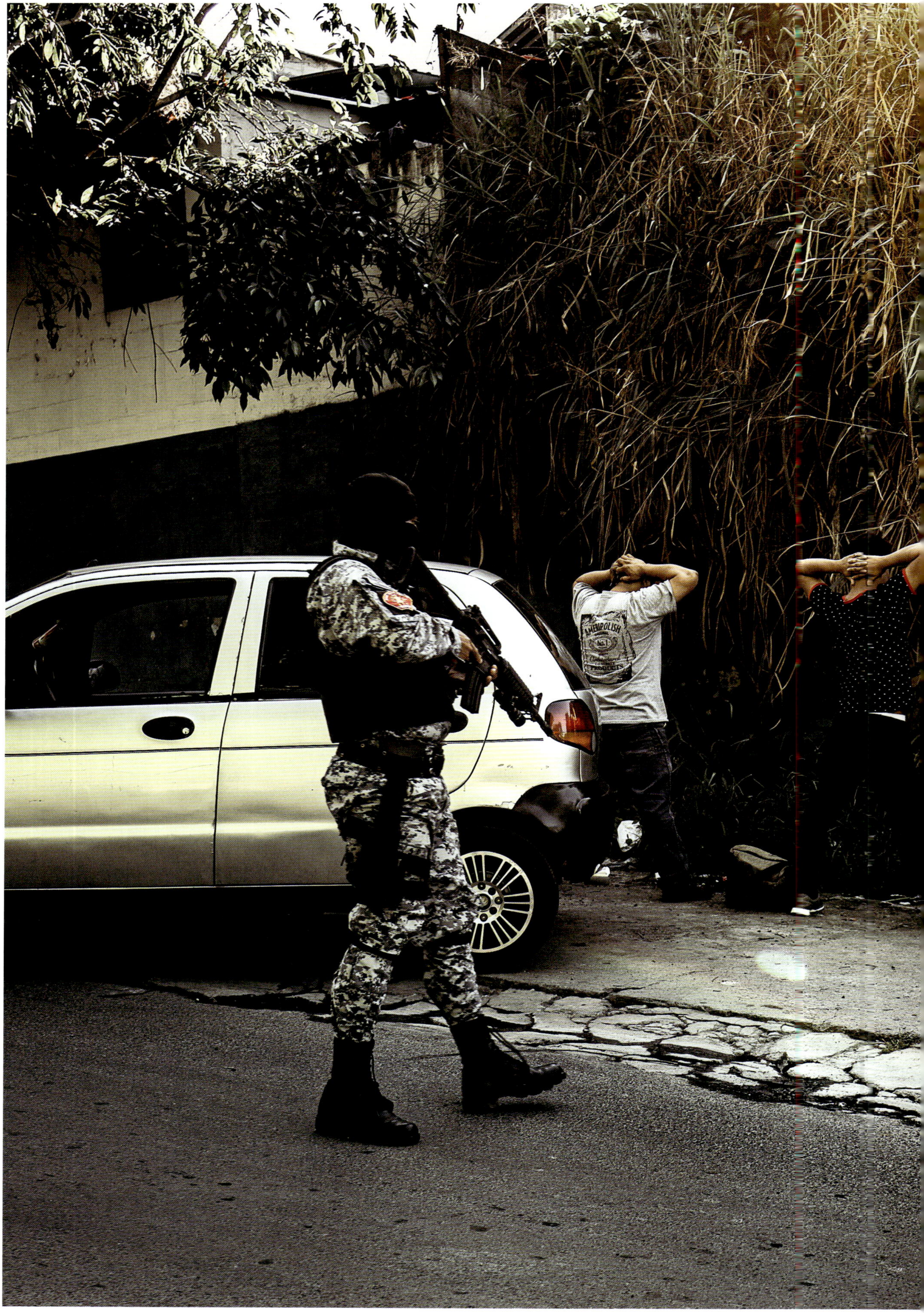

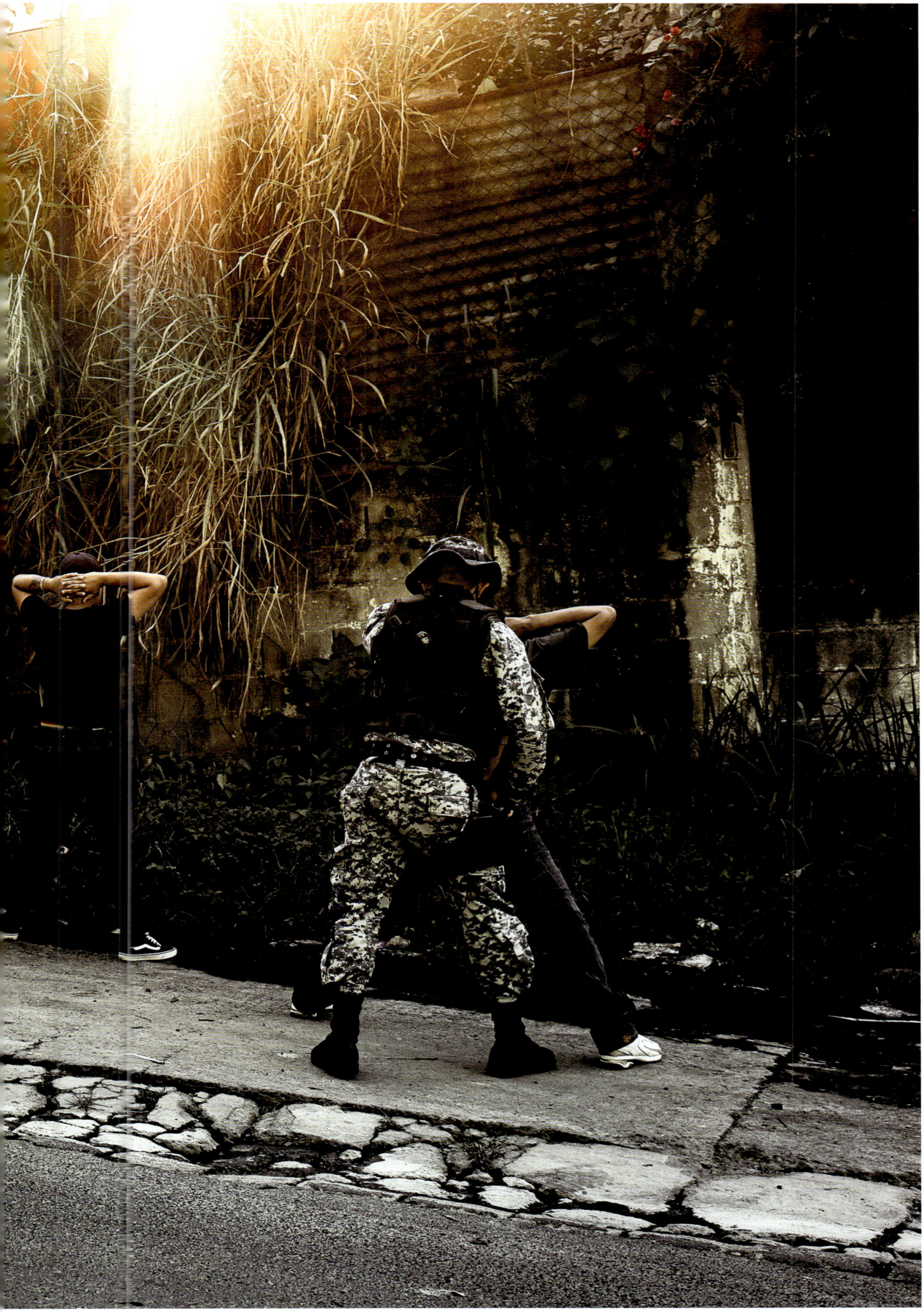

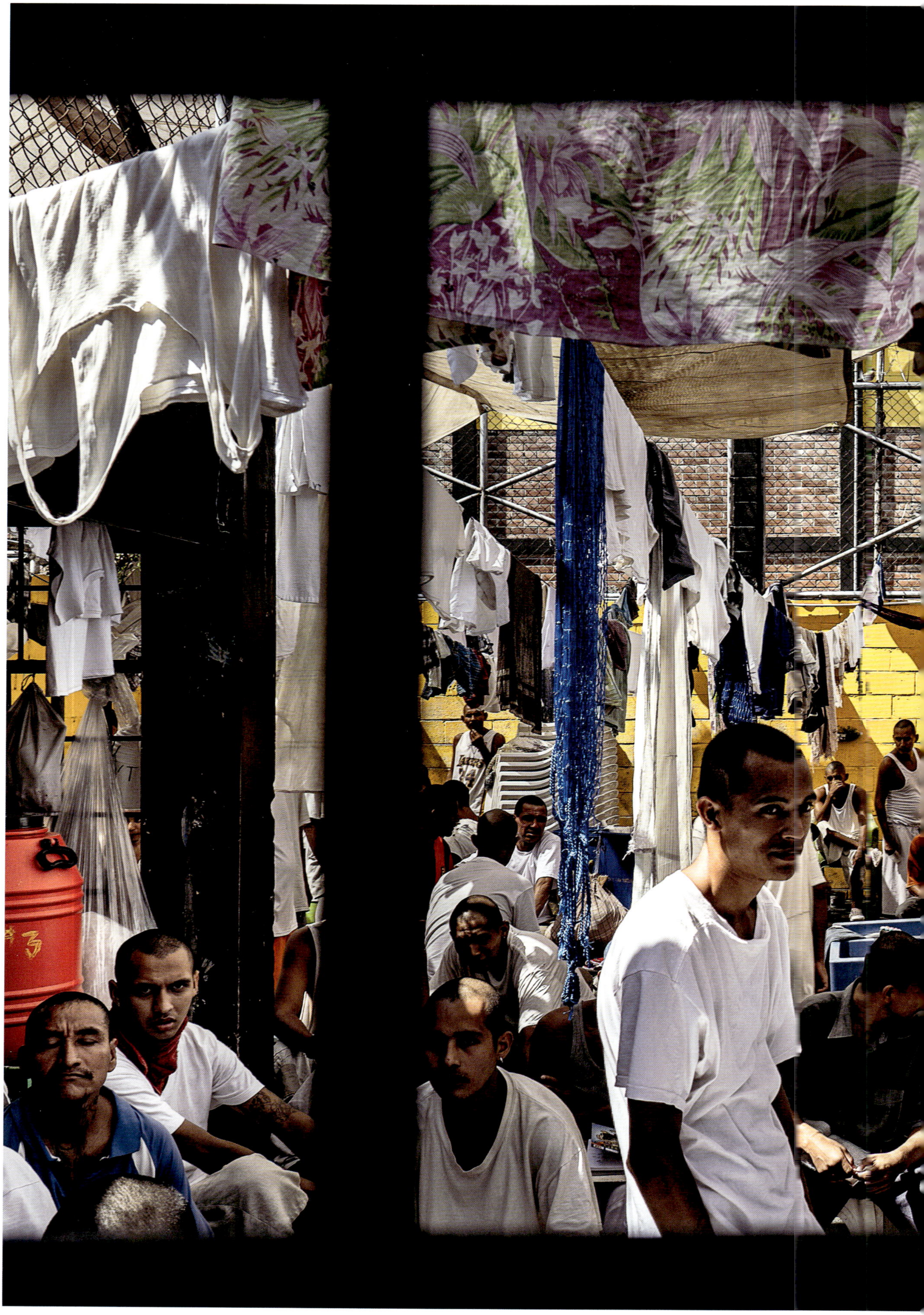

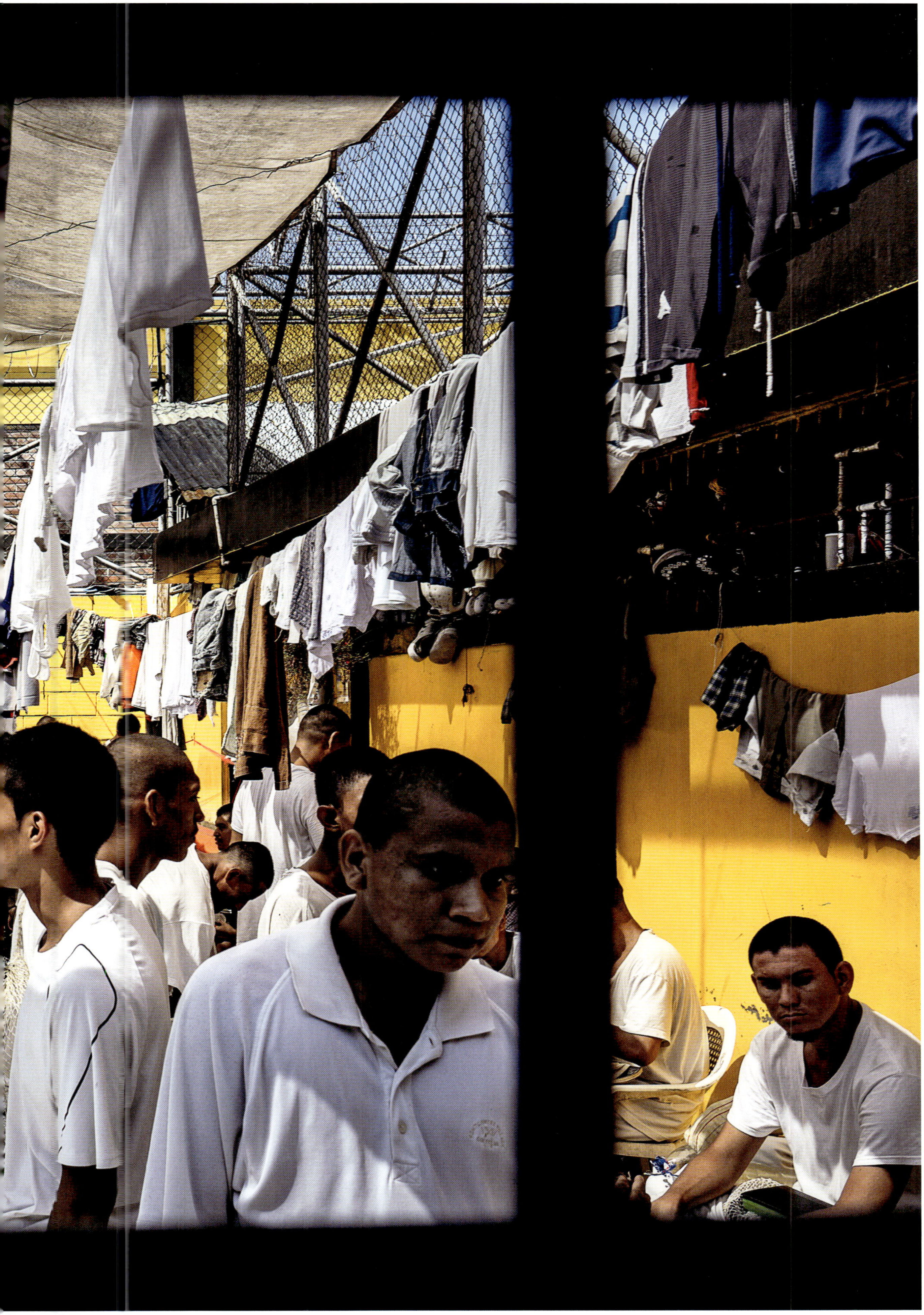

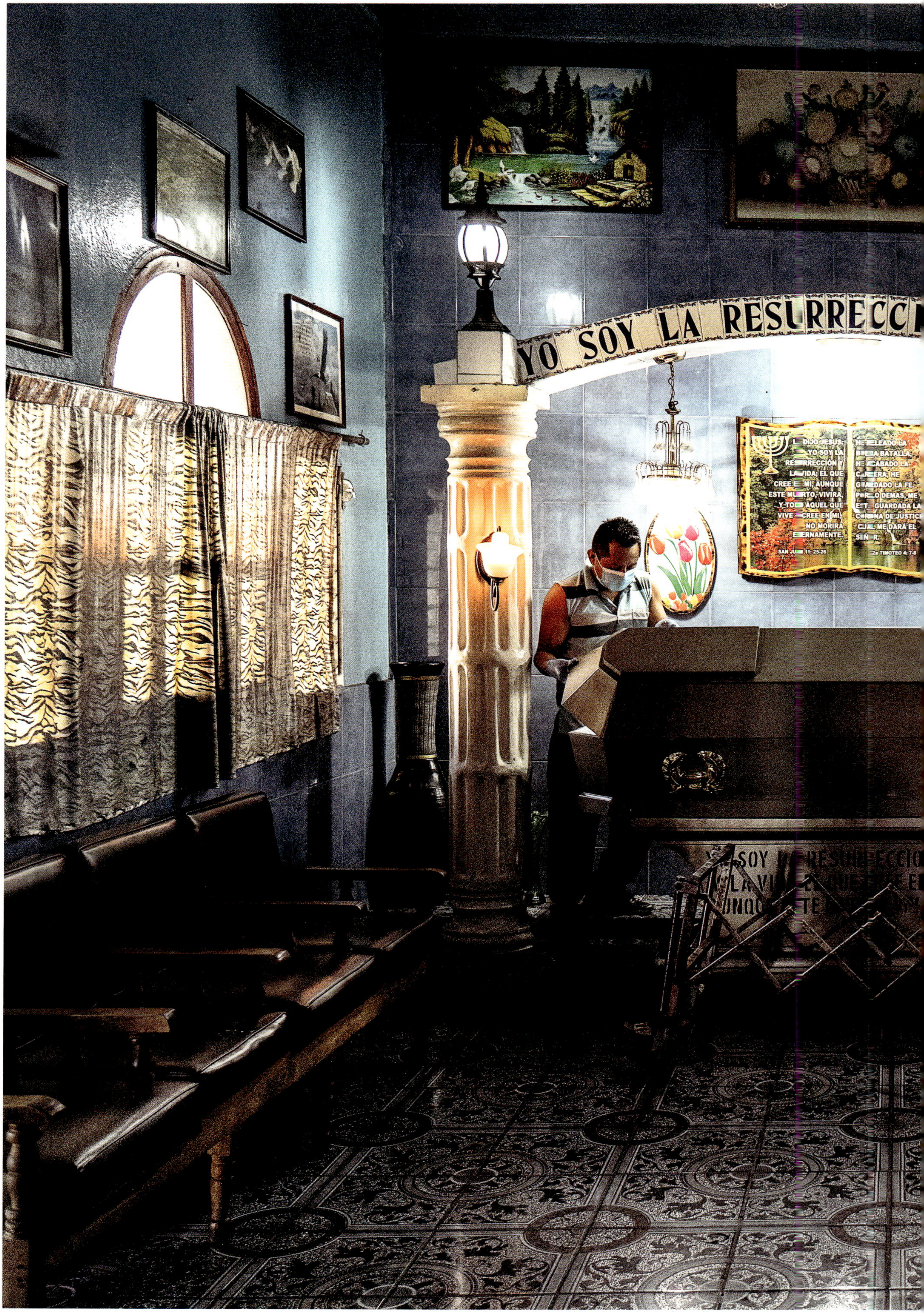
YO SOY LA RESURRECC

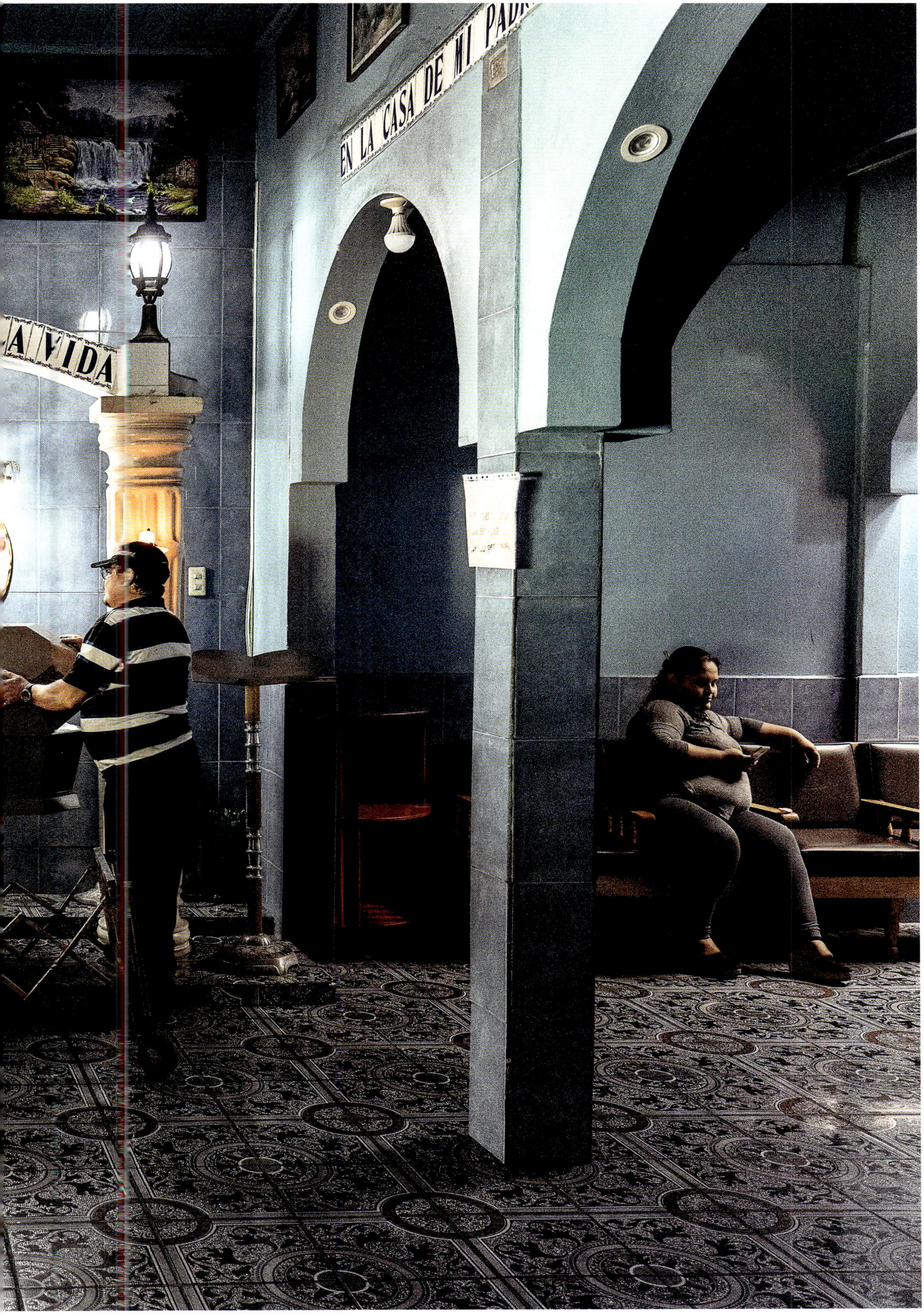
EN LA CASA DE MI PADR
A VIDA

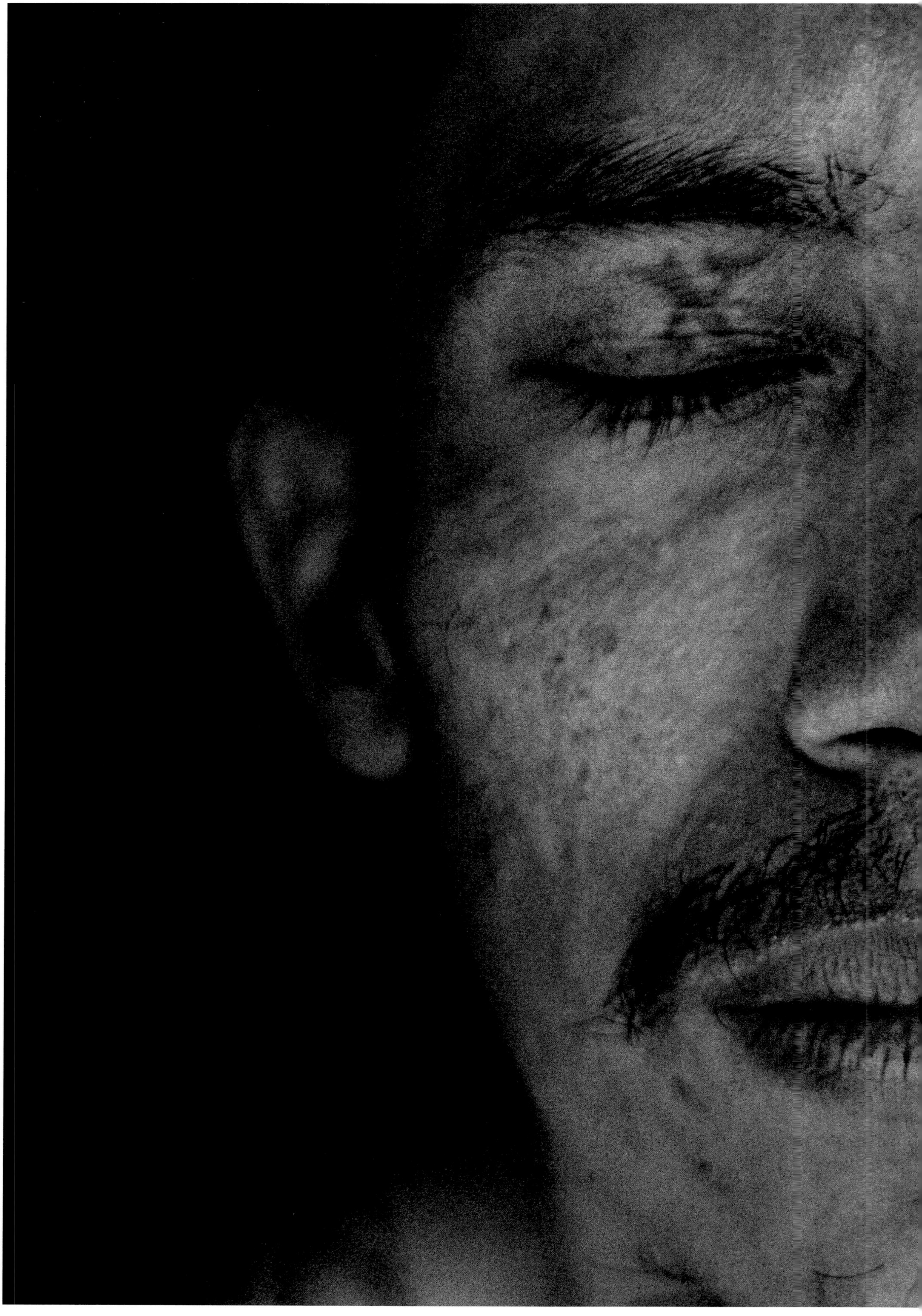

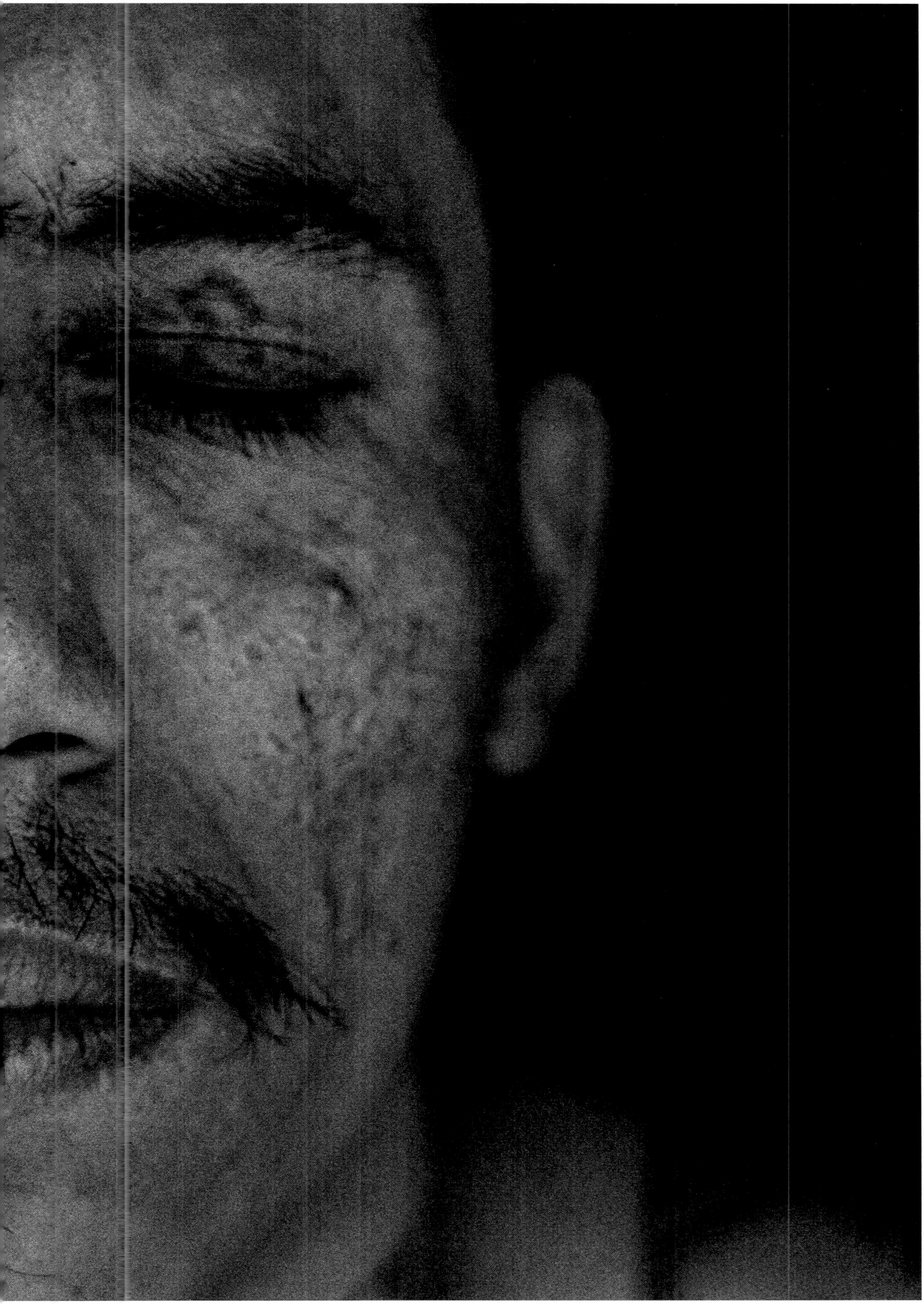

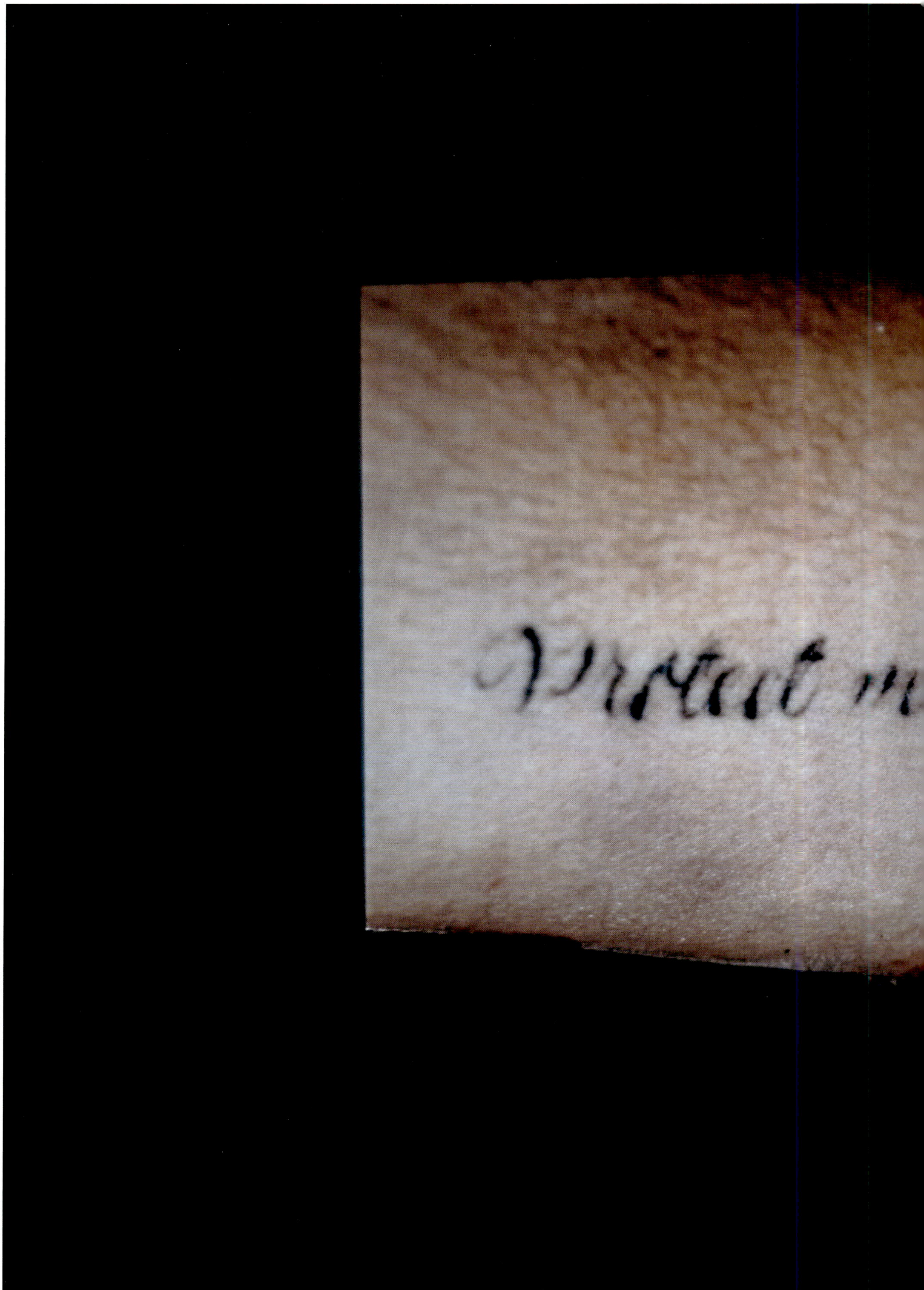
Verlaat

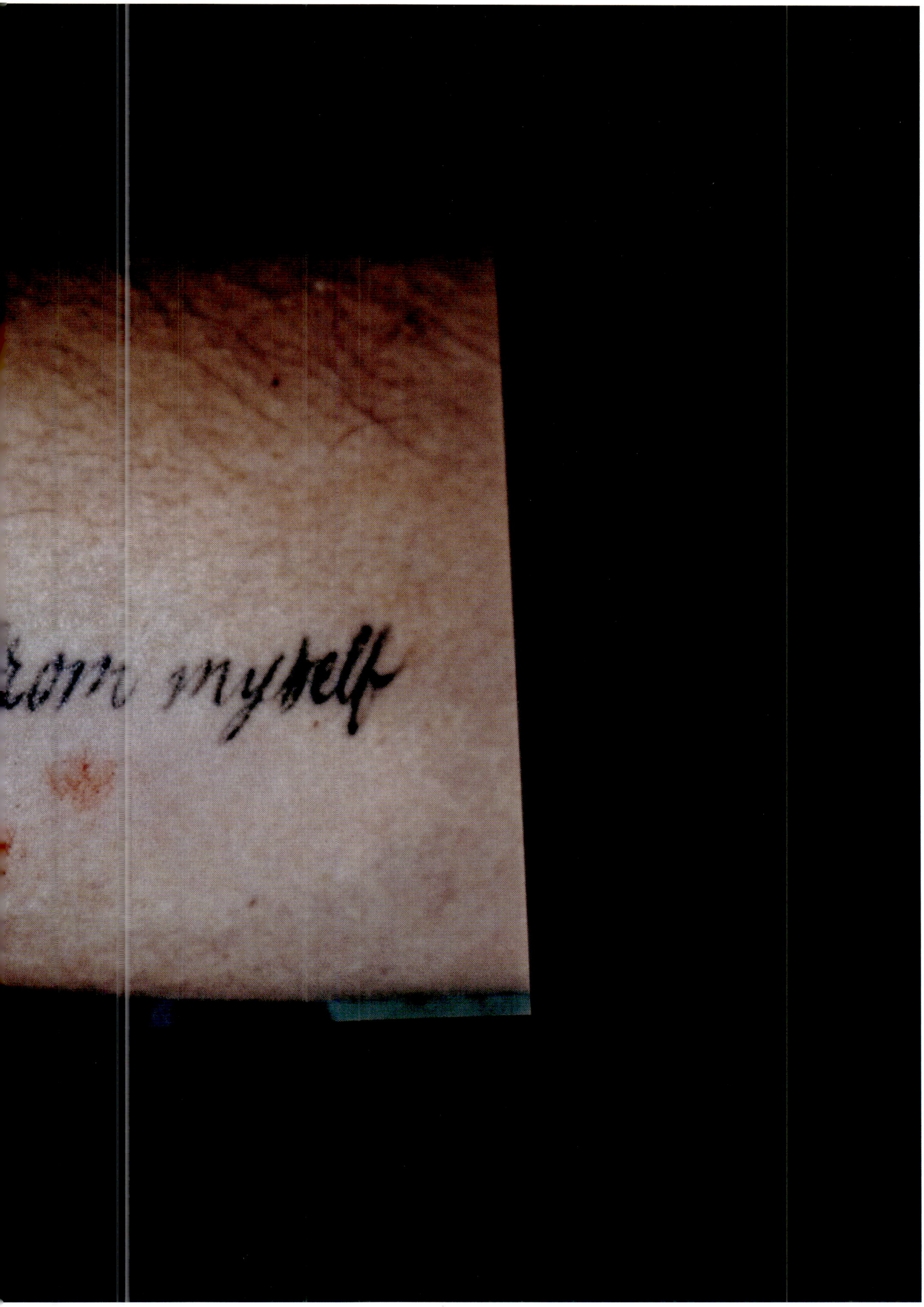
rom myself

SINCE COMING TO POWER IN 2019,

the administration of President Bukele has, for the most part, continued the policies of its predecessors—governing with La Mano Dura ('iron fist'). The policies were originally introduced in 2003 as a part of the government's tough-on-crime course of action and has been extended ever since, eventually being made permanent by Congress in August 2018.

The measures include transferring the leading gang members to maximum-security prisons, the holding of judicial proceedings in prisons (therefore reducing the need to transfer prisoners to and from courtrooms), the restriction of visitation rights and telecommunication rights, and mandatory participation in rehabilitation and work skills programmes.

President Bukele promised to eradicate gang violence within four years of coming to power and since his election, violence has significantly subsided. The murder rate fell 50% during his first year in office, and although Bukele has argued that his tough prison policies and increased police presence have been behind the drop, some observers have alleged it is possible an informal 'pact' exists between the government and leading gang leaders.

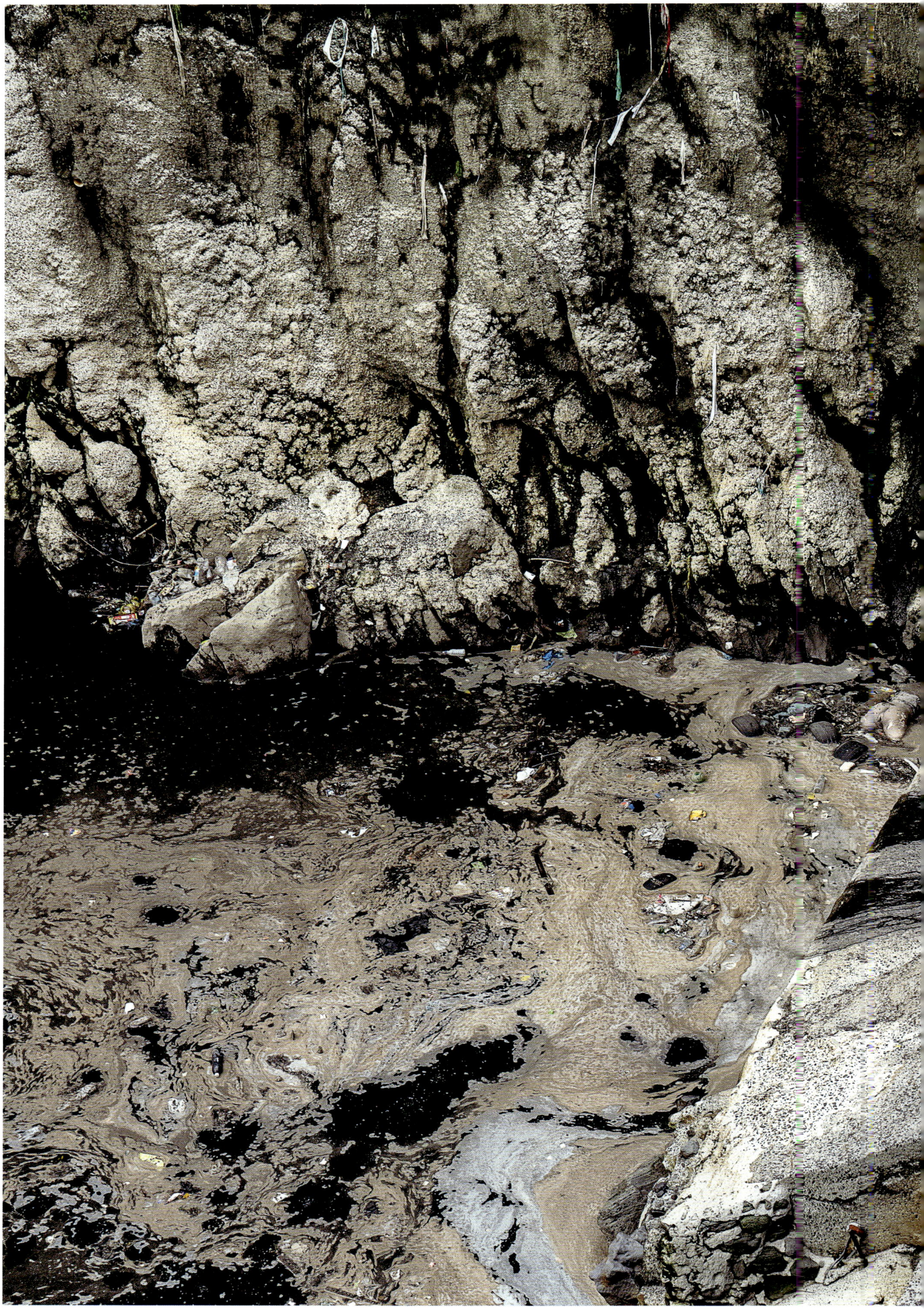

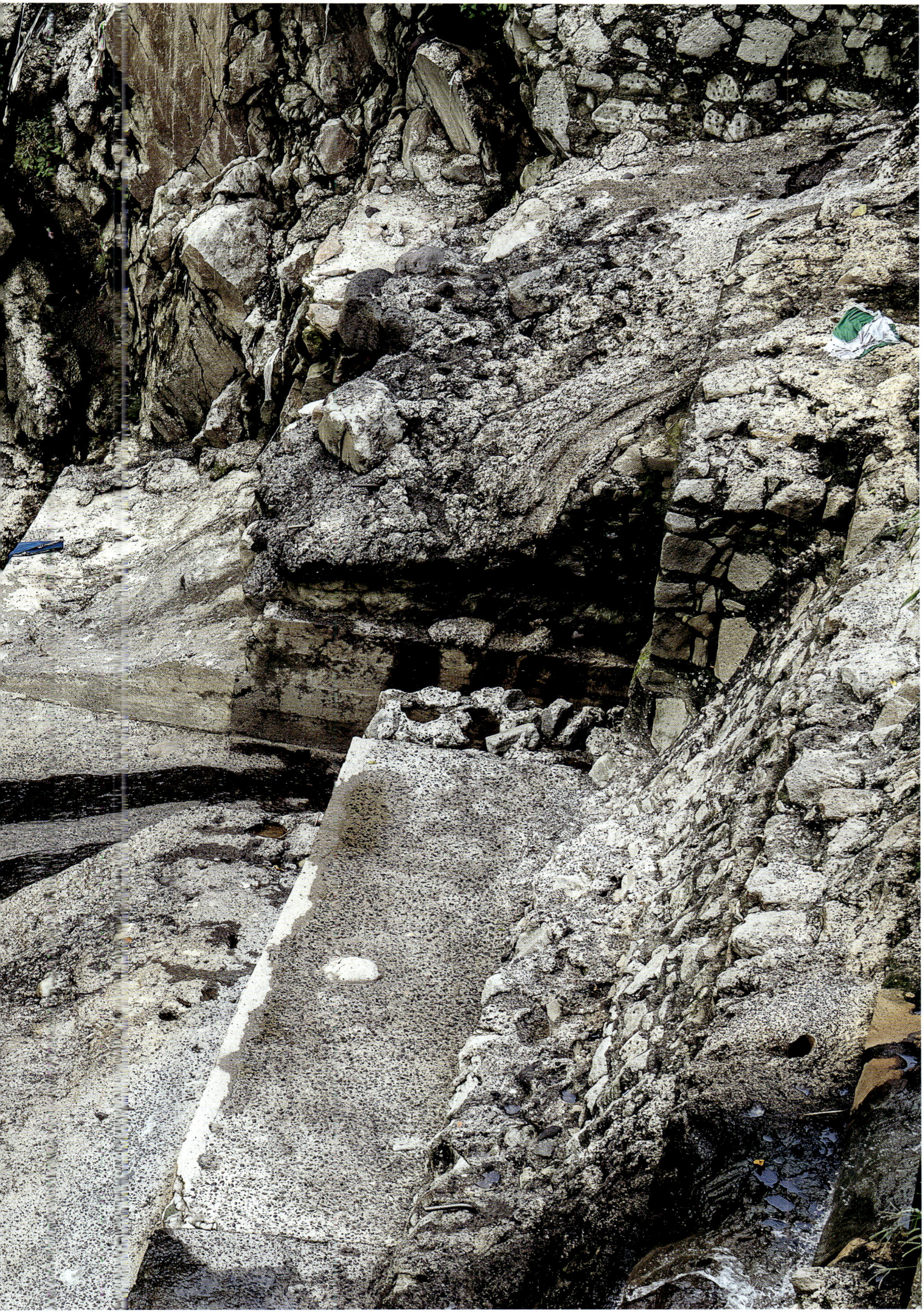

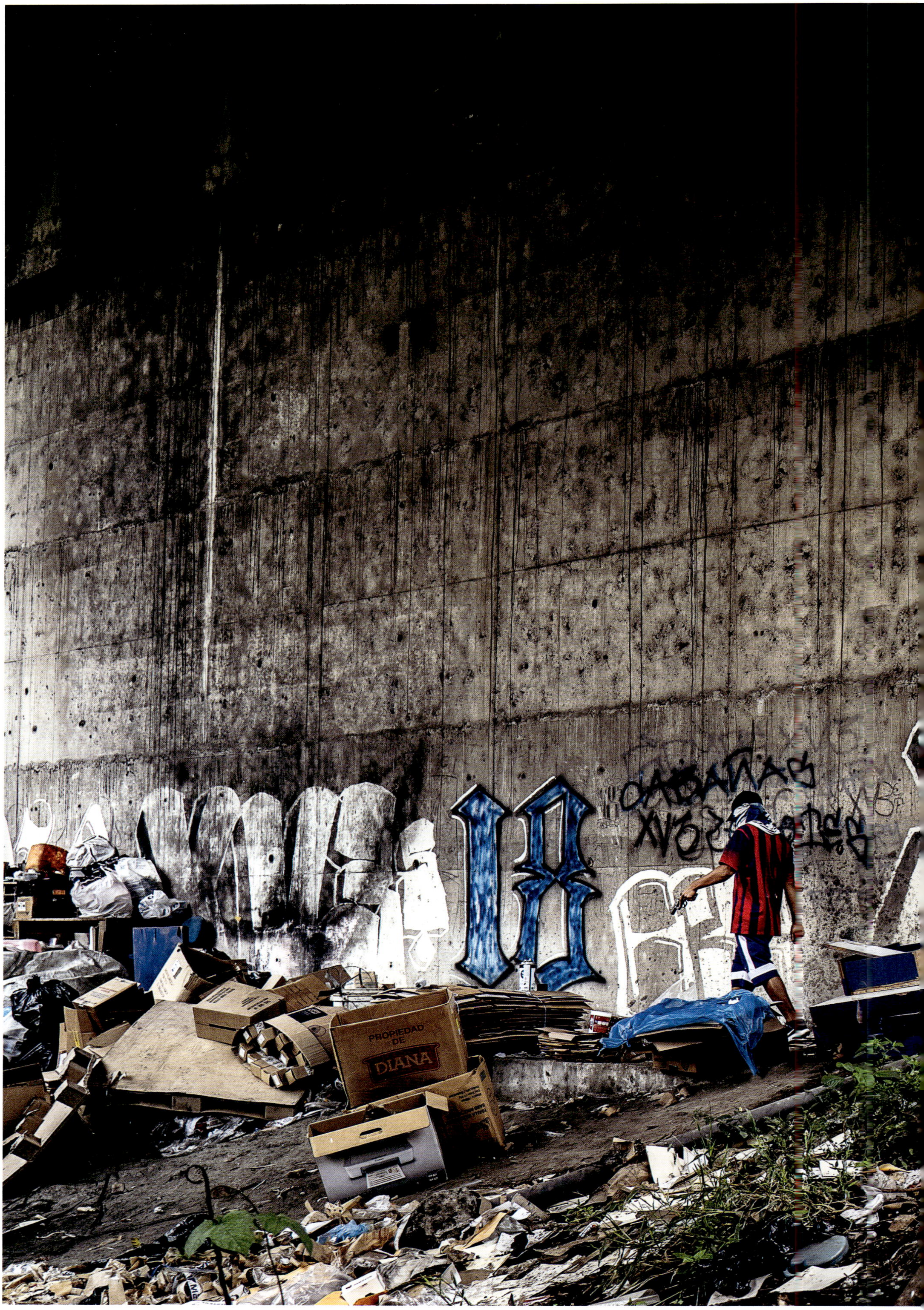
18
PROPIEDAD
DE
DIANA

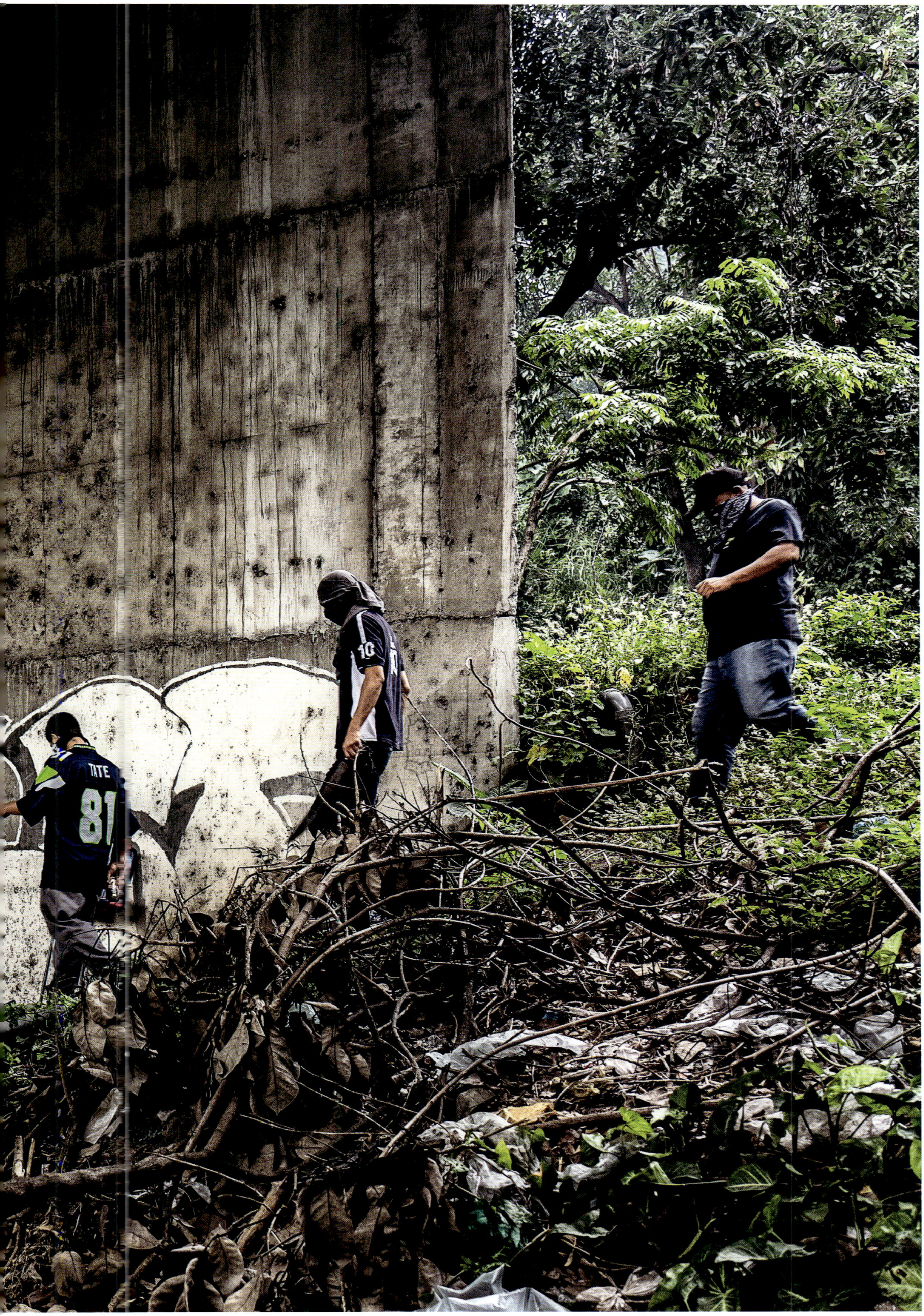

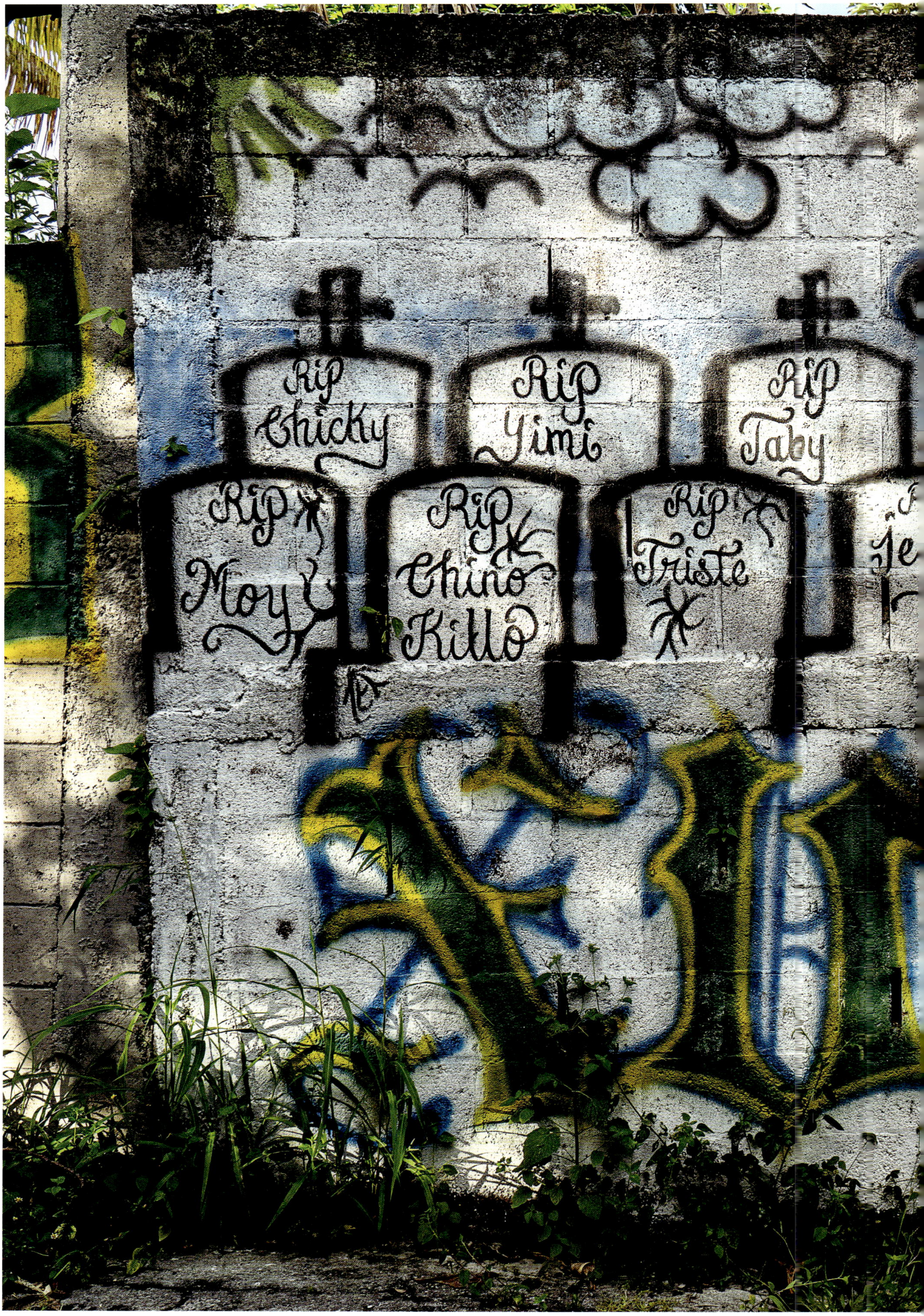
Rip Chicky
Rip Yimi
Rip Taby
Rip Moy
Rip Chino Killo
Rip Triste

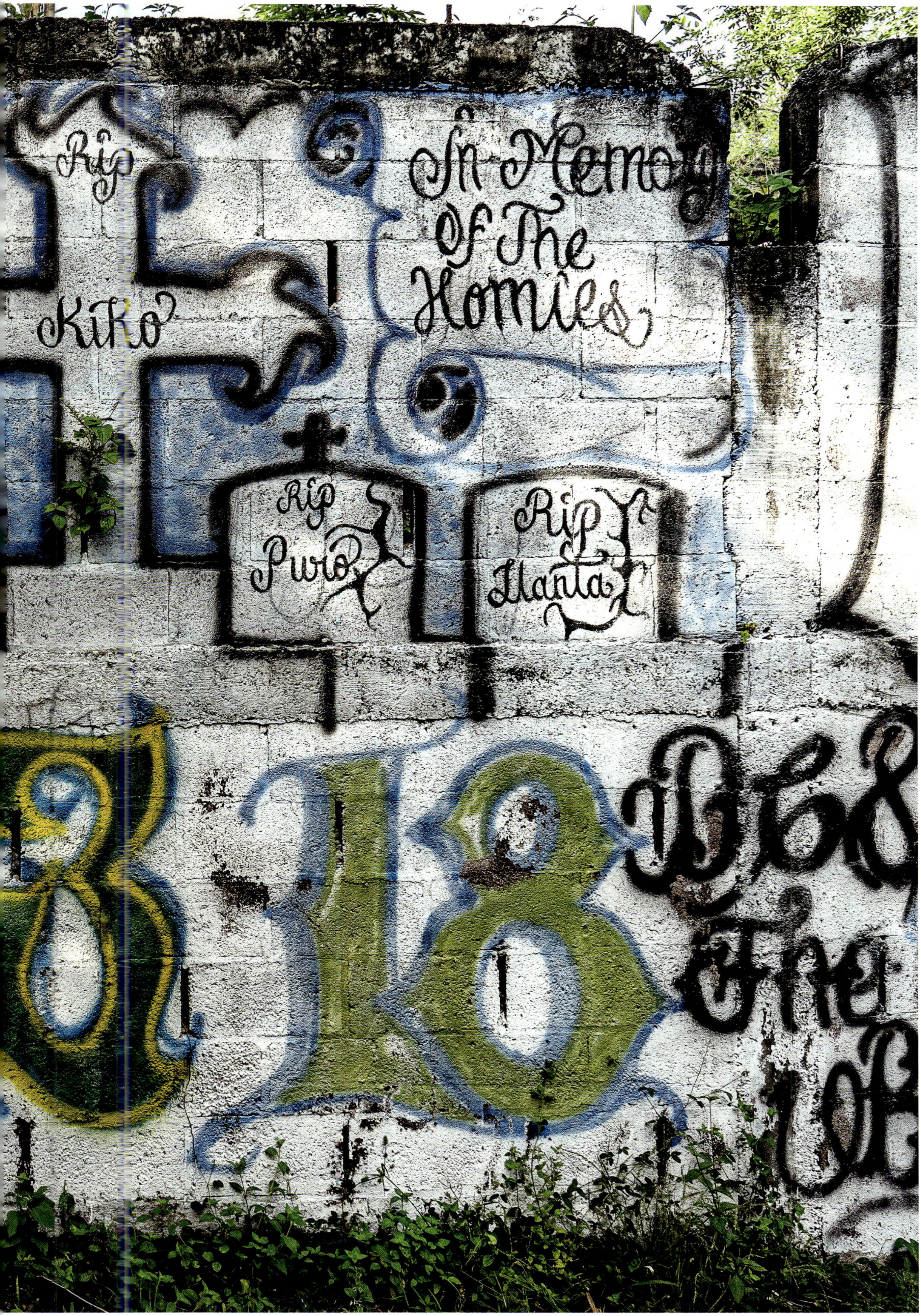
Rip
KiKo
In Memory
Of The
Homies
Rip
Puro
Rip
Llanta
18

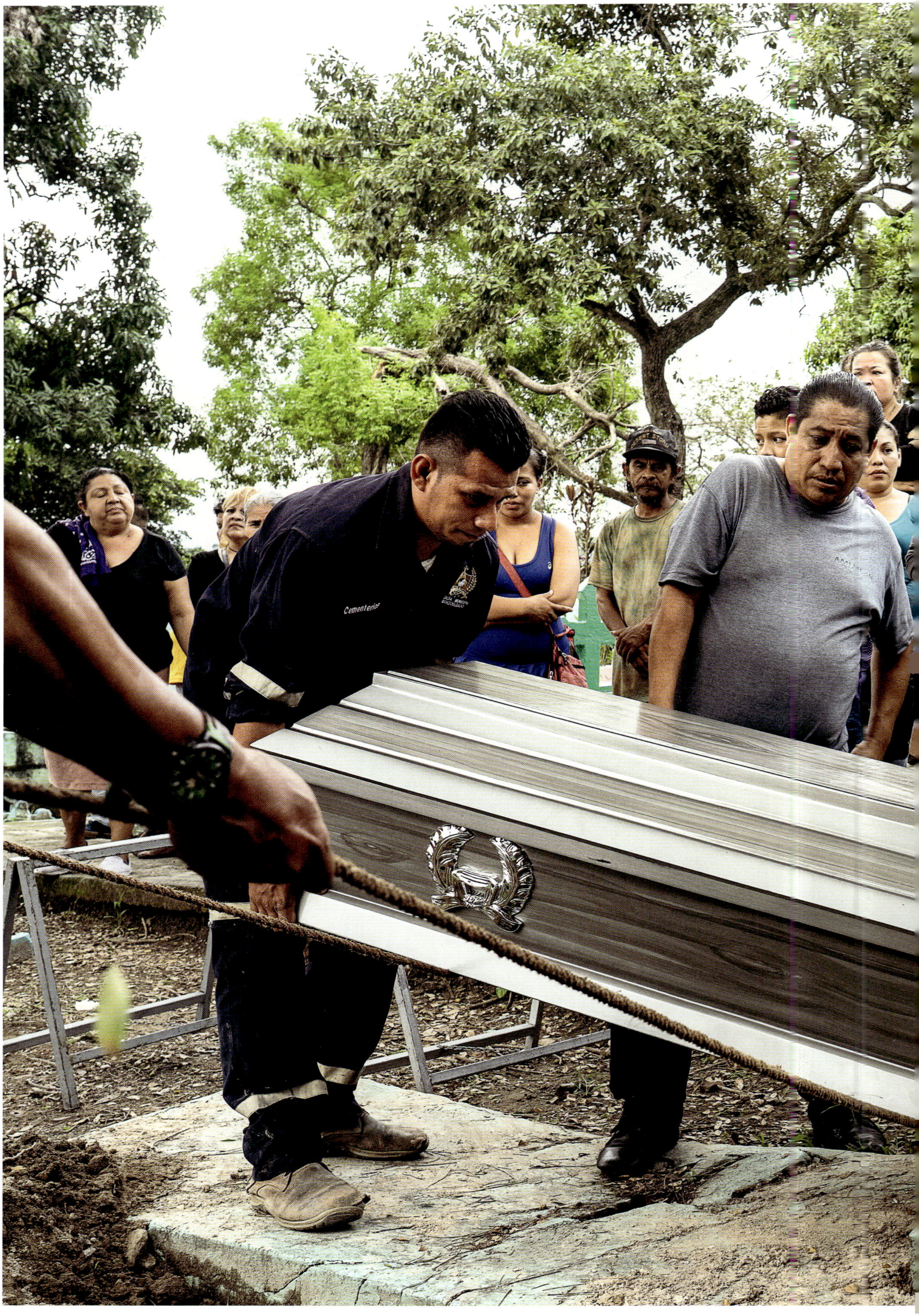
Cementerio

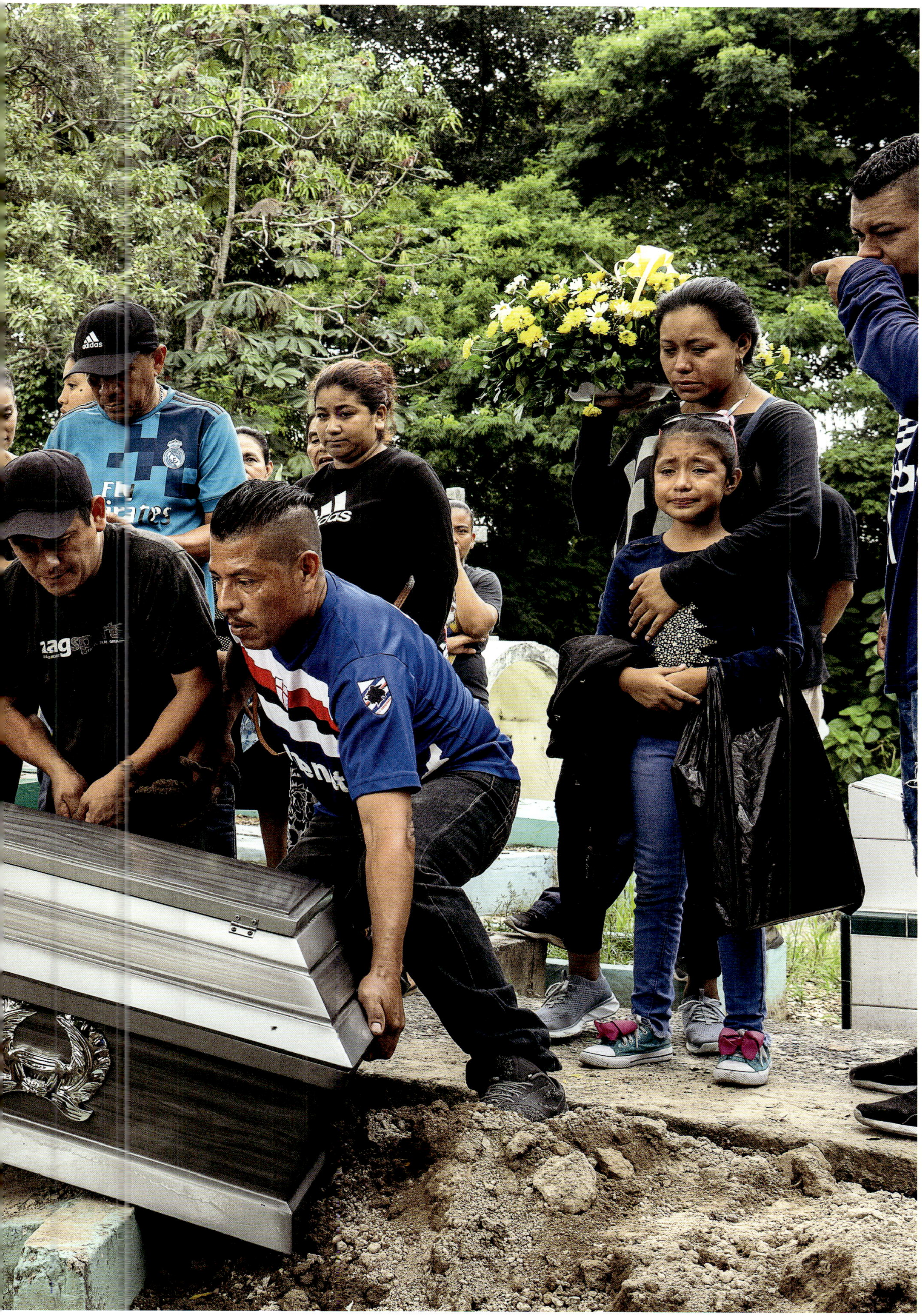
adidas

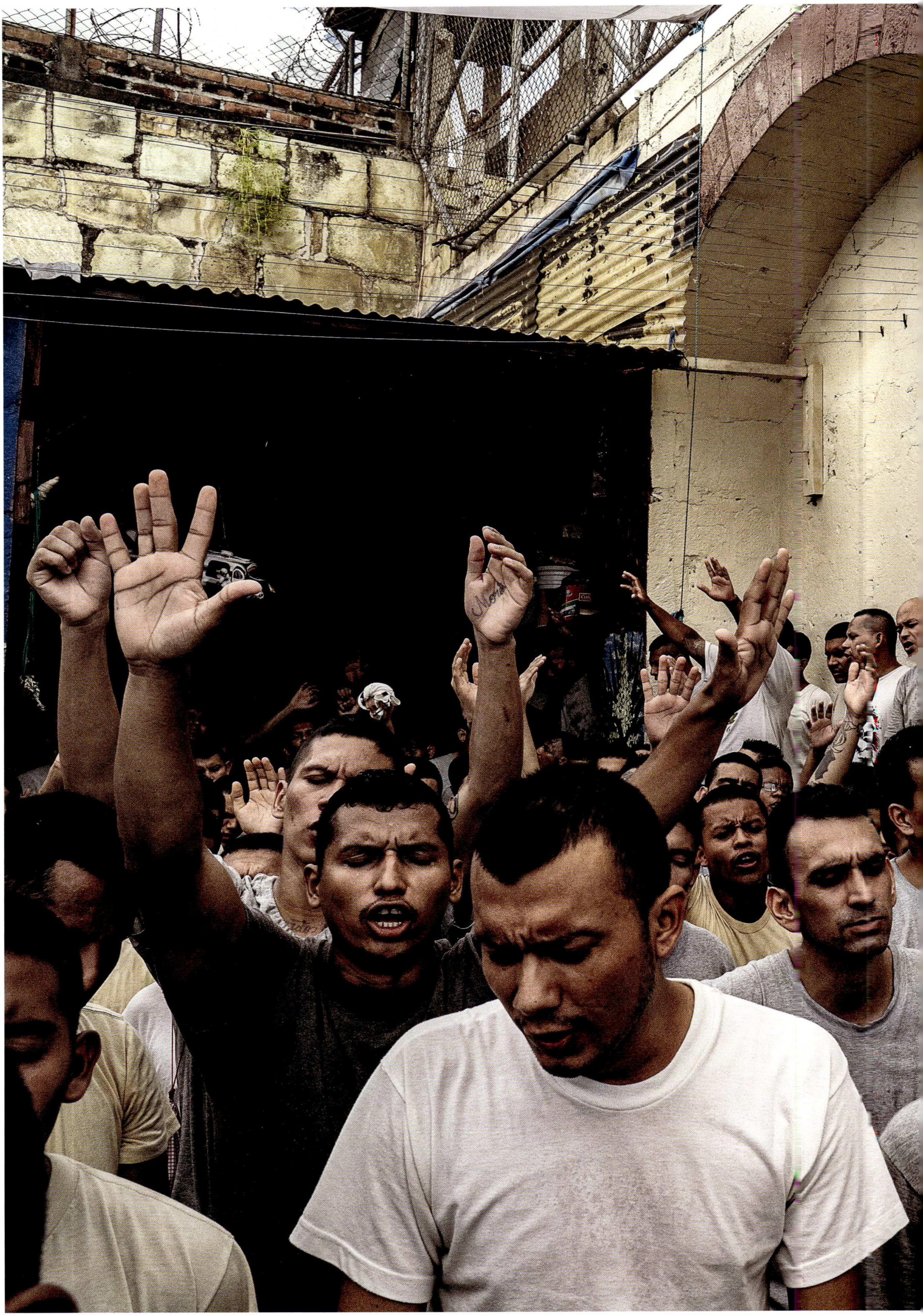

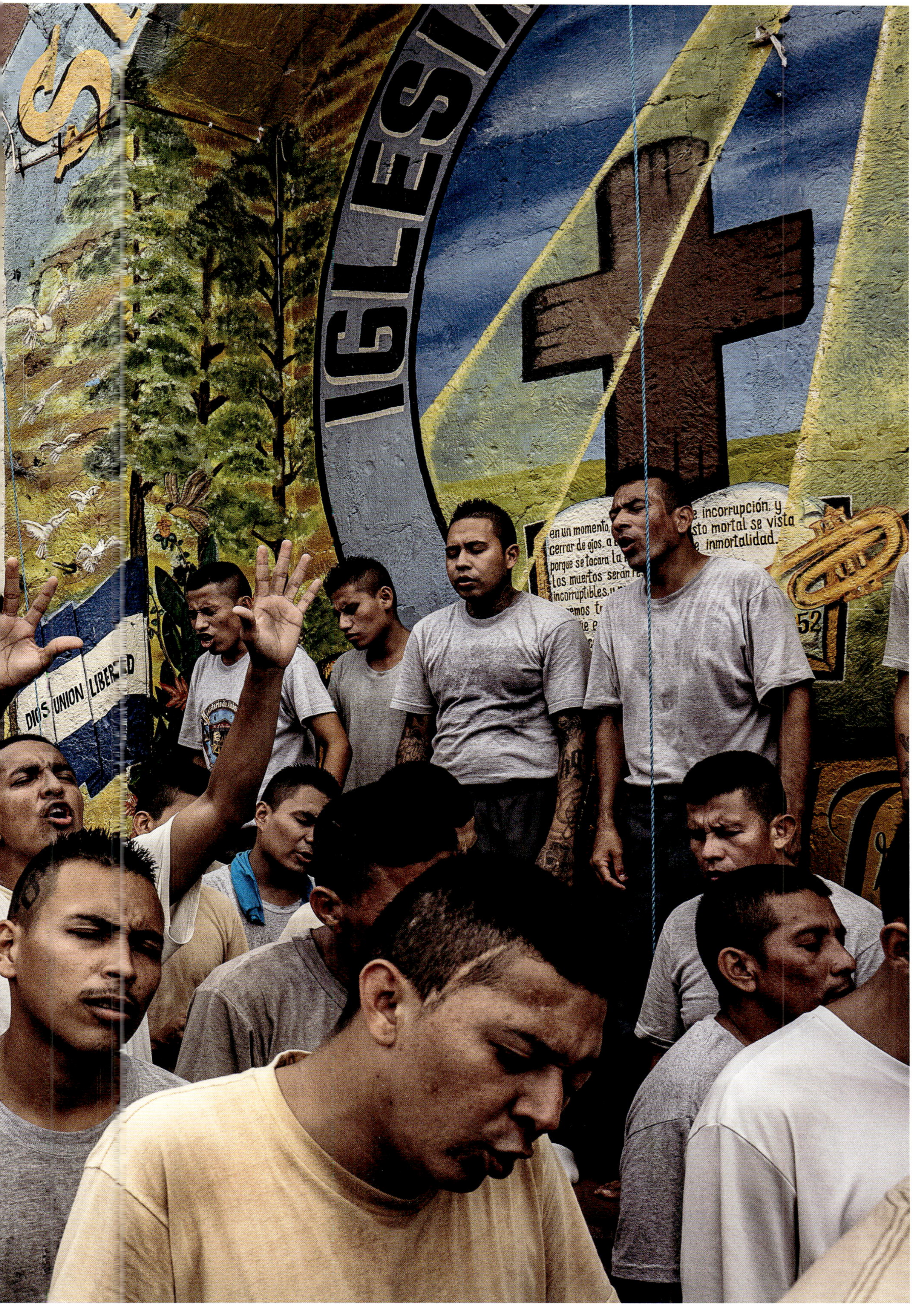
IGLESI
DIOS UNION LIBERTAD

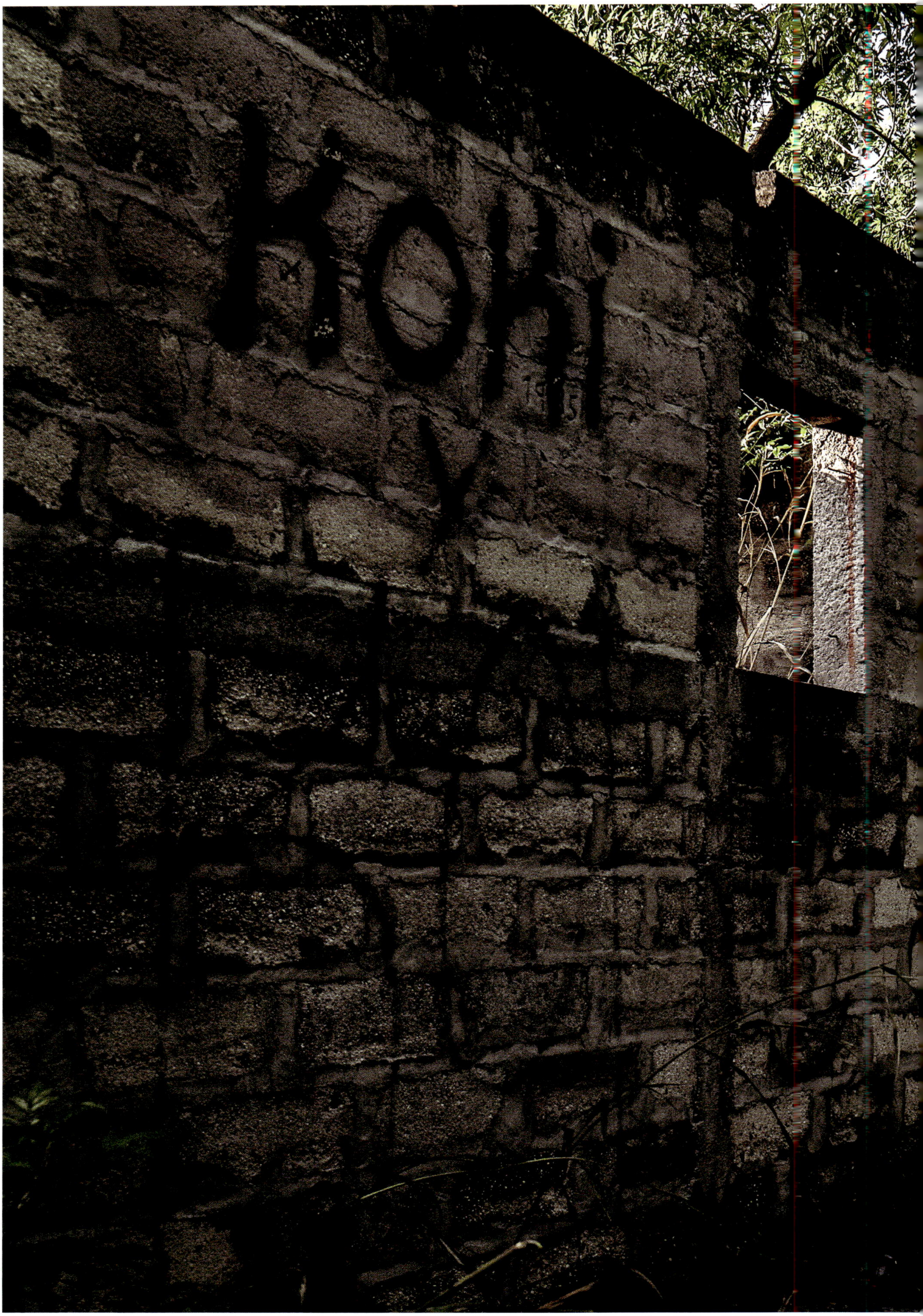

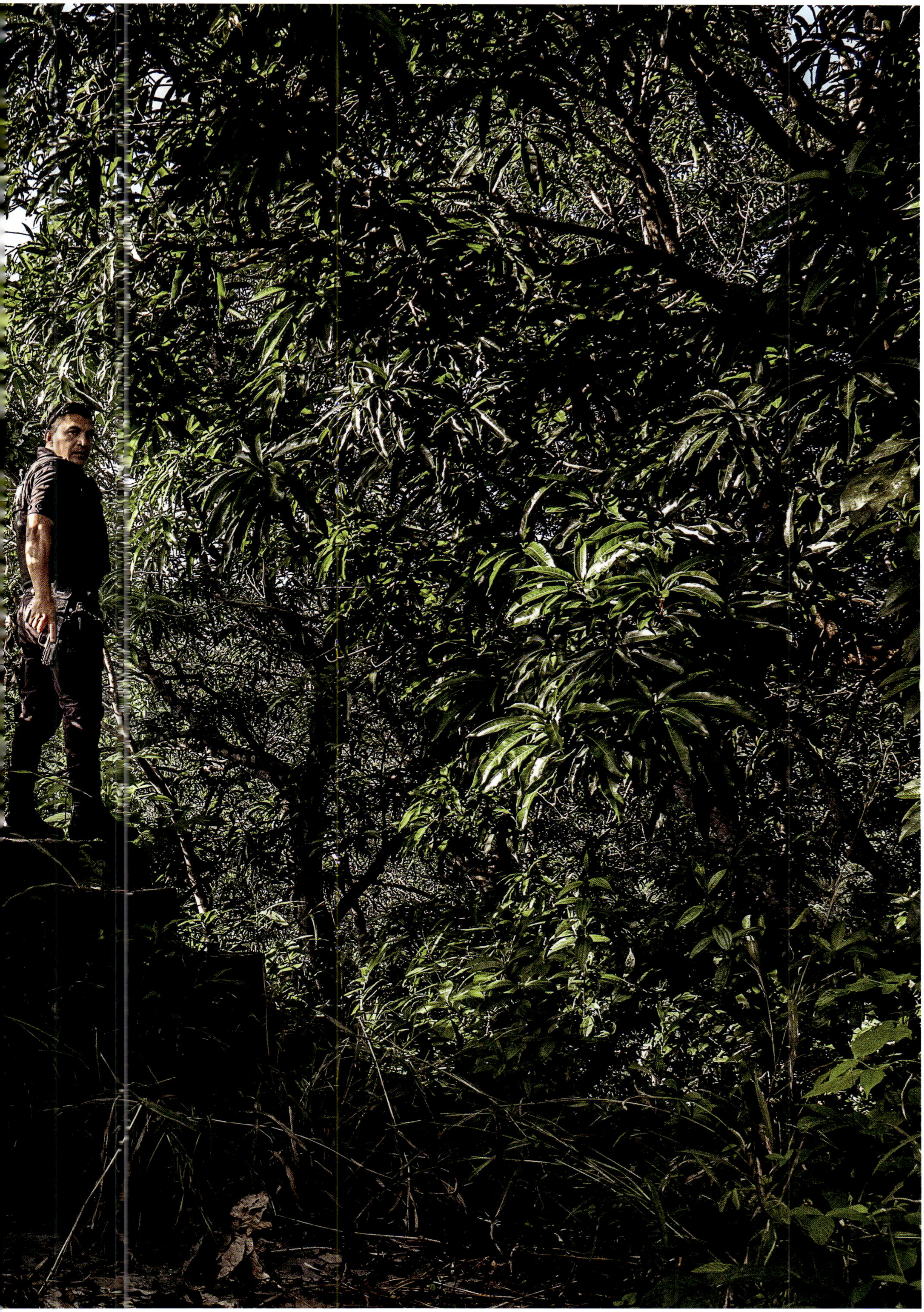

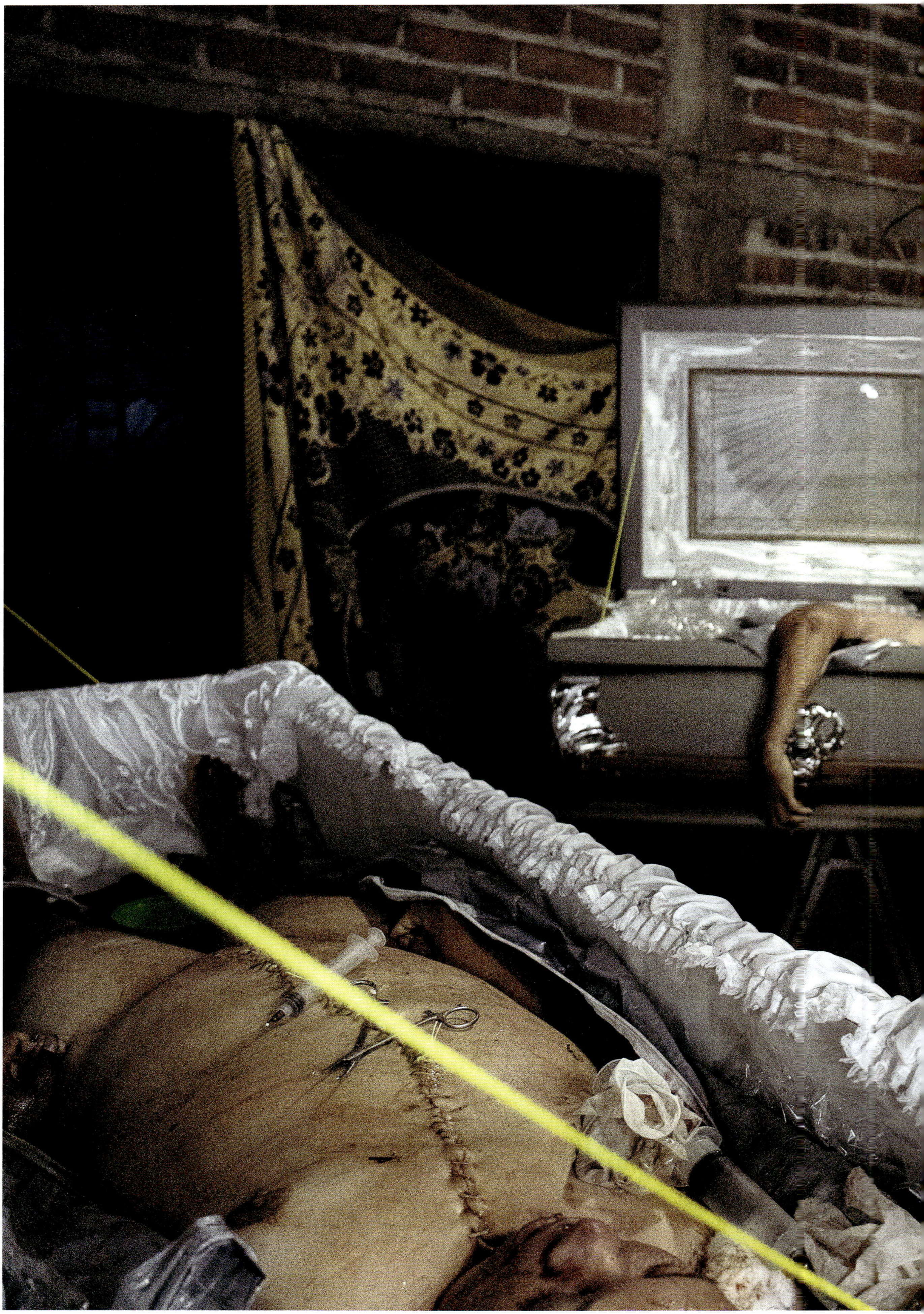

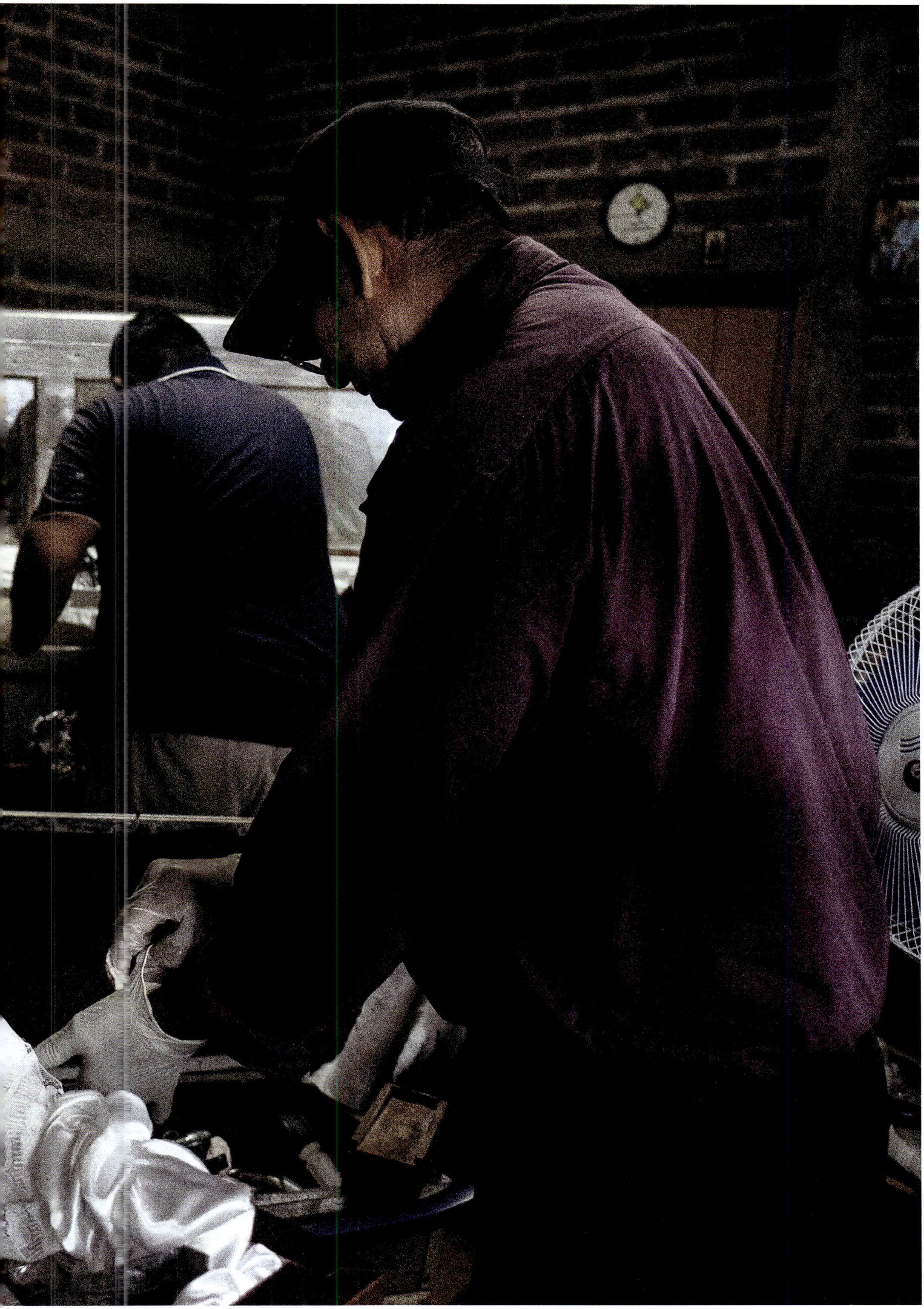

PRISONS HAVE BEEN AT THE CENTRE OF THE BUKELE ADMINISTRATION'S APPROACH TO DRIVE DOWN GANG VIOLENCE.

According to the former Minister of Justice and Security Rogelio Rivas, gang leaders inside prisons reportedly still play a large role—from behind bars—in outside gang activity. The focus of the government's measures has been on the major maximum-security gang prisons, where many leading gang members have been held.

There are different prisons for members of MS-13 and Barrio 18, but there is one prison, Penal San Francisco Gotera, where members of both gangs mix. Typically anti-Christian with gang references to satanism, the inmates here are evangelical Christians who have disavowed their gangs.

Previous administrations have attempted various prisoner reform schemes—the most notable one, Yo Cambio (I Change), attempts to rehabilitate prisoners through education and skills training. Initiated in June 2014, it has become a new model for prison management. With many different methods of rehabilitation including cultural initiatives, spiritual teaching and work training, the long-term goal for the programme is to release prisoners back into society with renewed socialisation and work skills.

On 26 December 2019 President Bukele announced the Chalatenango Penal Center—one of the largest gang prison's in El Salvador—would close. That day, six hundred inmates were transferred to other prisons and the remaining 730 were transported shortly after.

Following an explosion of gang-related violence in April 2020, Bukele's administration made an unprecedented change: they placed members of rival gangs MS-13 and La 18 together in six prisons across the country—many sharing the same cells. The president then ordered the suspension of all activities in the prisons—total isolation for 24 hours. Shortly after the prison restructuring was in place, he commented via his Twitter account: 'They will be inside, in the dark, with their friends from the other gang.'

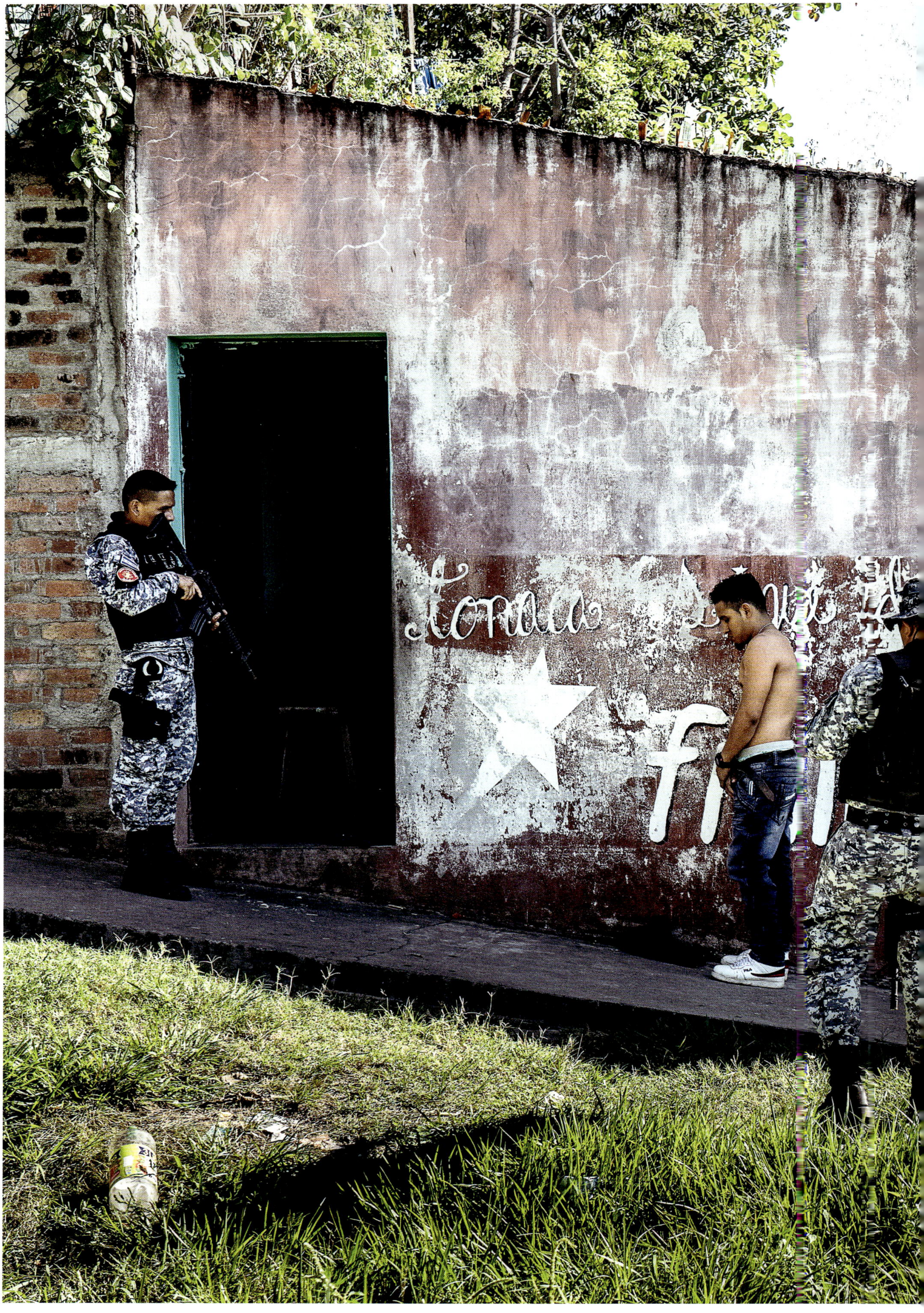

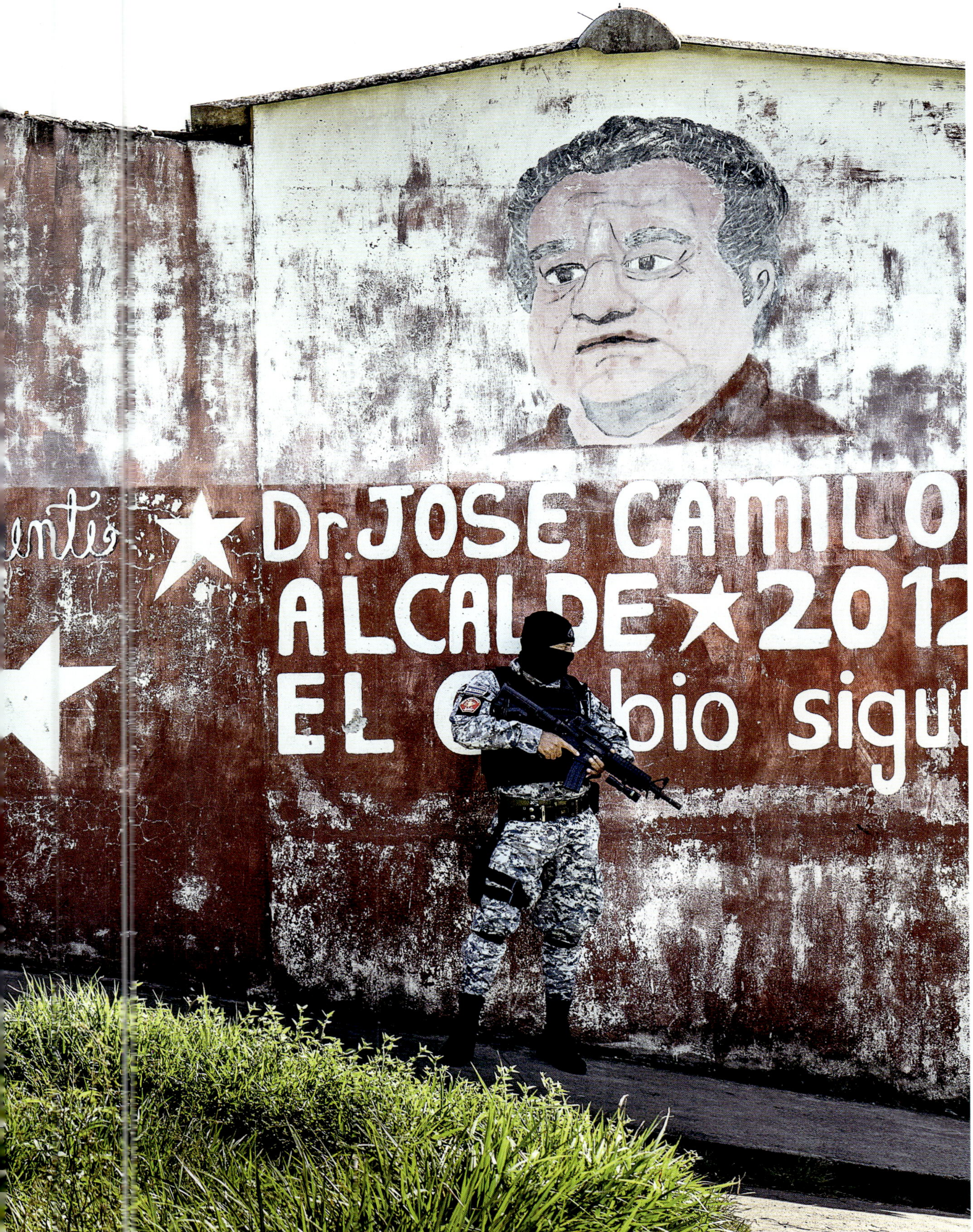
Dr. JOSE CAMILO
ALCALDE
EL

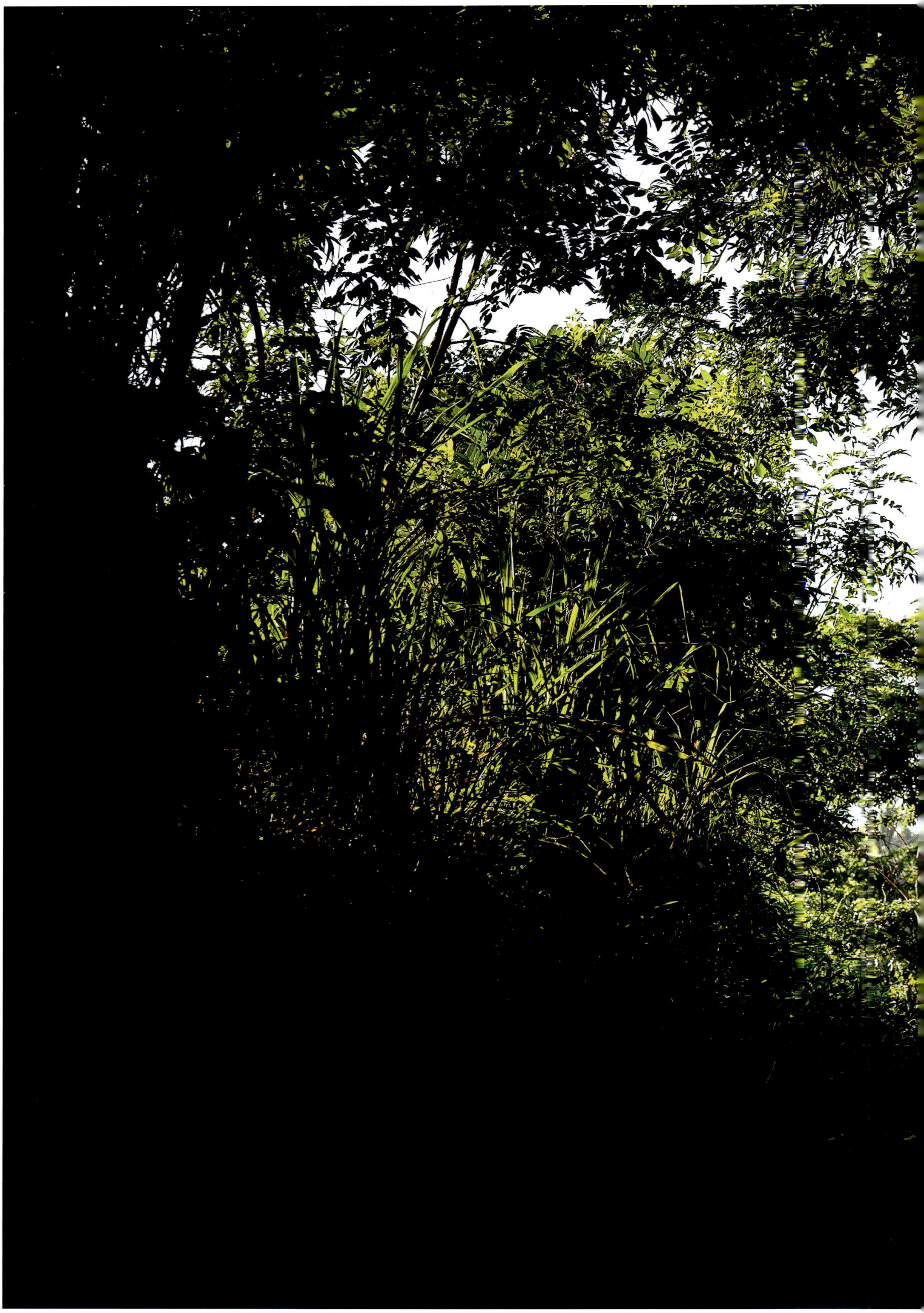

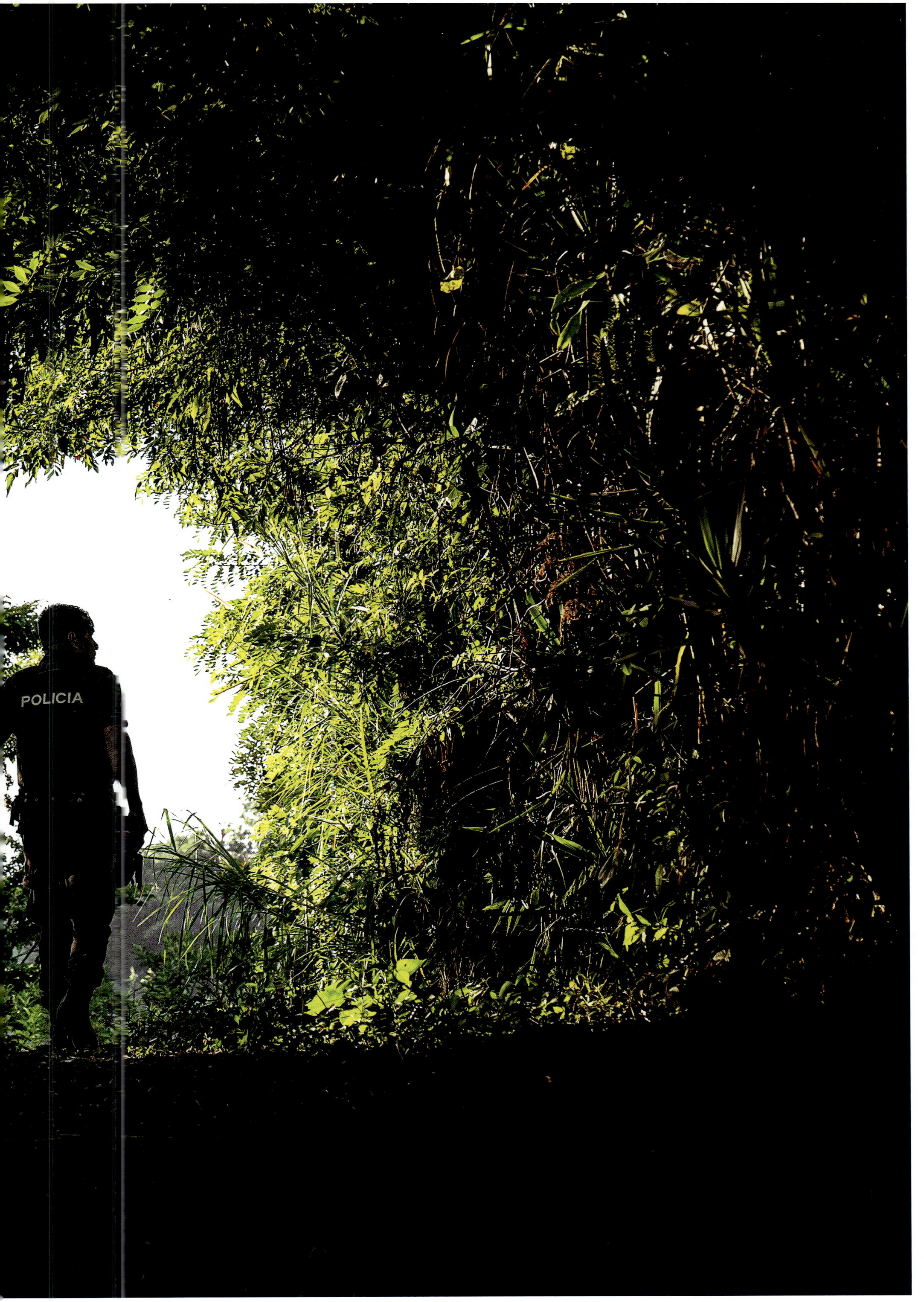
POLICIA

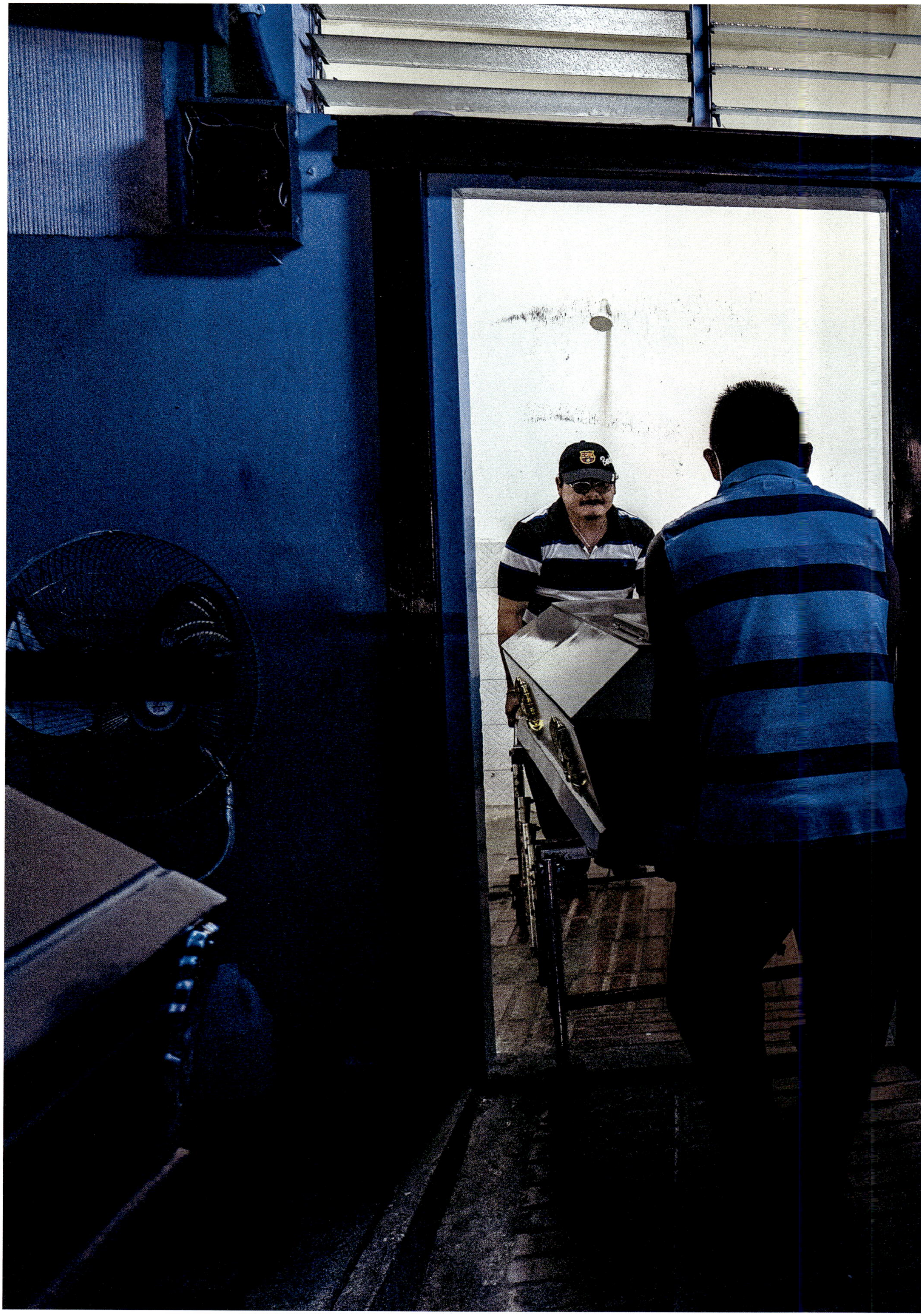

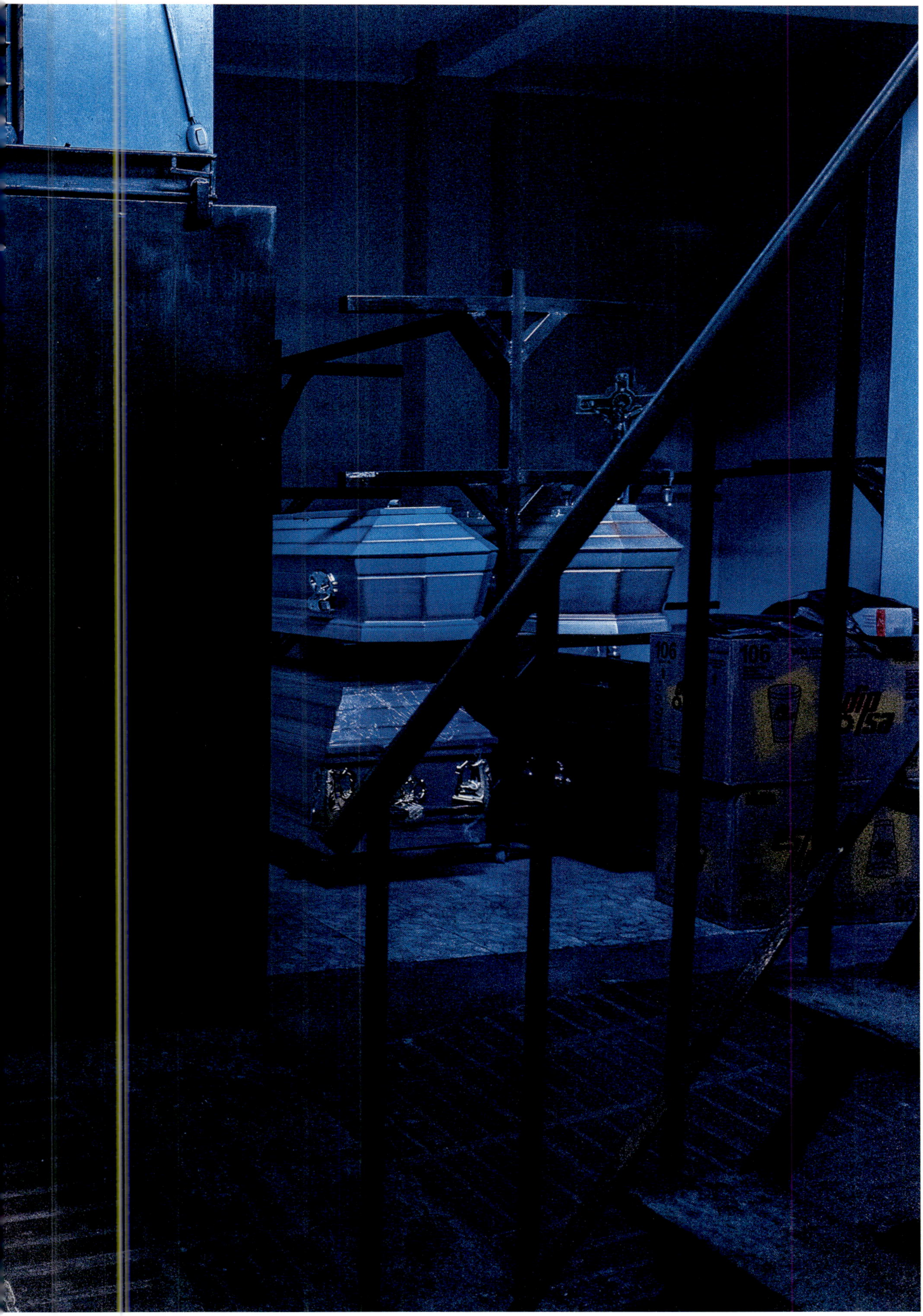
106
106

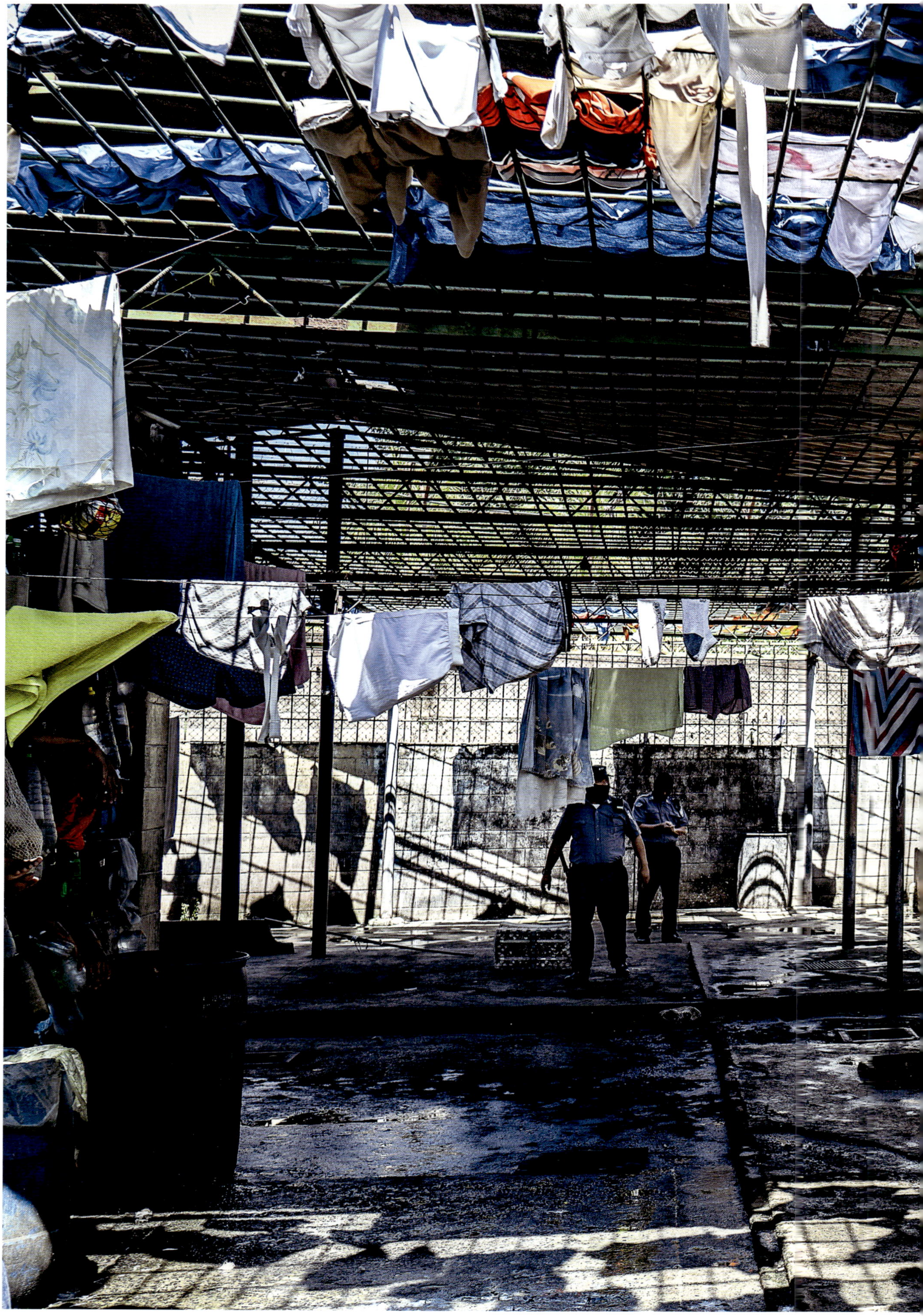

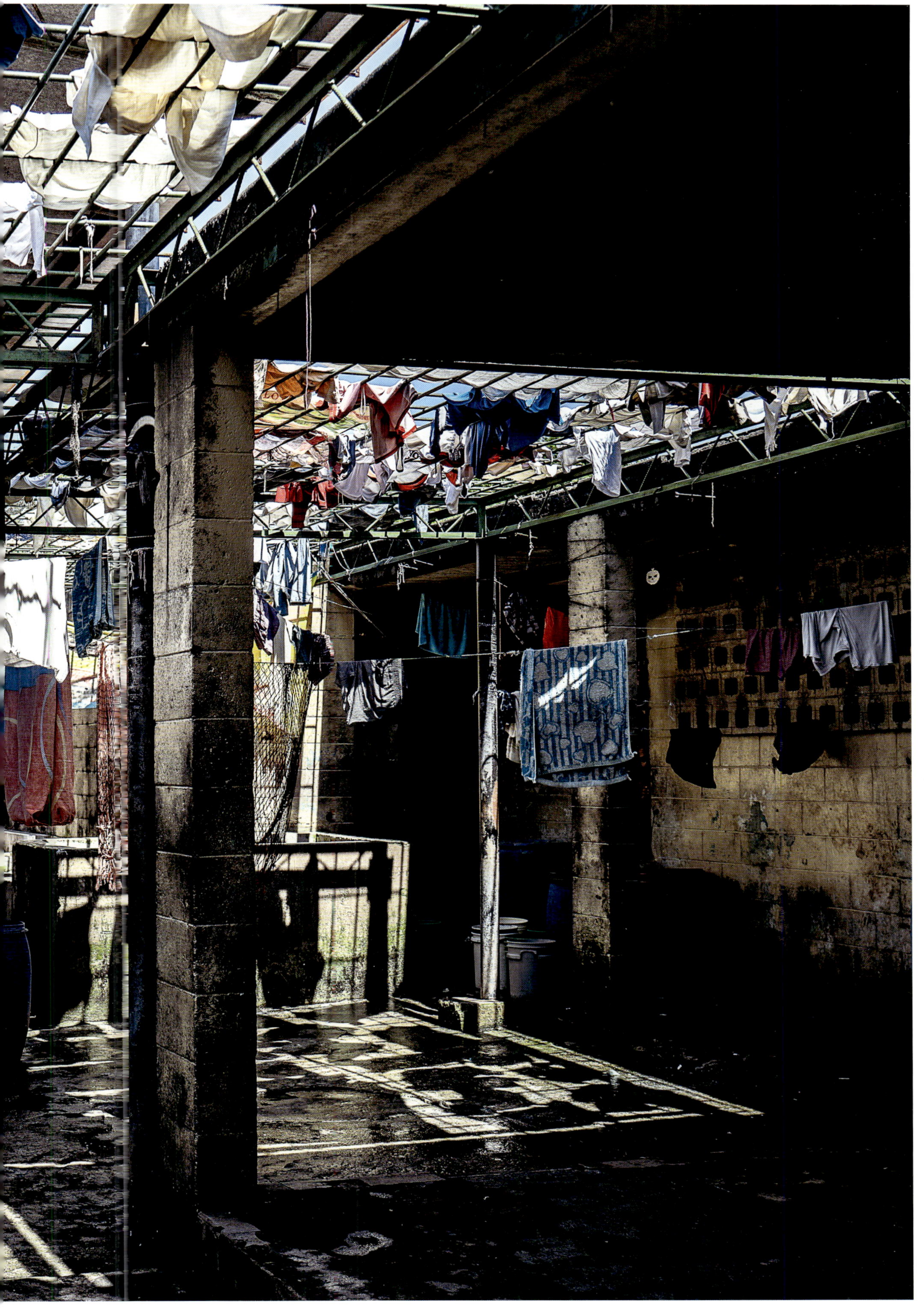

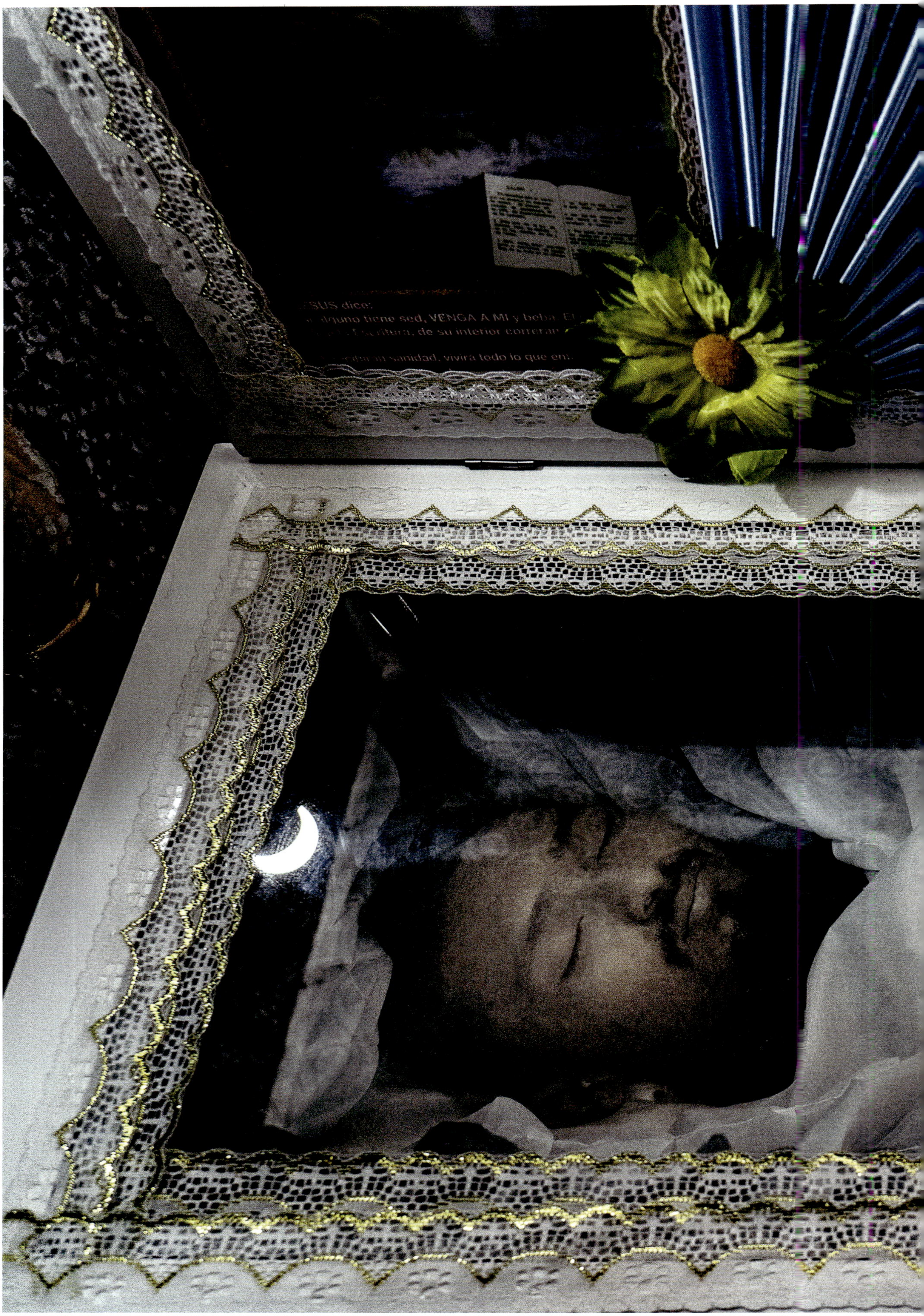

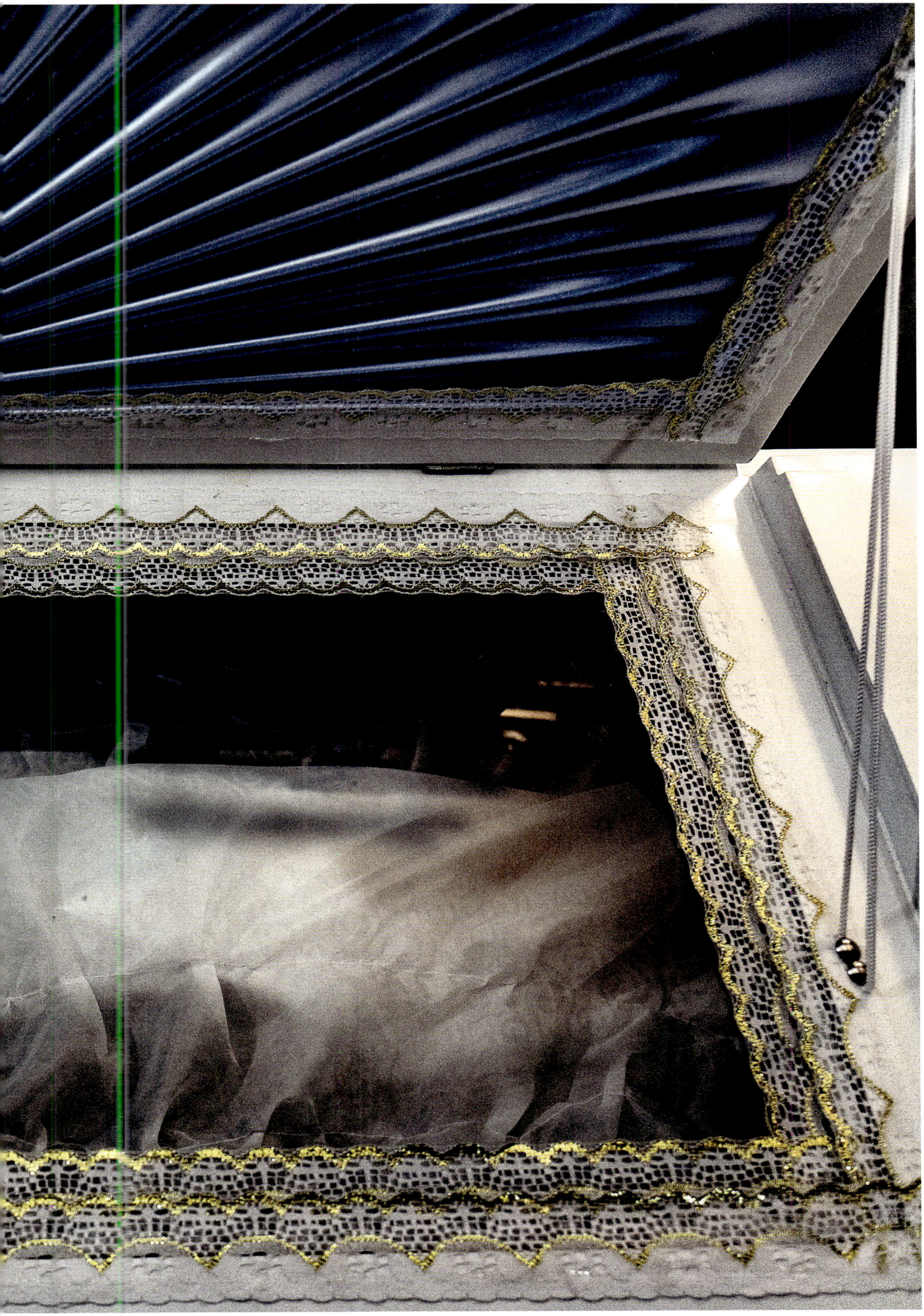

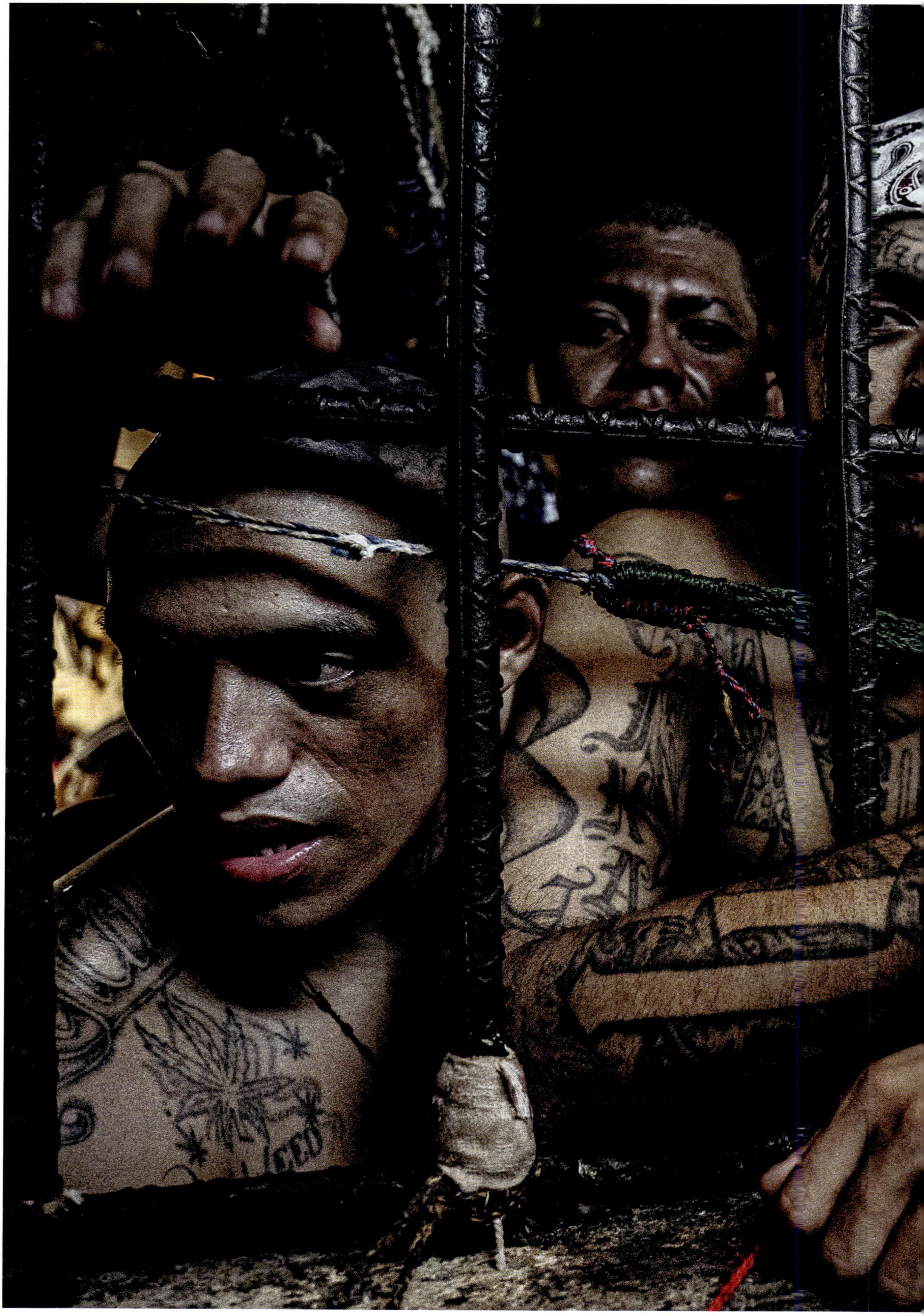

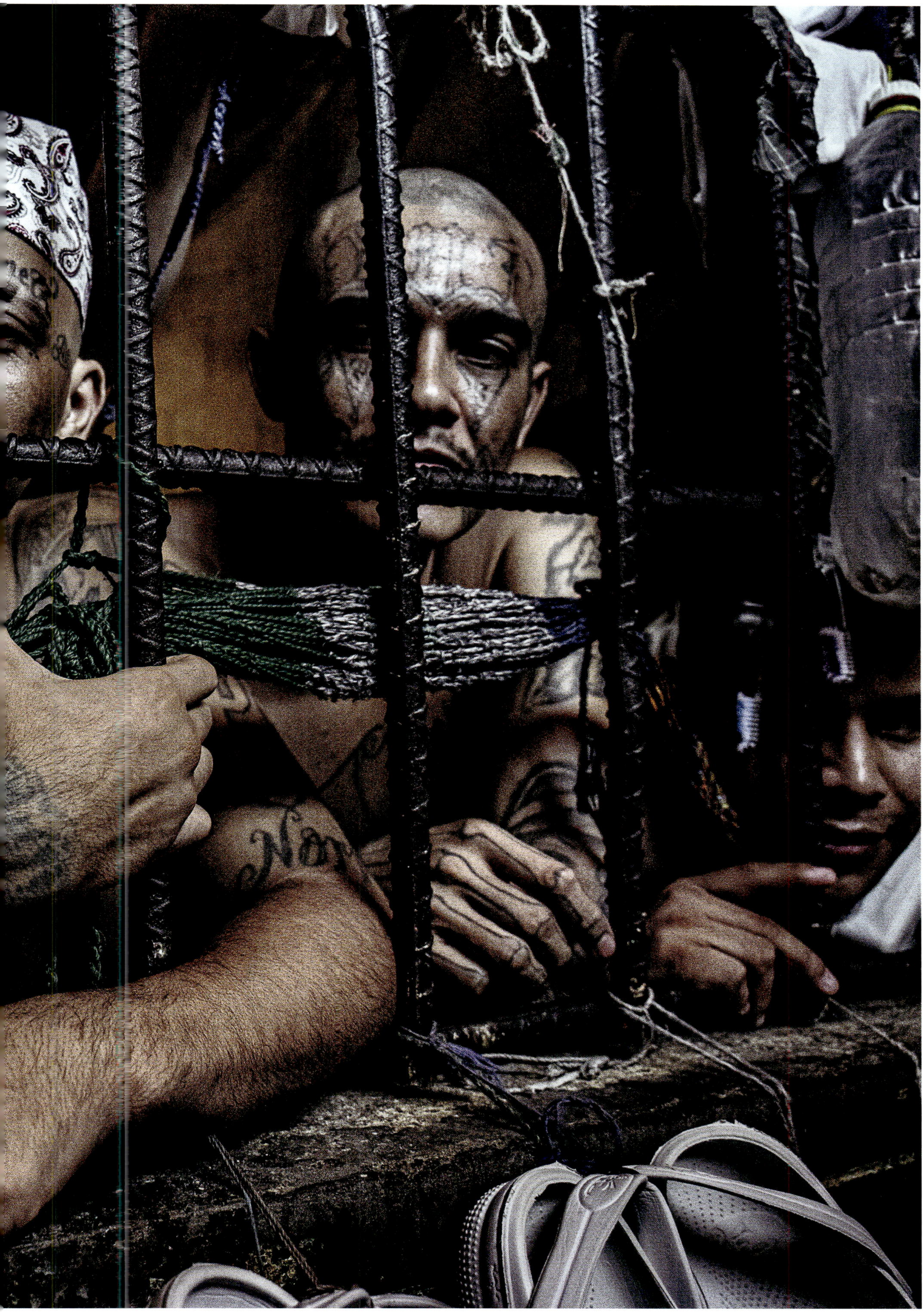

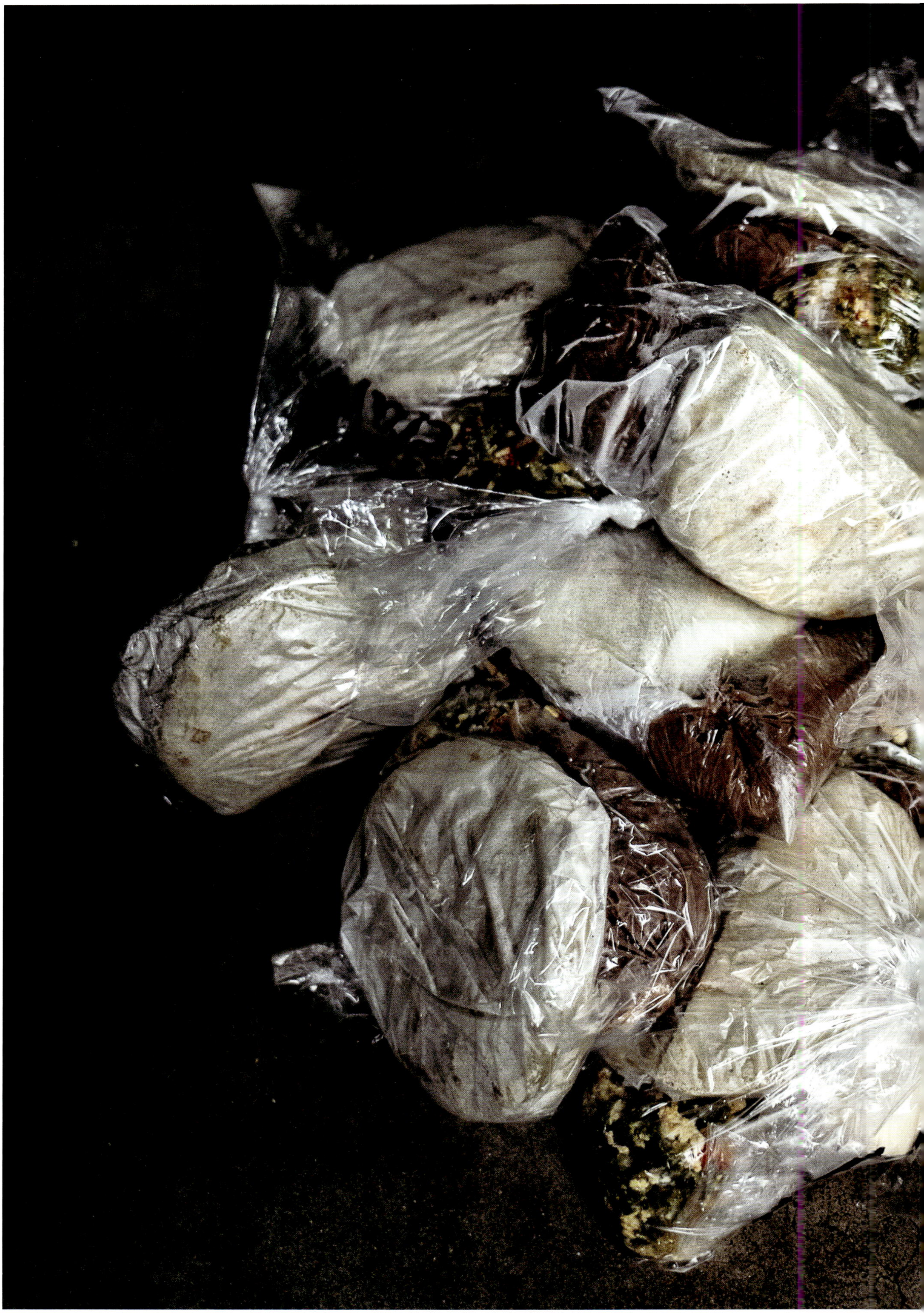

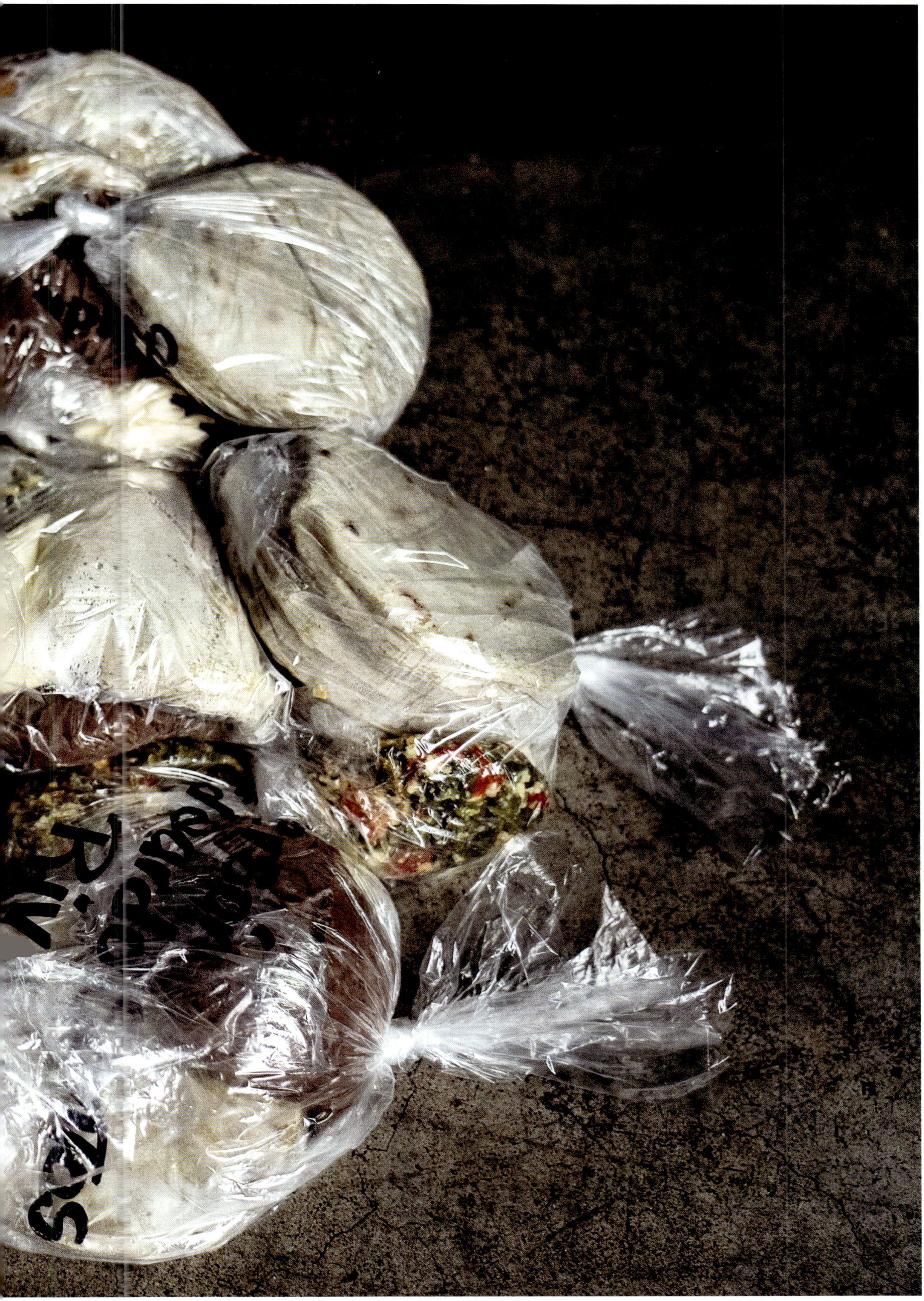

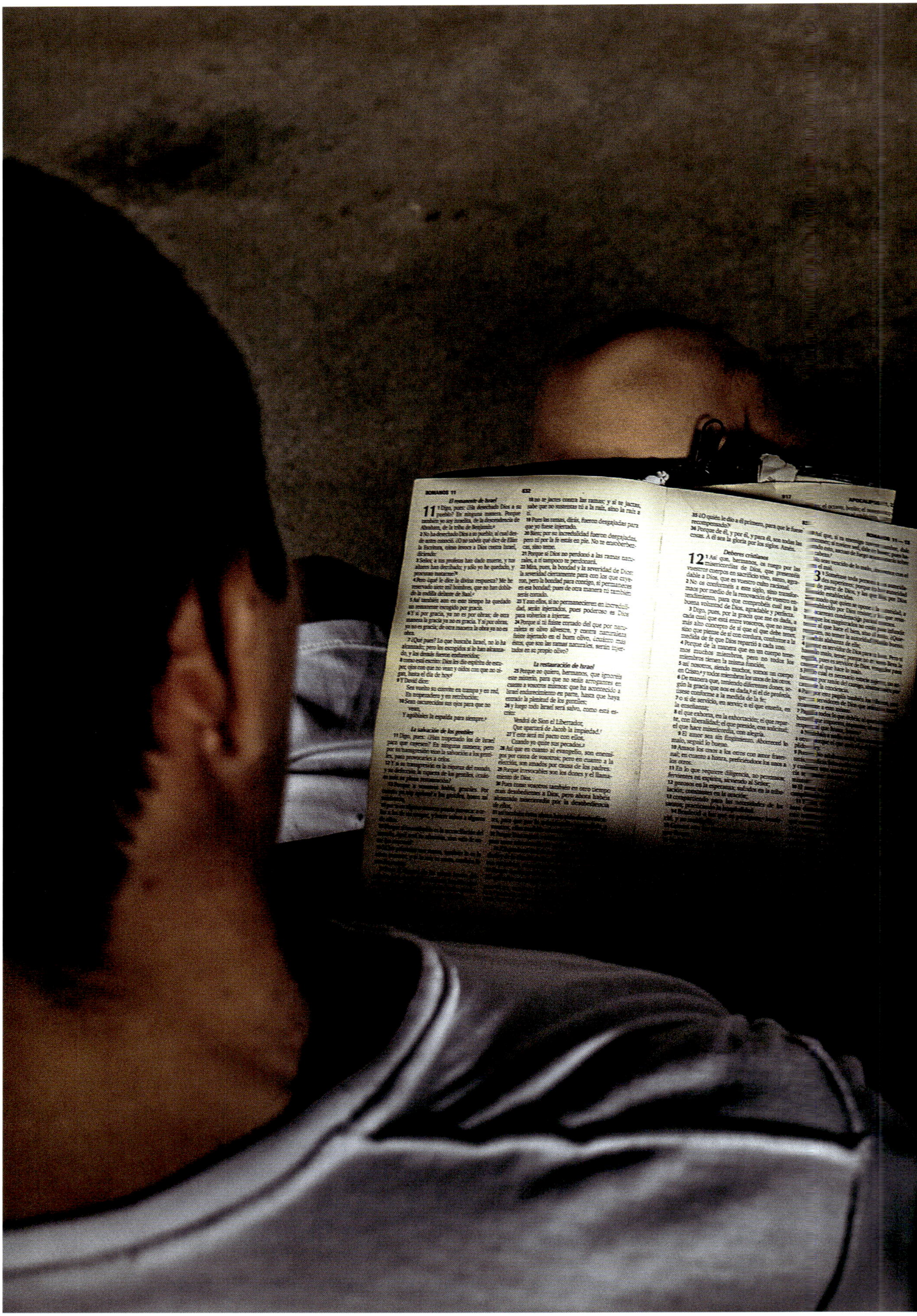

La restauración de Israel
Deberes cristianos

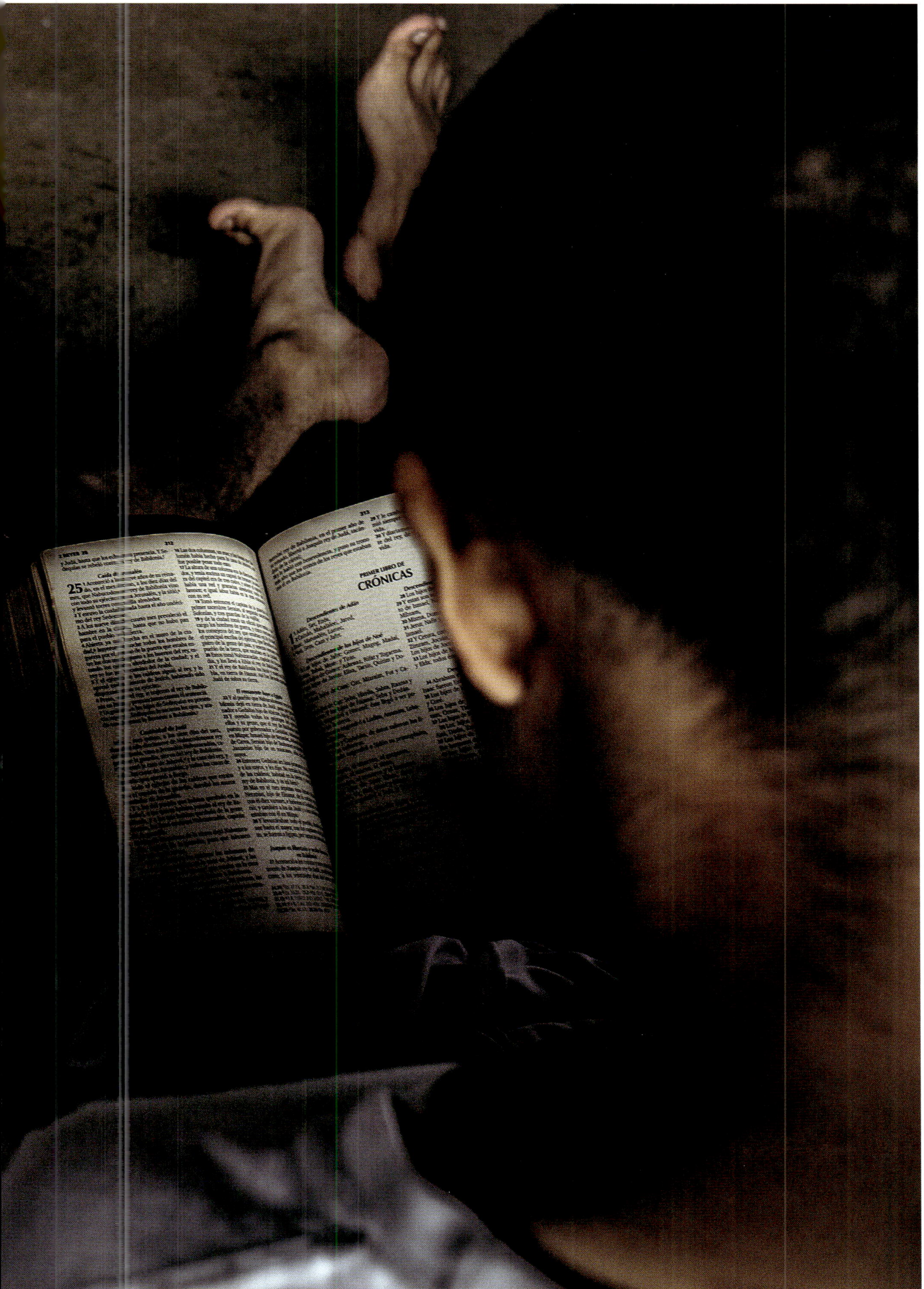
PRIMER LIBRO DE
CRÓNICAS

PART OF THE REASON WHY THE ERADICATION OF GANG VIOLENCE HAS BEEN SUCH A CHALLENGE IS THE MANNER IN WHICH GANGS OPERATE IN EL SALVADOR.

Unlike other global extortion organisations like Japan's Yakuza or the Italian Camorra, El Salvador's gangs more closely resemble internationally franchised street gangs than centrally led organisations. Local chapters or 'cliques' operate largely independently, and even rival chapters of the same gang are often at odds with one another. In 2021, there were as many as 250 individual cliques in El Salvador, all operating at a local, neighbourhood level.

Despite the clashes that exist, there is some leadership that directs these cliques. The 2012 truce for instance, was led by gang leaders, but had a major impact at the street level. The truce was mediated by a Catholic bishop, Father Fabio Colindres, and a former FLMN guerrilla, Raul Mijango. The government allowed the two mediators access to maximum-security prisons where gang leaders of both MS-13 and Barrio 18 were serving sentences. Leaders of both gangs agreed to cease attacks on police and civilians, and in turn, demanded their members be rehabilitated into society and not be discriminated against for tattoos identifying them as gang members. They also requested an affirmative action law for former gang members looking for work.

El Salvador's police chief stated in 2014 that turf wars between the gangs—which had not been fully addressed in the truce—were behind the rise in attacks. In response, gang leaders argued the government had stopped cooperating with the gangs and had reduced communication between incarcerated gang leaders and local chapters.

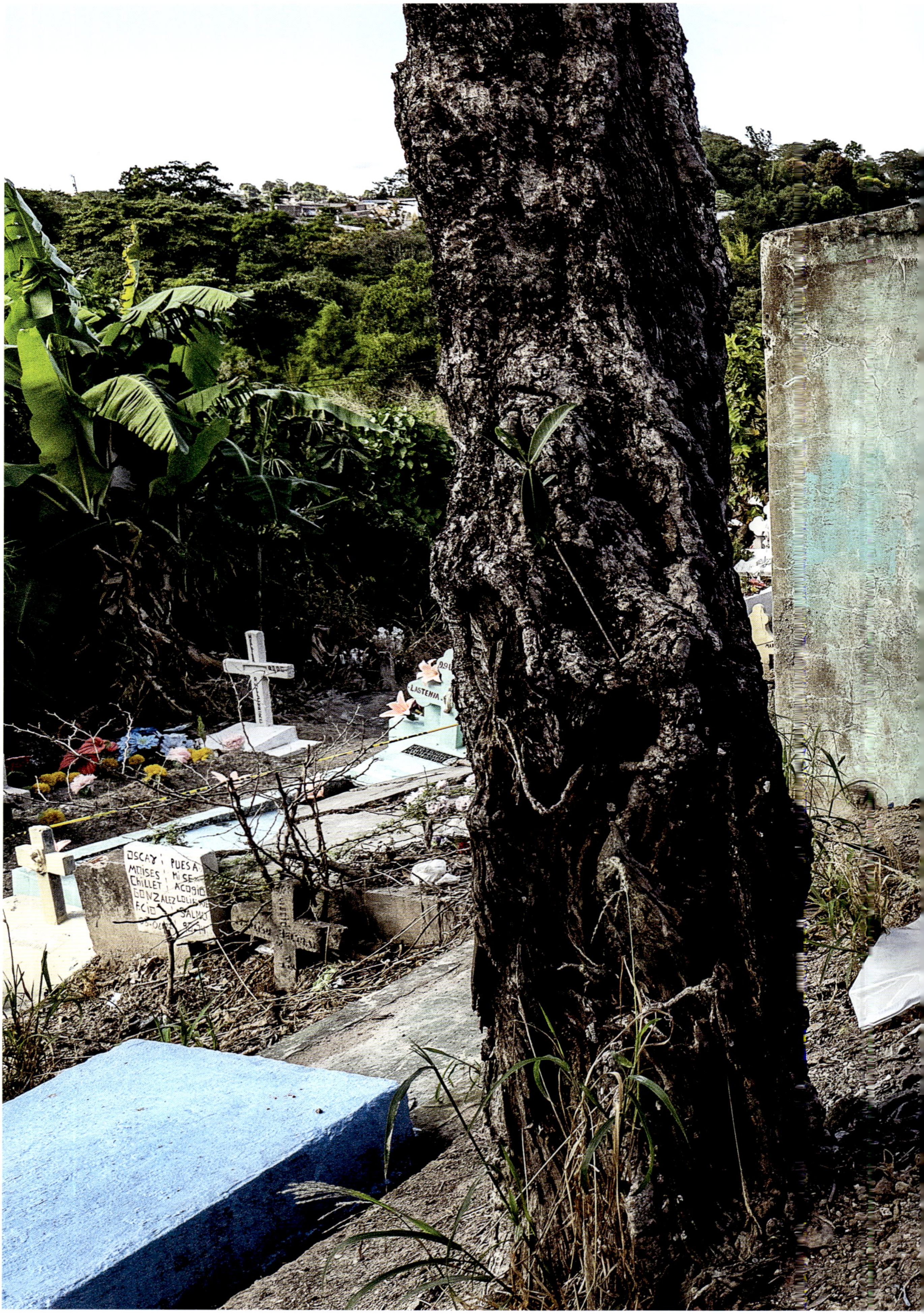
OSCAR MOISES CHILLET GONZALEZ F.CIO
PUES A MI SE ACOGIO
LASTENIA

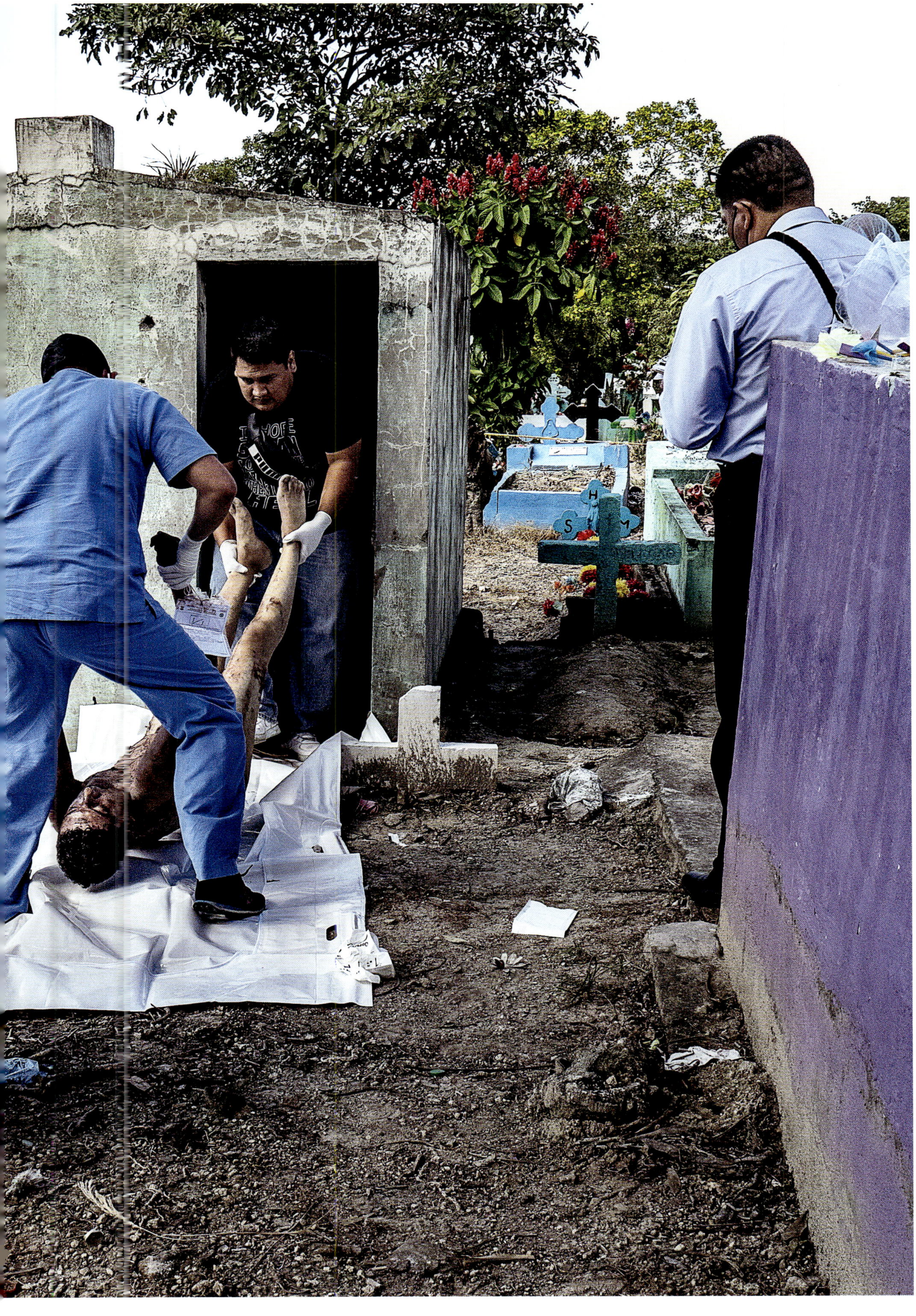

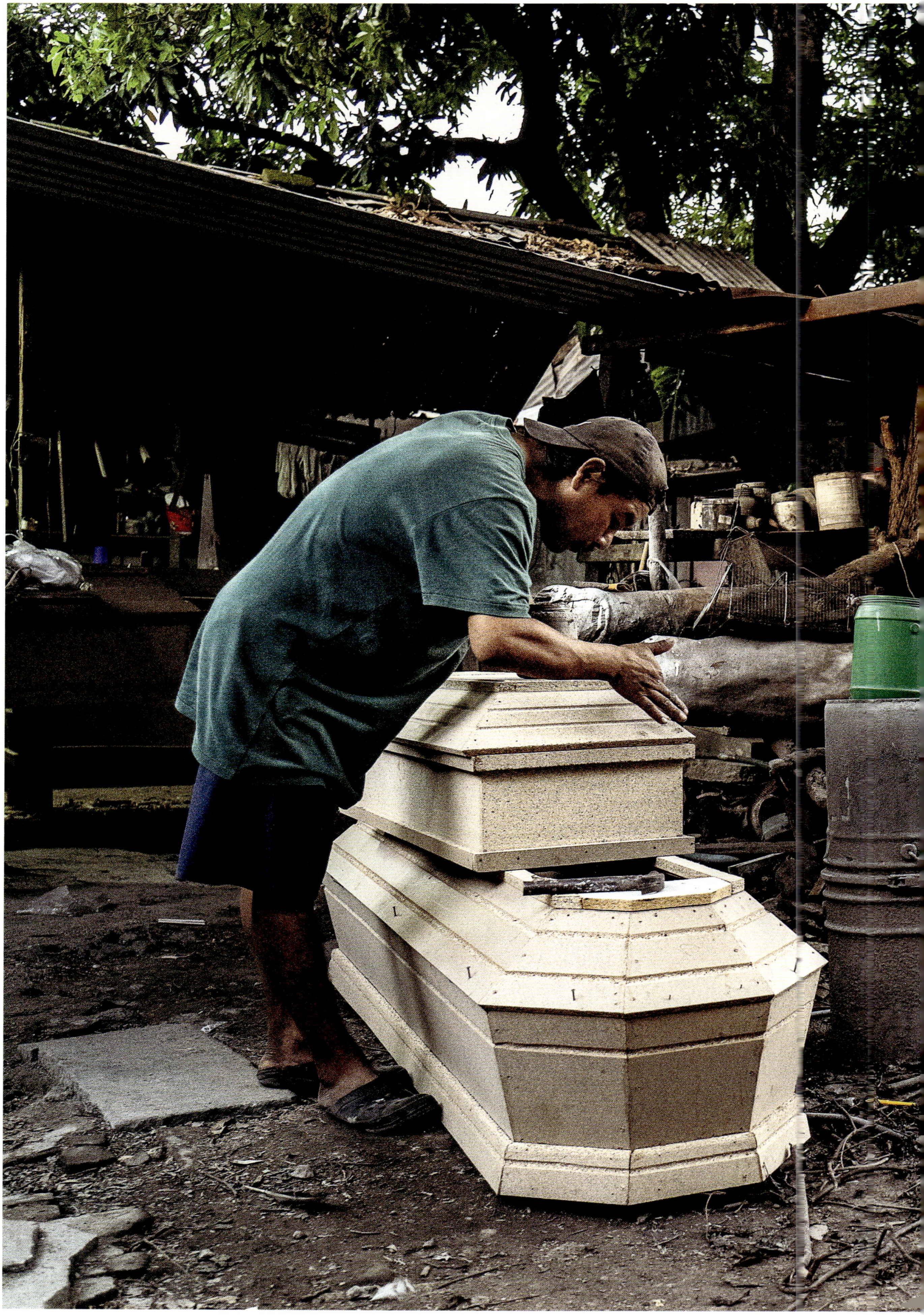

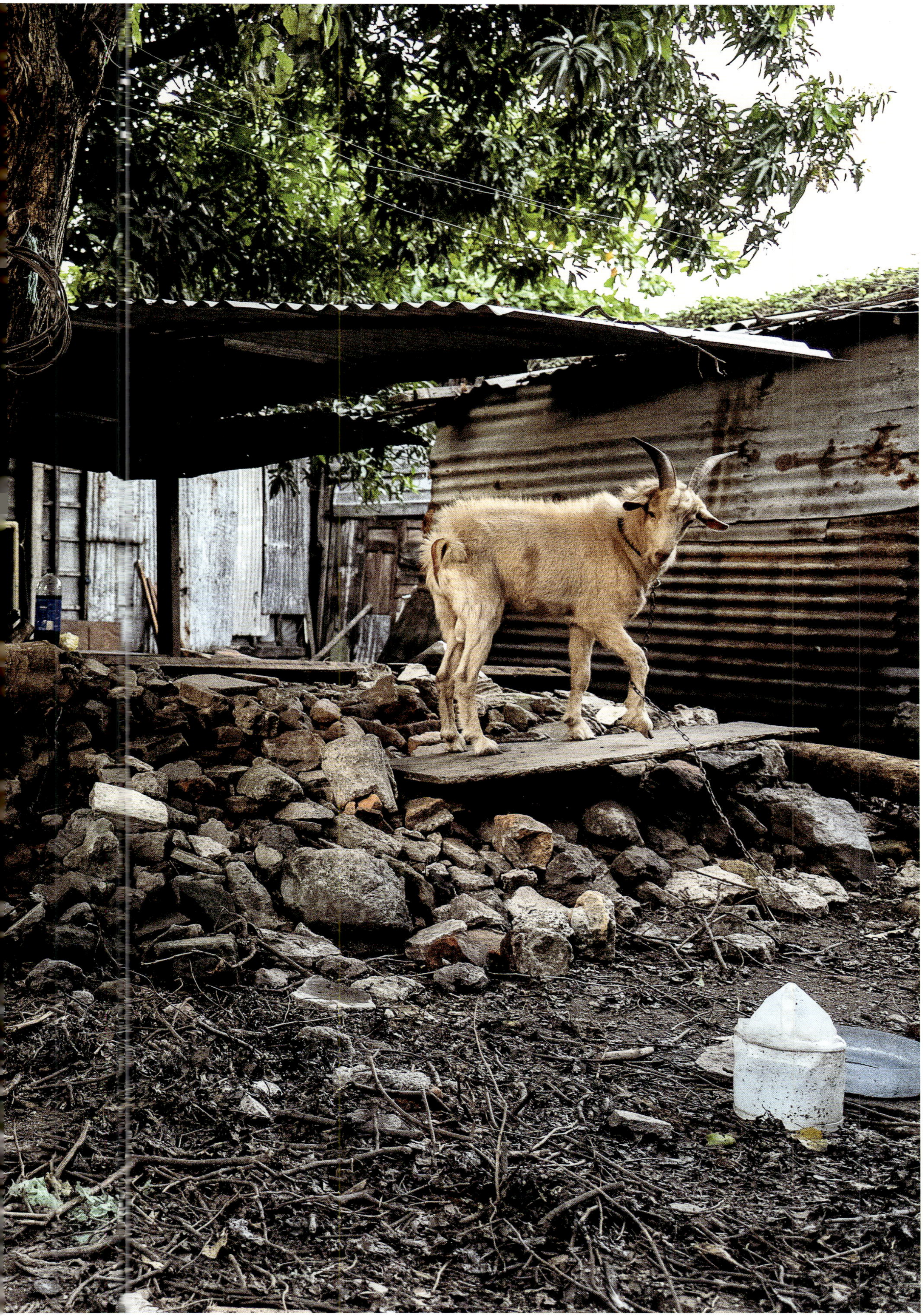

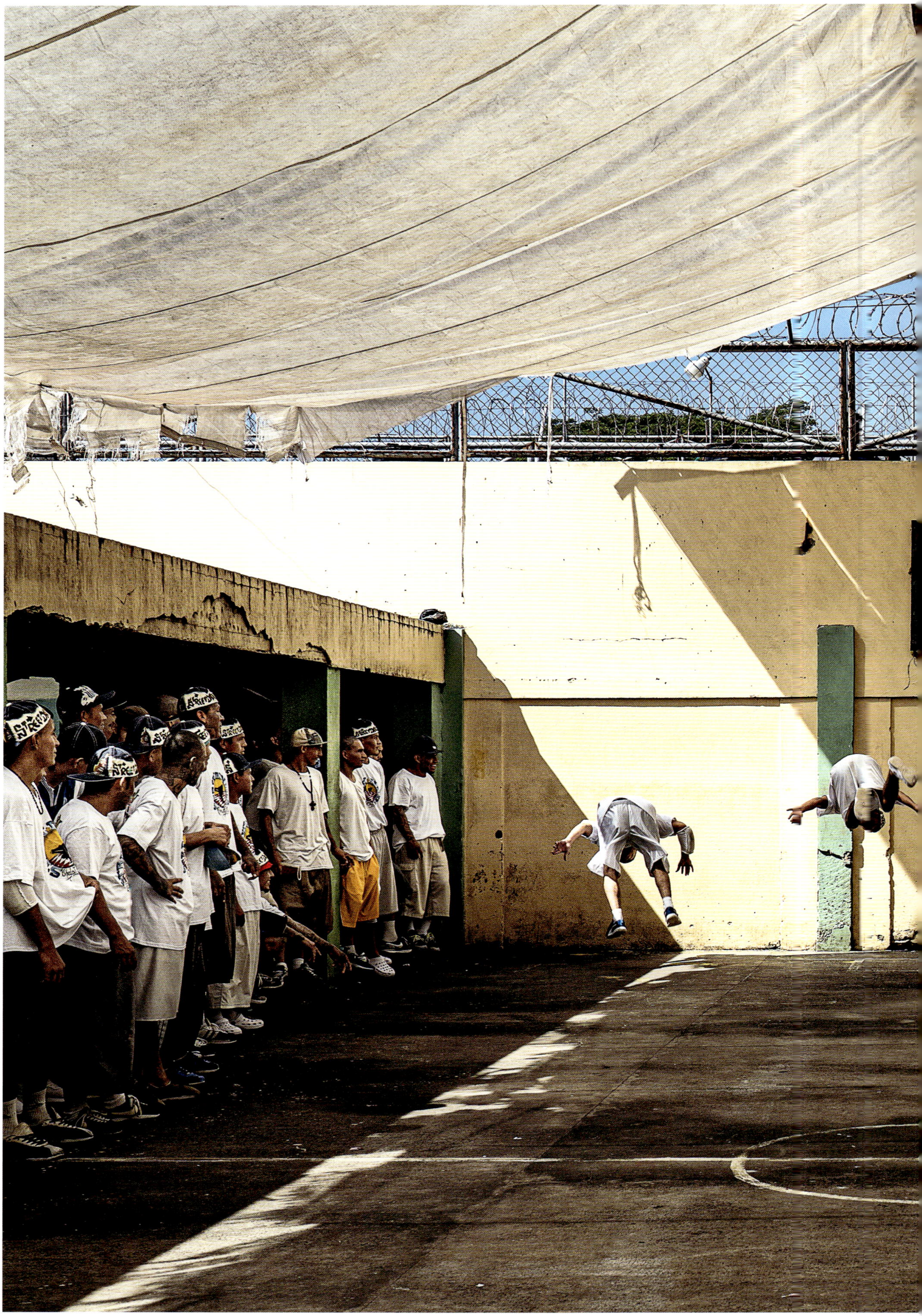

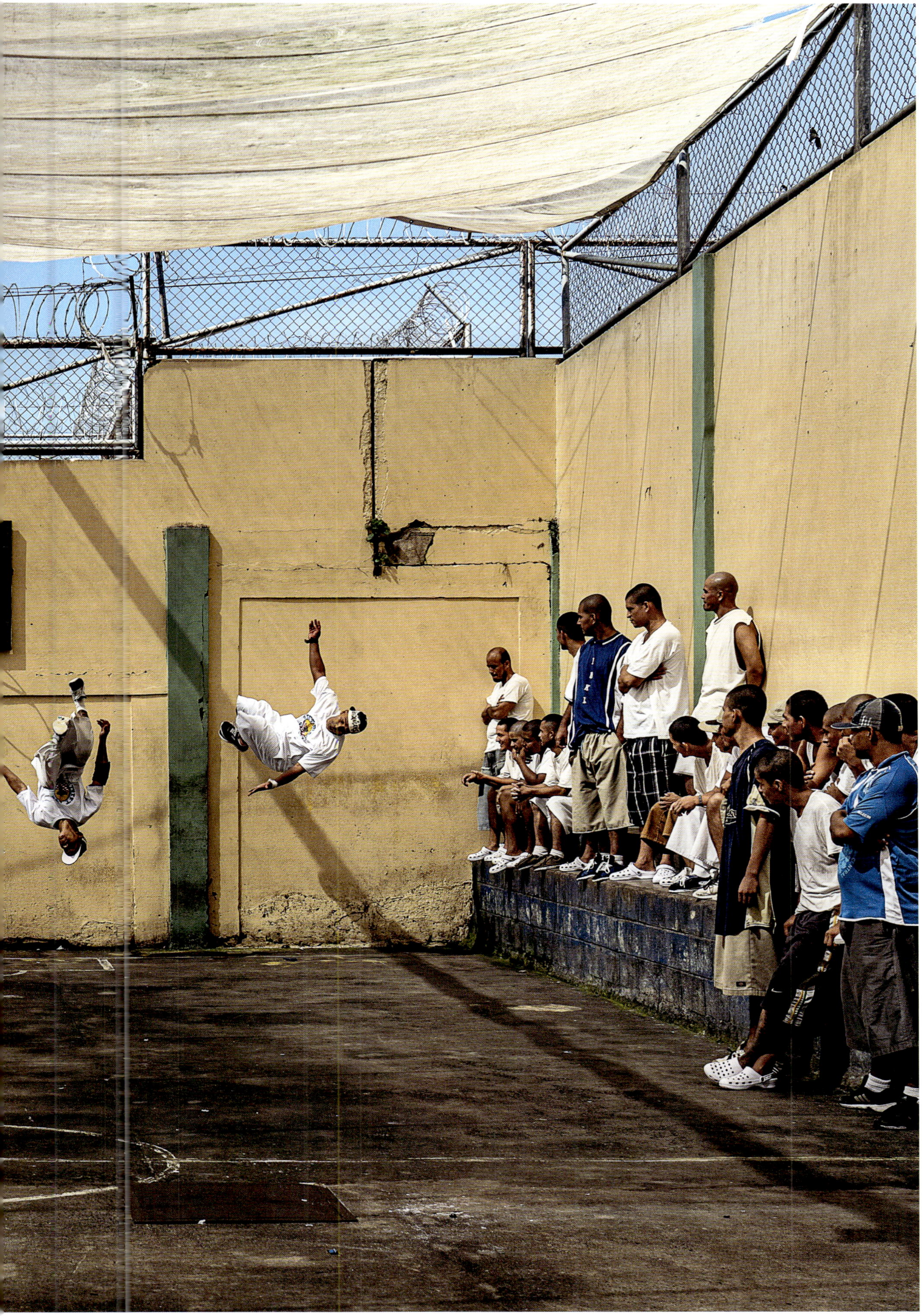

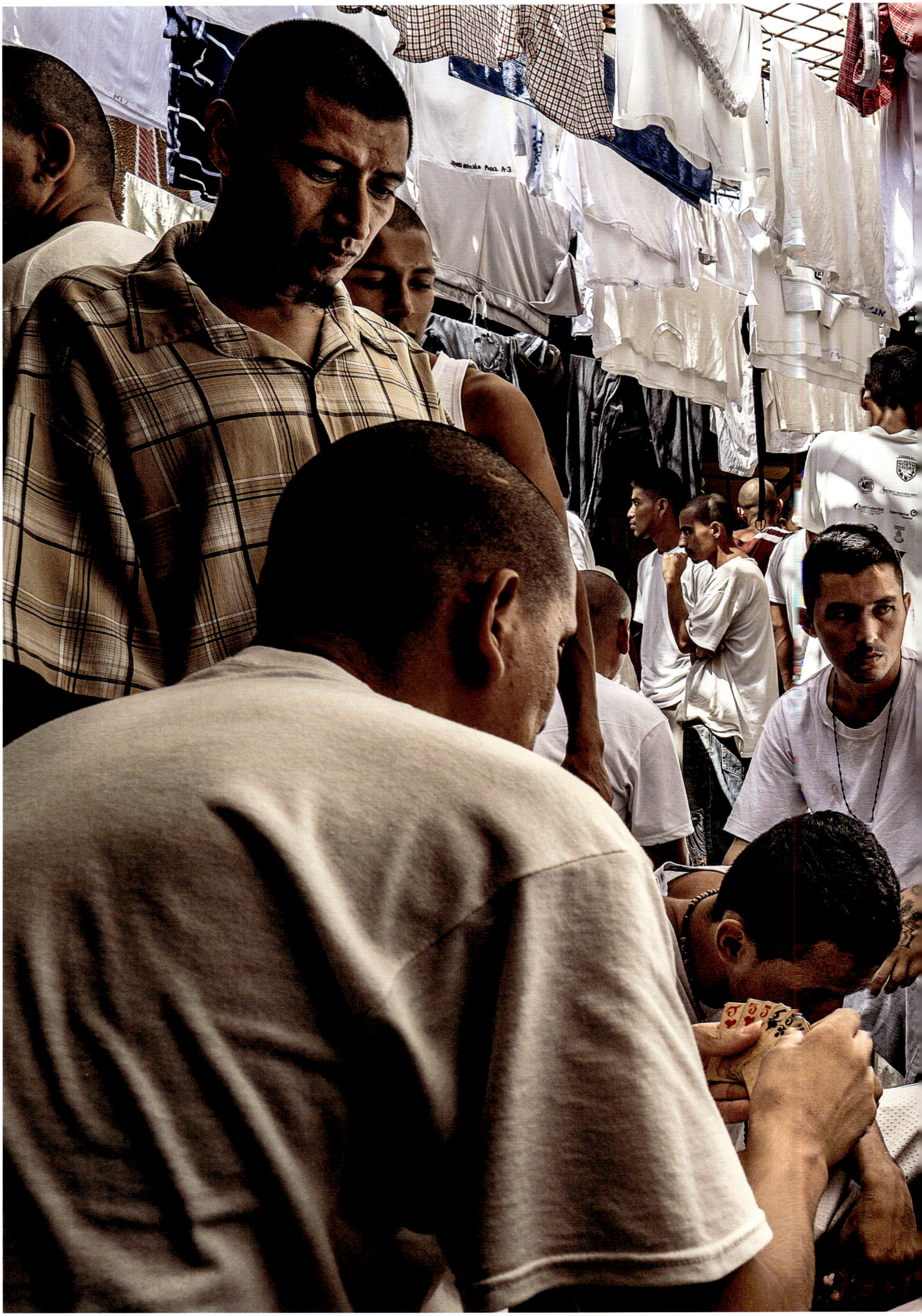

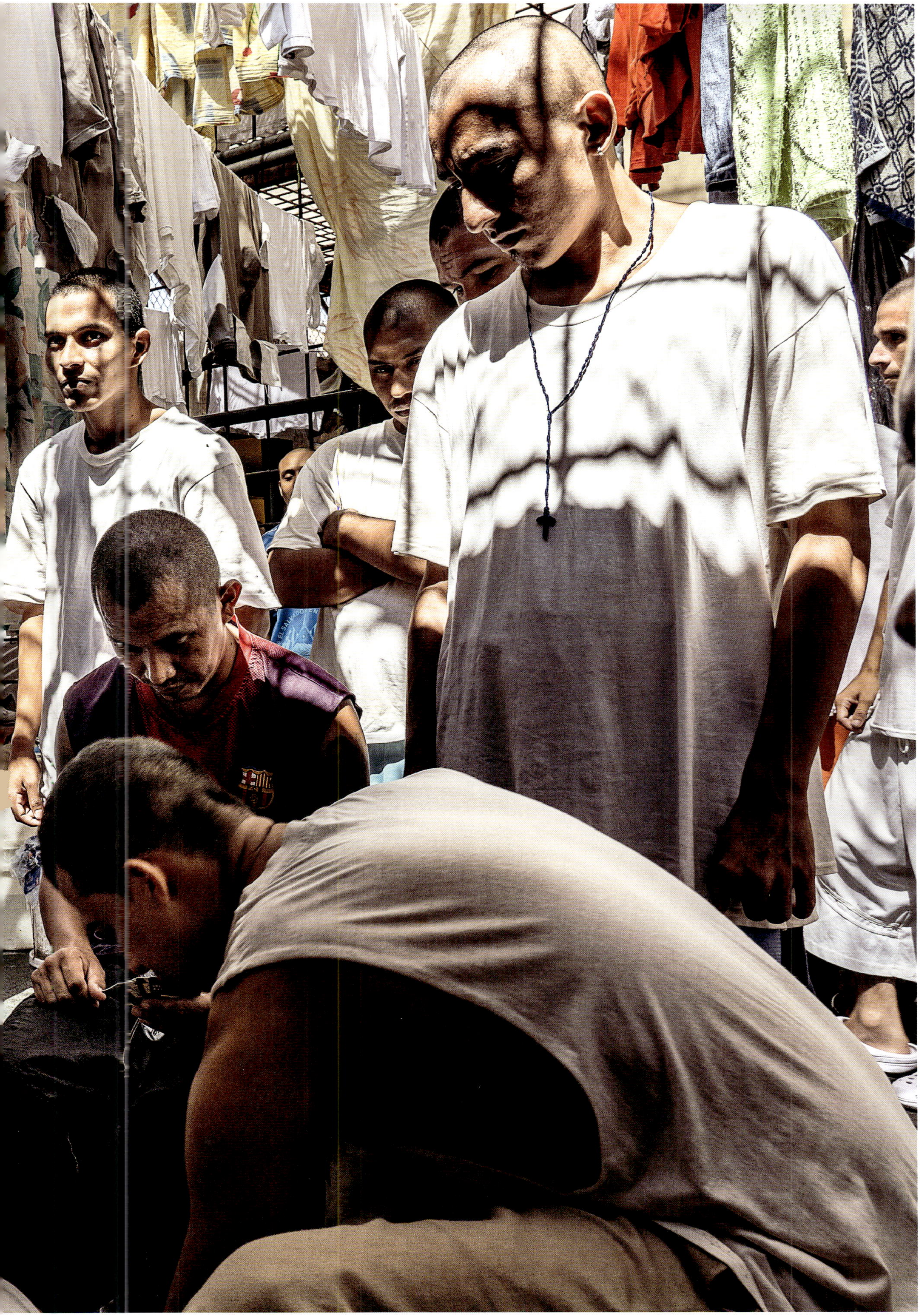

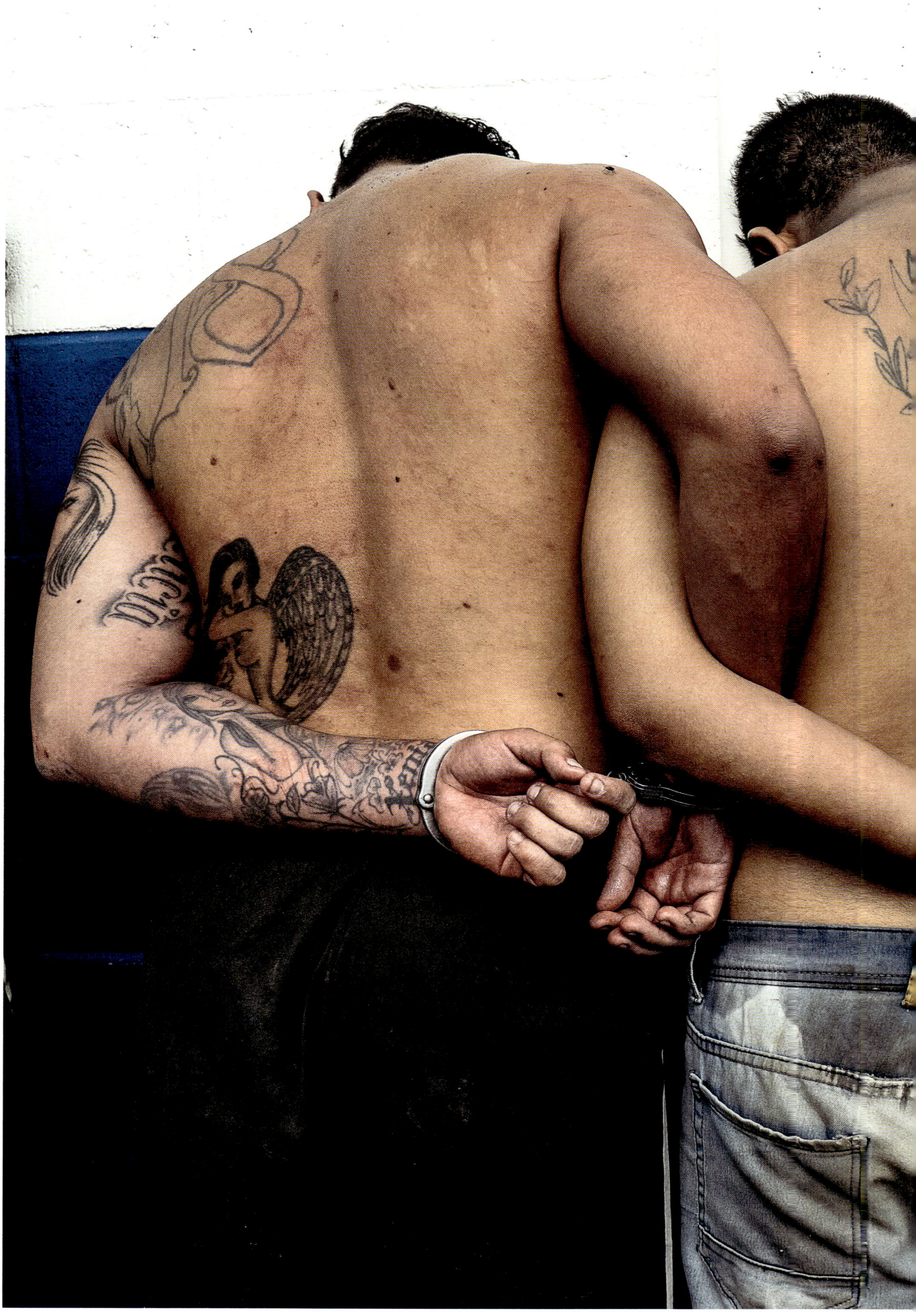

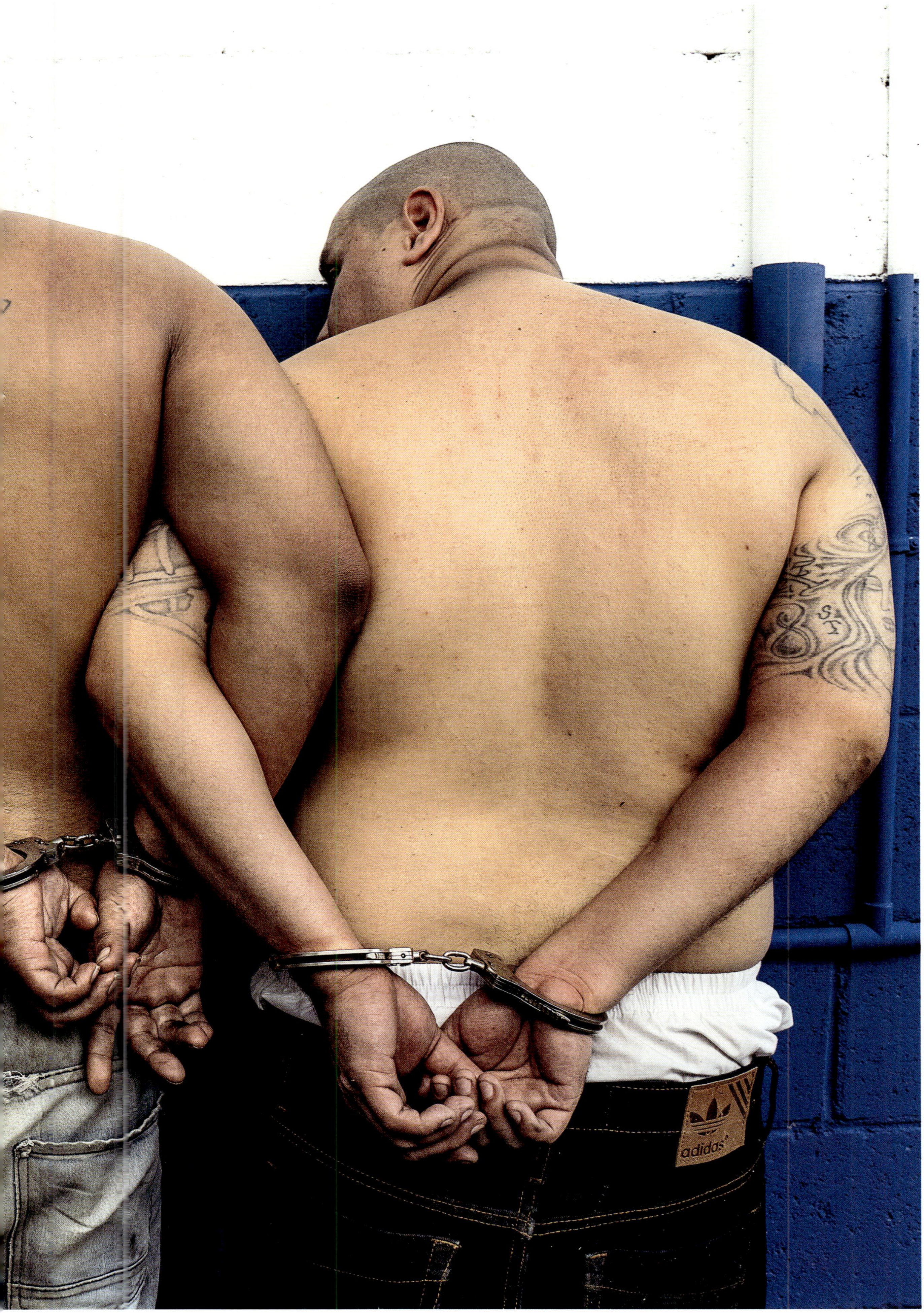
adidas

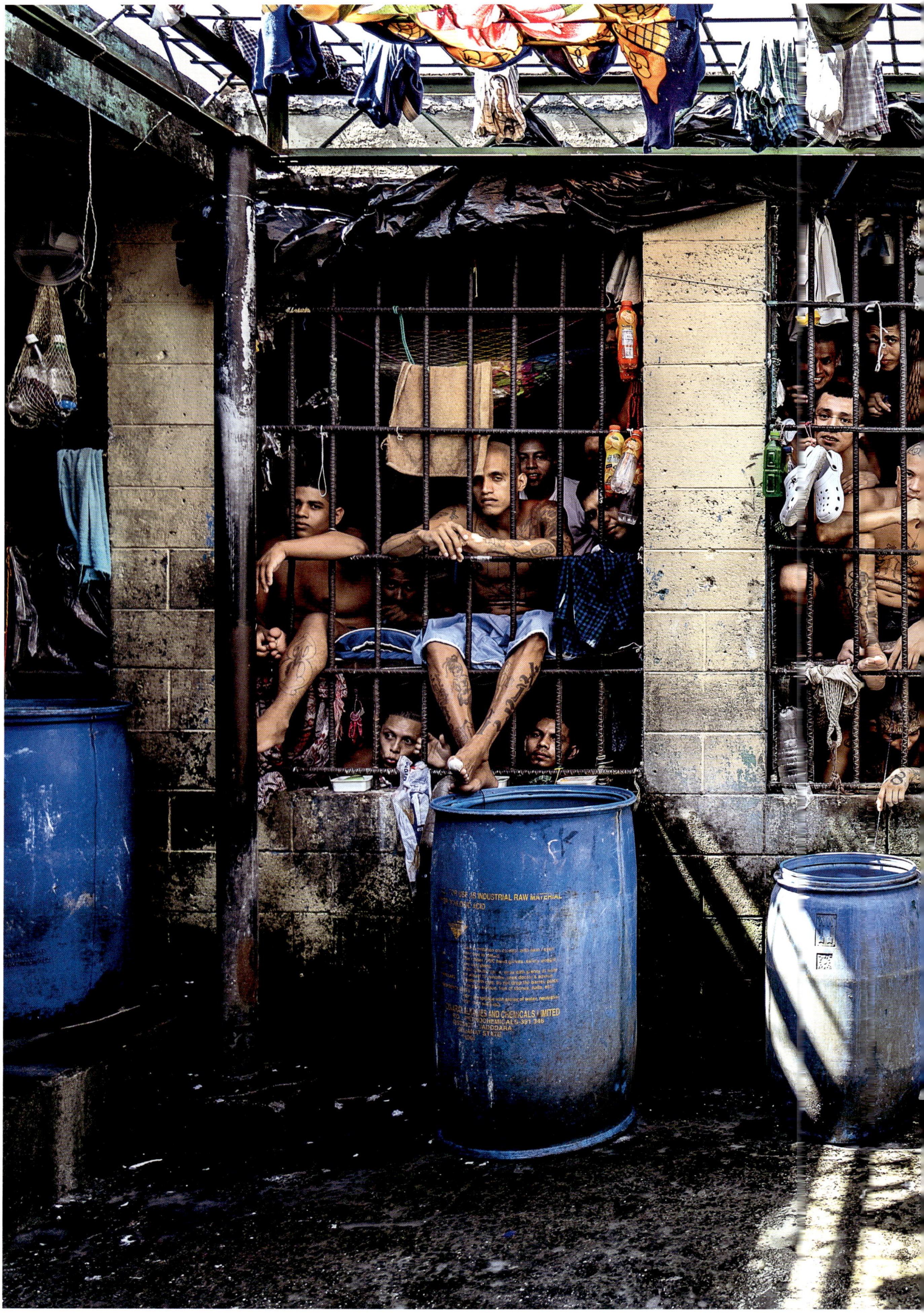
INDUSTRIAL RAW MATERIAL
ACID
AND CHEMICALS
VADODARA
STATE

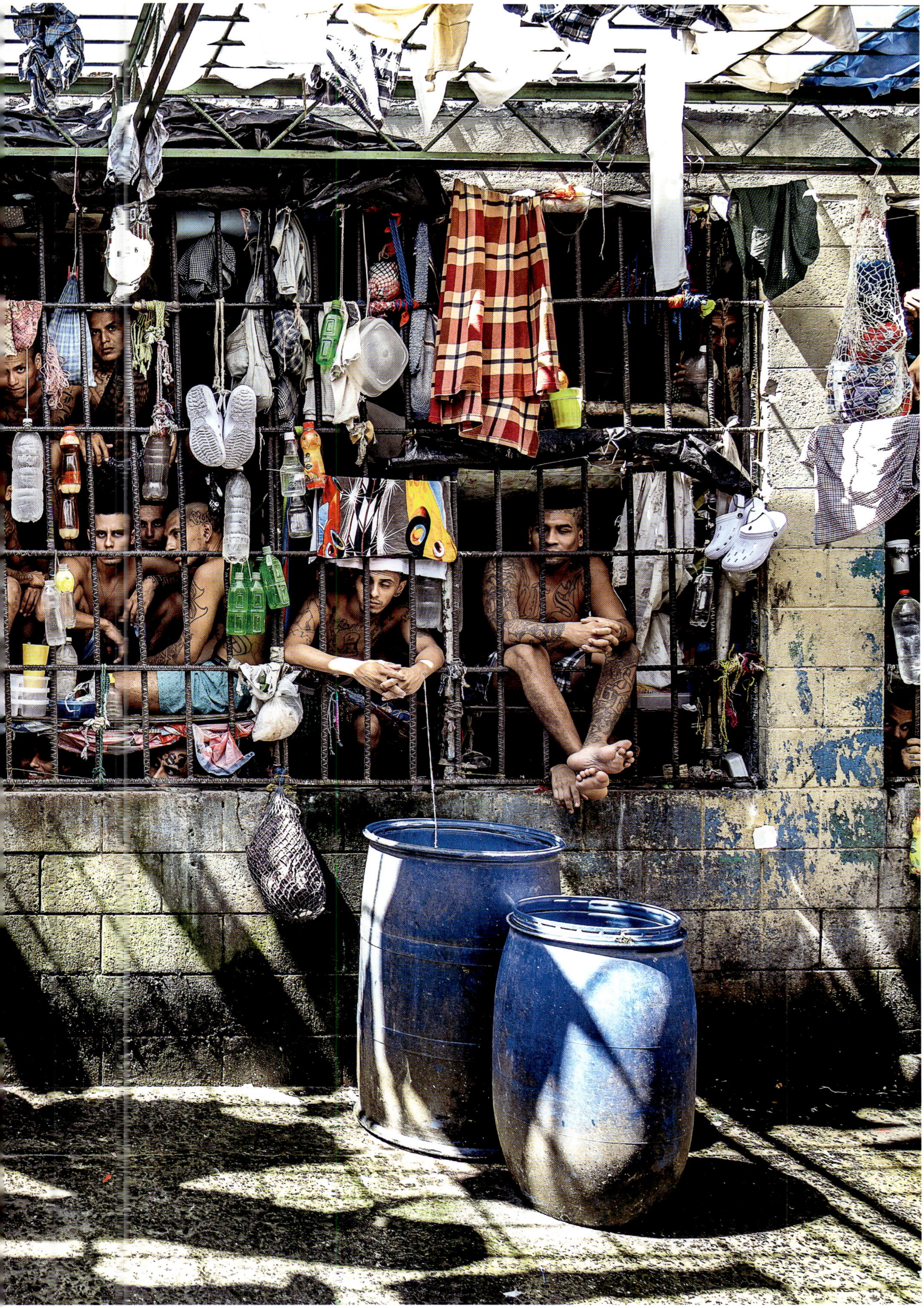

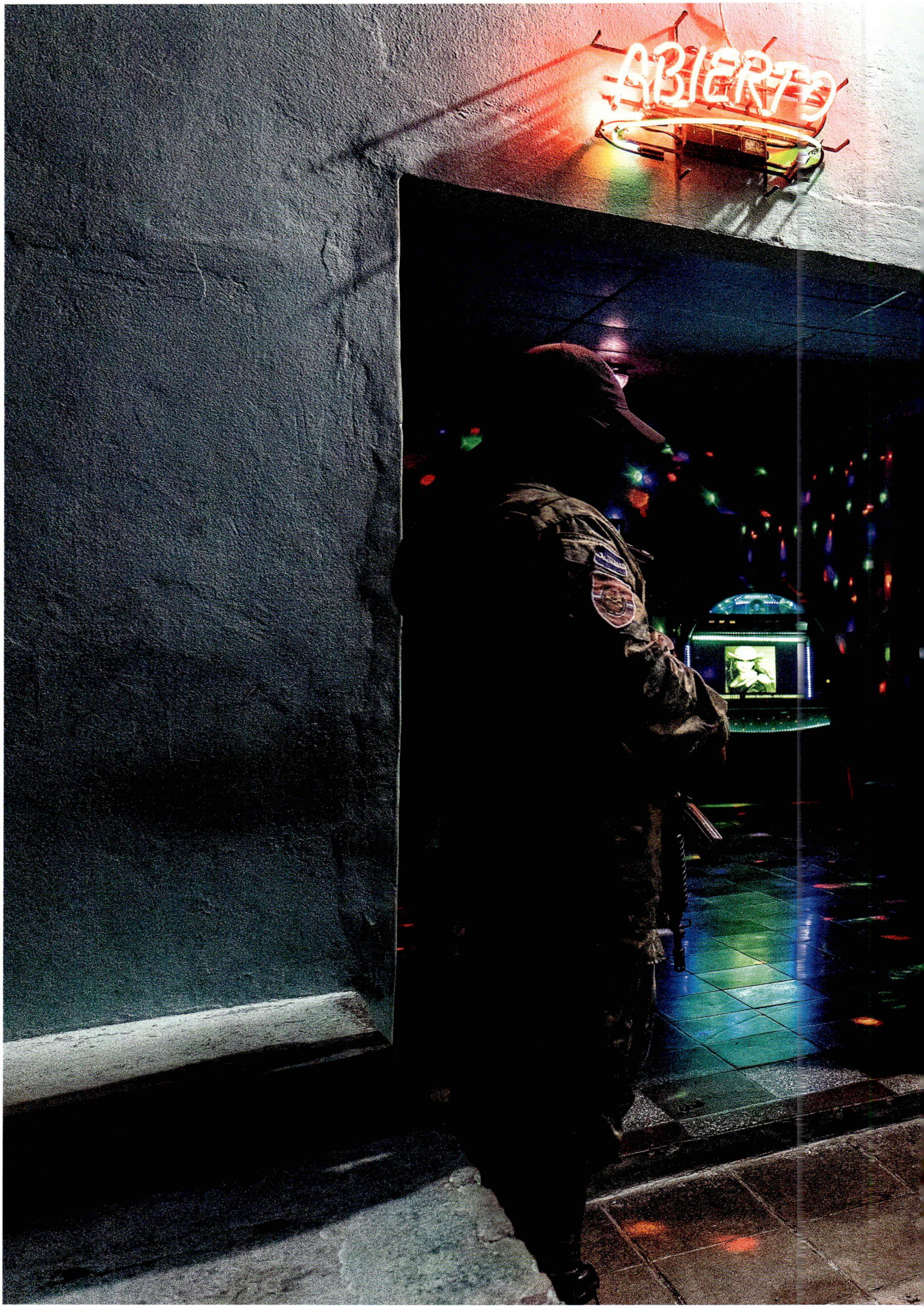
ABIERTO

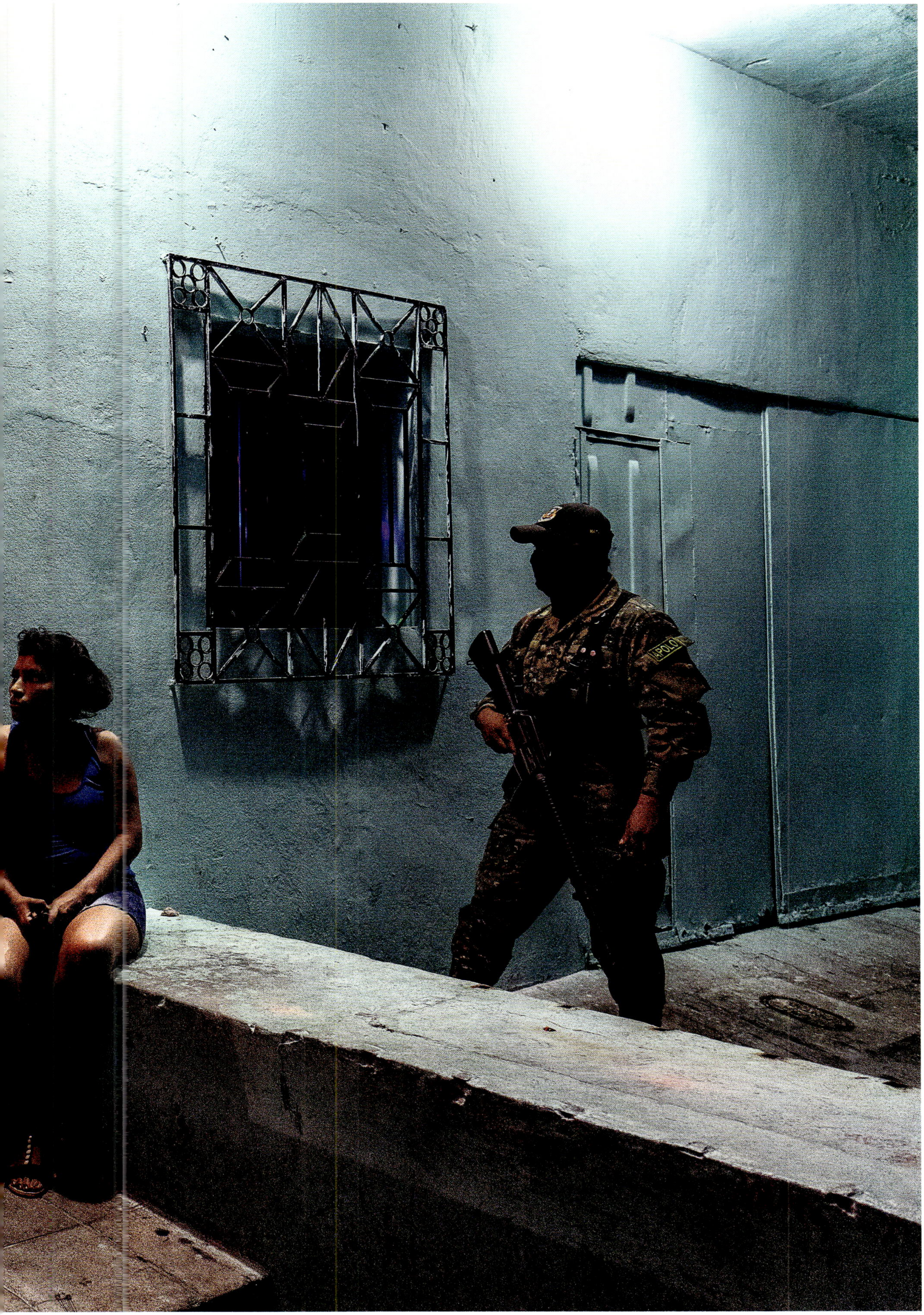

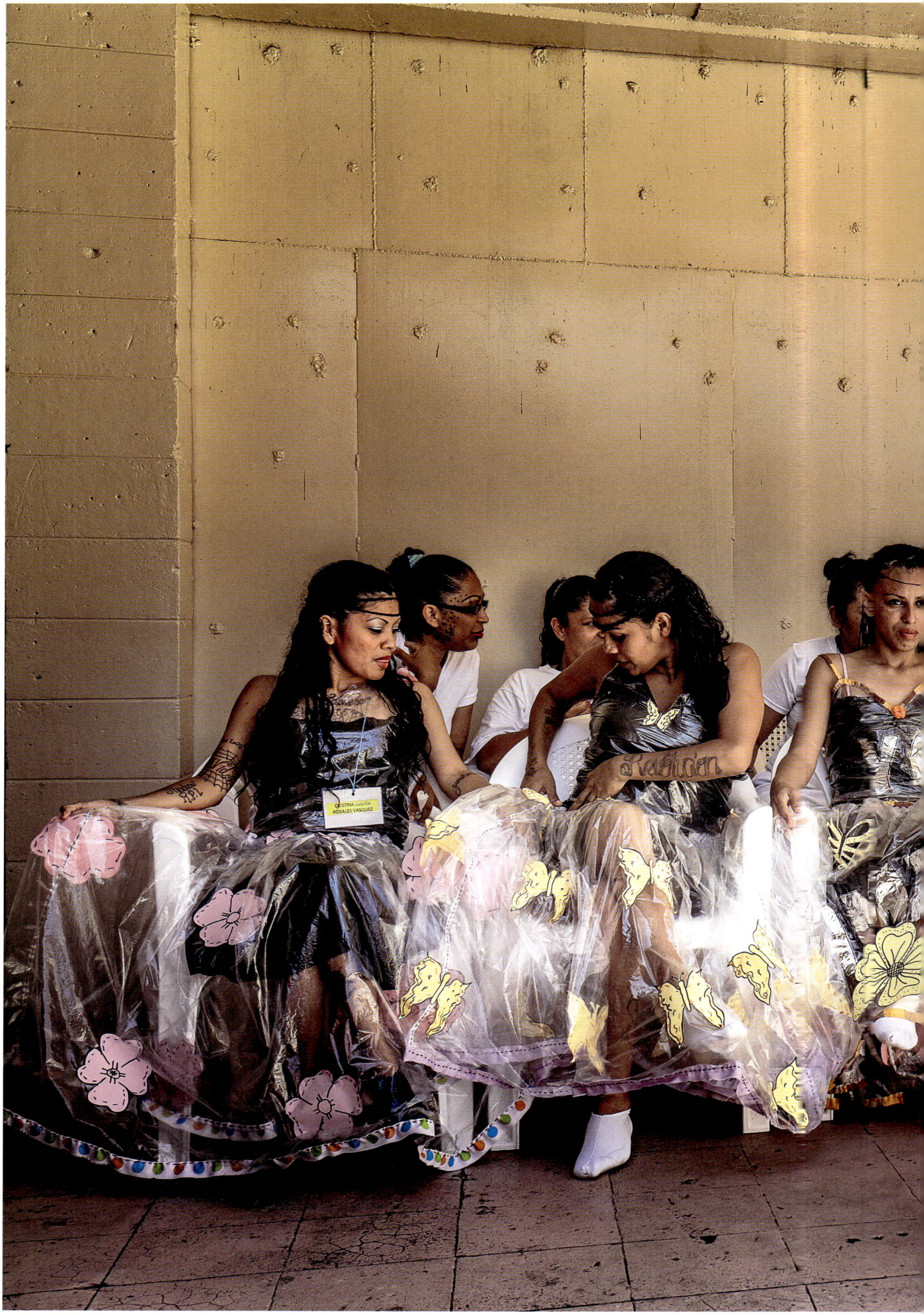
CRISTINA JUDITH
ROSALES VASQUEZ

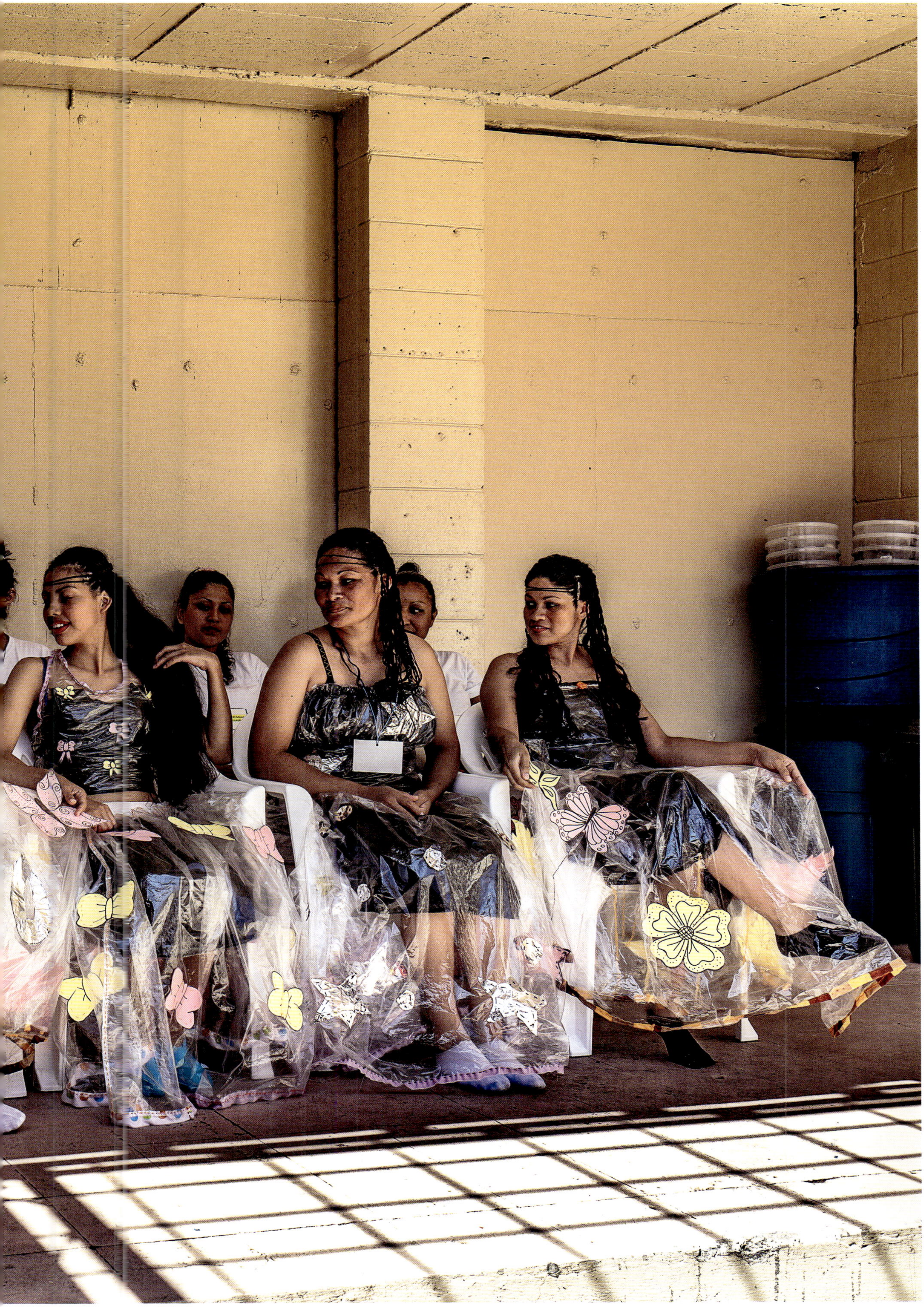

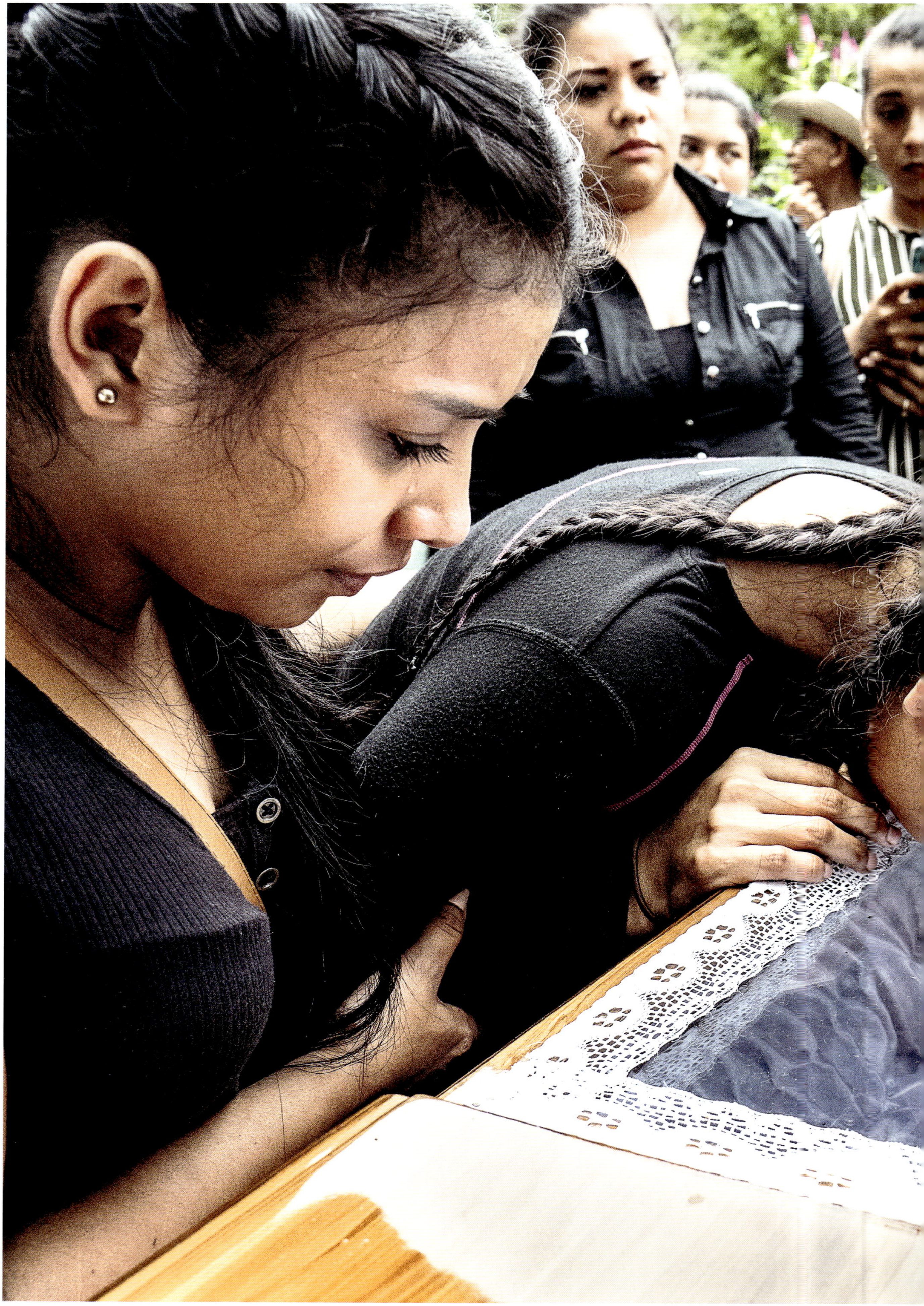

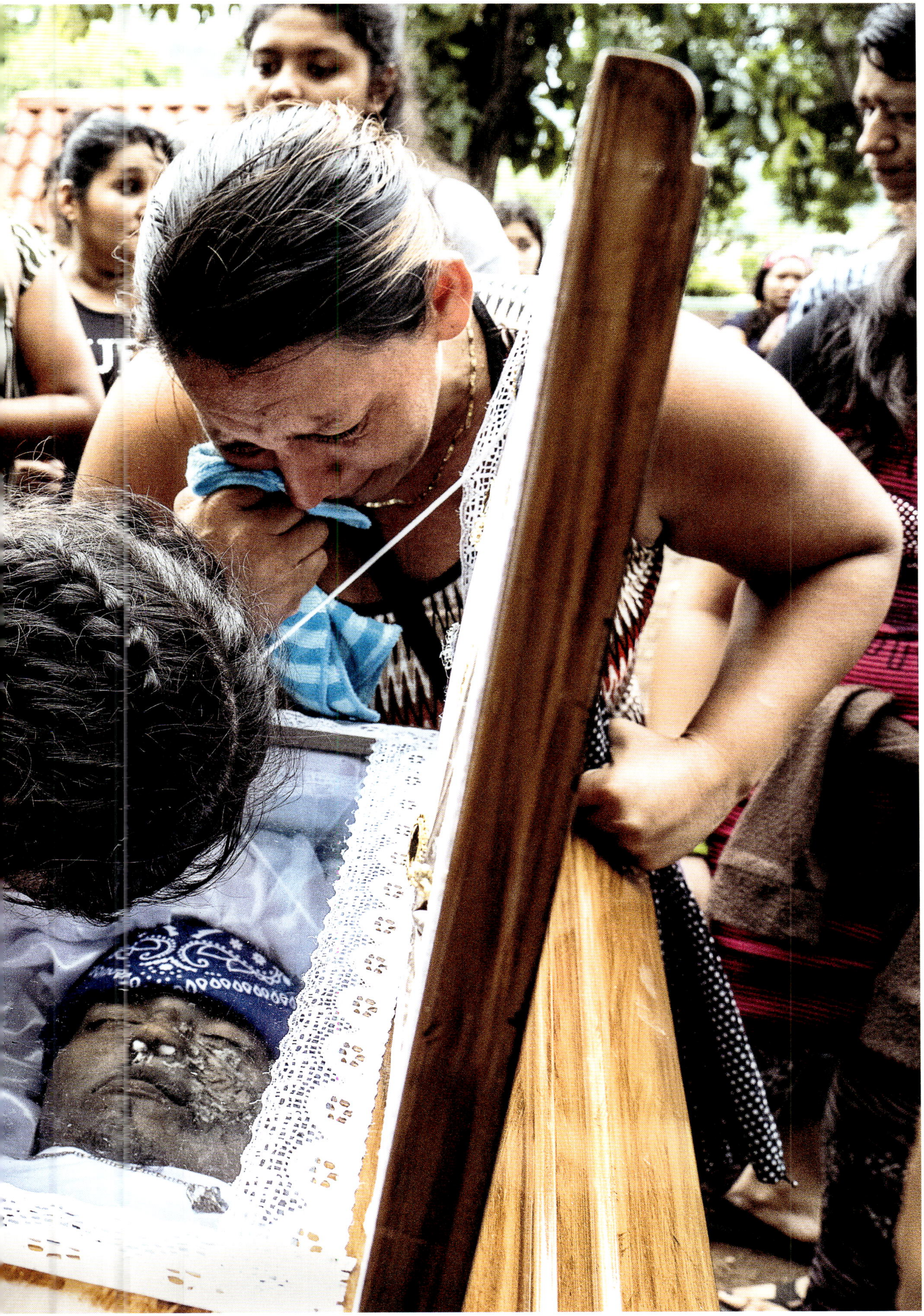

A MULTI-YEAR RESEARCH INITIATIVE BY INSIGHT CRIME AND AMERICAN UNIVERSITY

into the inner workings of MS-13 revealed a complex organisational structure—one that has grown more sophisticated as the gang has expanded over the years.

There is a hierarchy within the gangs dependant on experience and time spent as a member. At the highest level is the 'ranfla,' where the most experienced veteran gang members or those who have shown deep loyalty to the gang often end up. The ranfla, form 'leadership councils' and beneath them, at a middle level, are 'programmes' of managers (also known as 'corredores' or 'runners'). They in turn control the lowest level, the 'cliques.' Programmes were initiated in the mid-2000s as a response to the growth in gang membership and allowed ranflas to exert greater control over cliques and make the gang economy more structured. Almost all the leaders in the ranfla are in prison, but through this network they maintain a level of control over gang policy.

Nearly thirty years of state failure and gang violence have created a situation unlike any other in the world, with a persistently high murder rate and culture of paranoia. While other countries suffer as a result of gang violence, the kind that has developed in El Salvador—with its satanism, brutality and relentlessness—is unique.

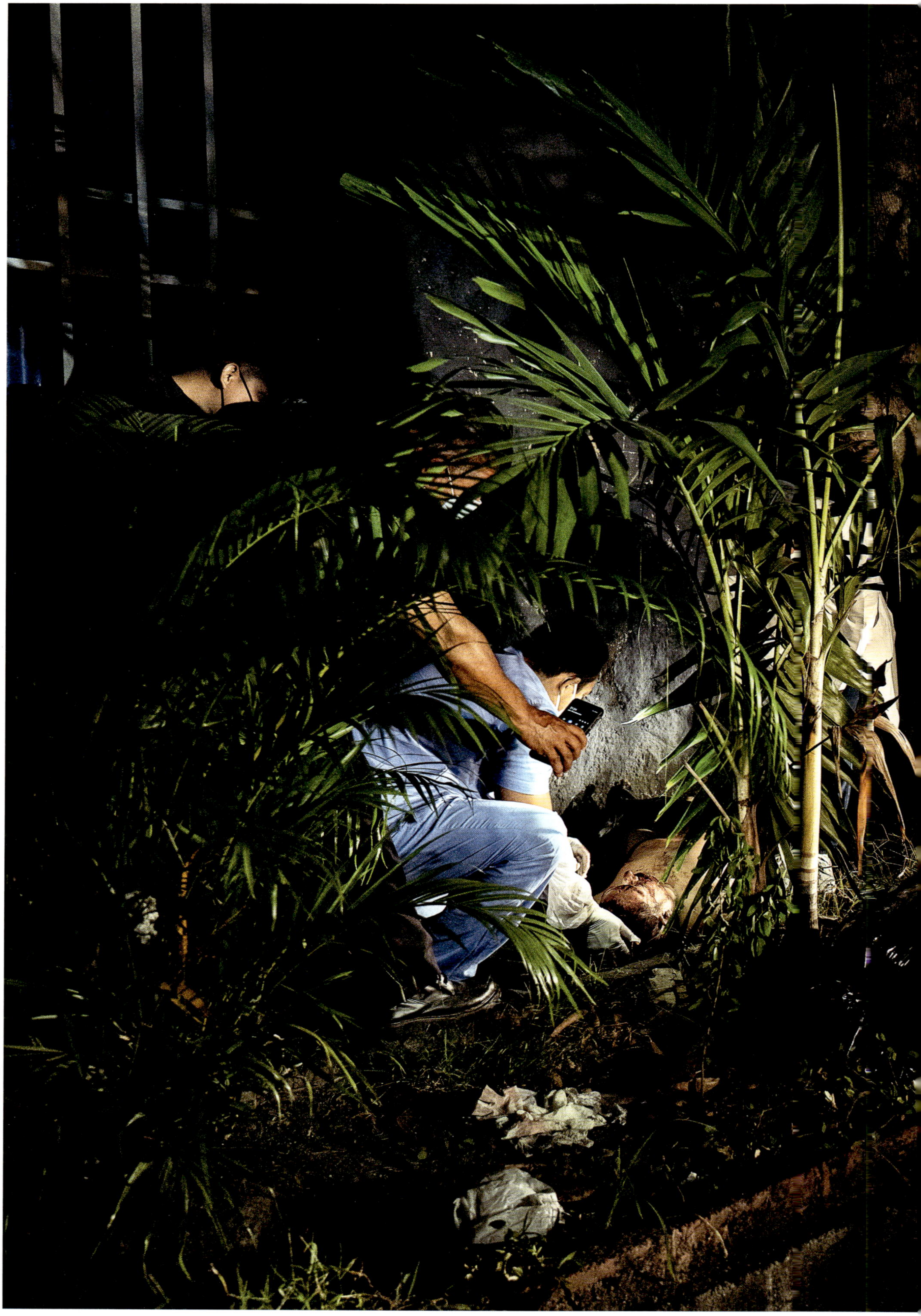

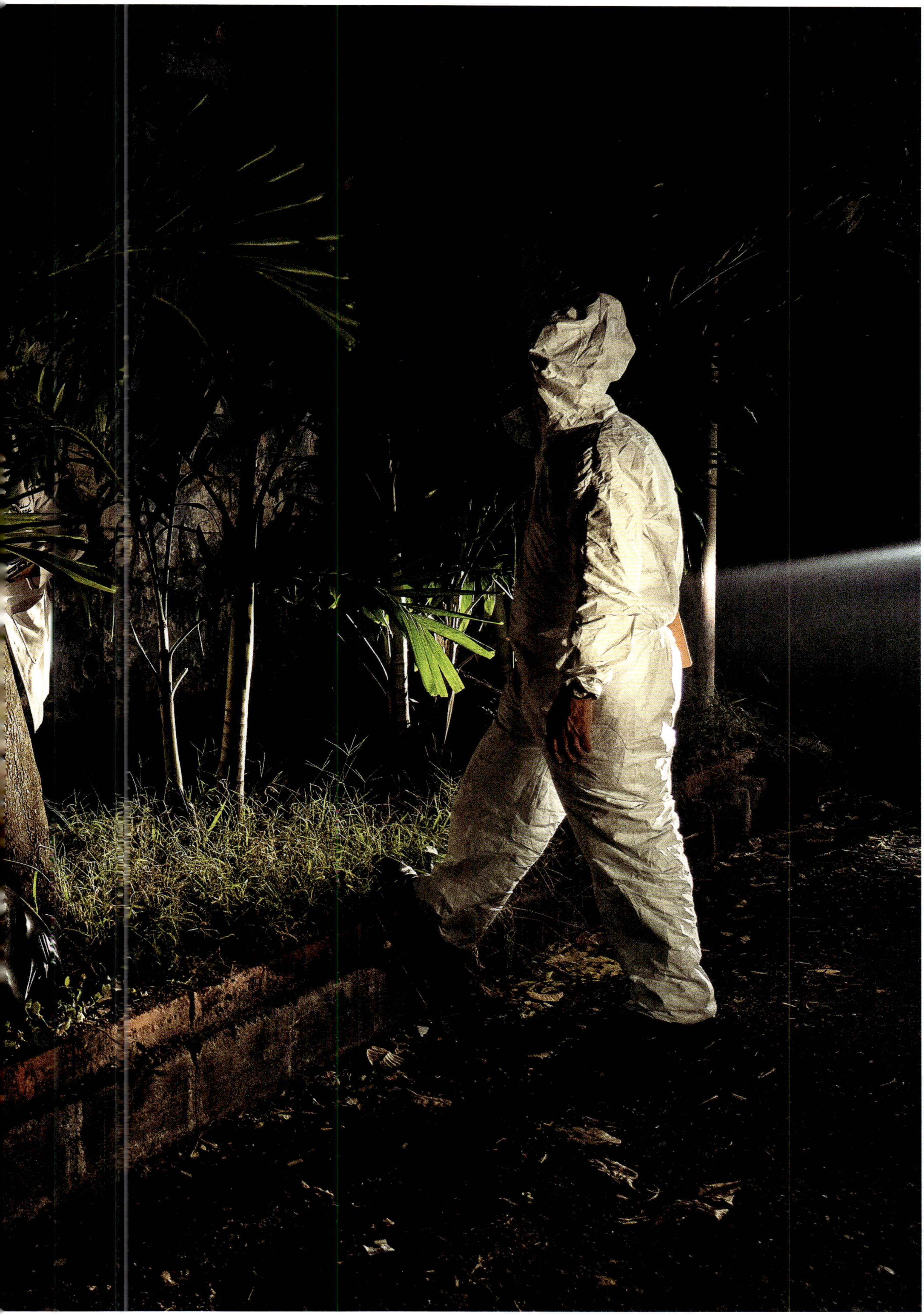

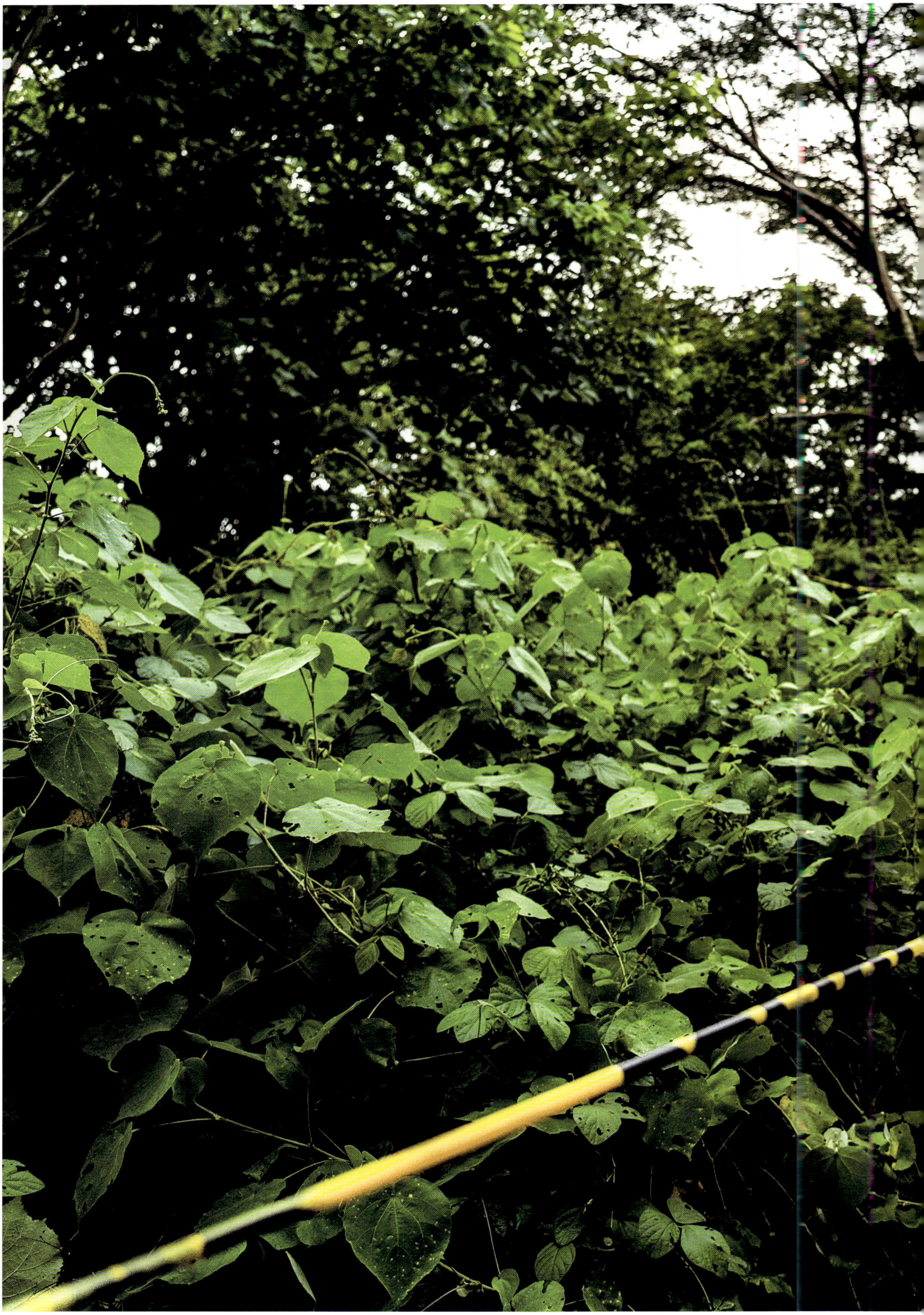

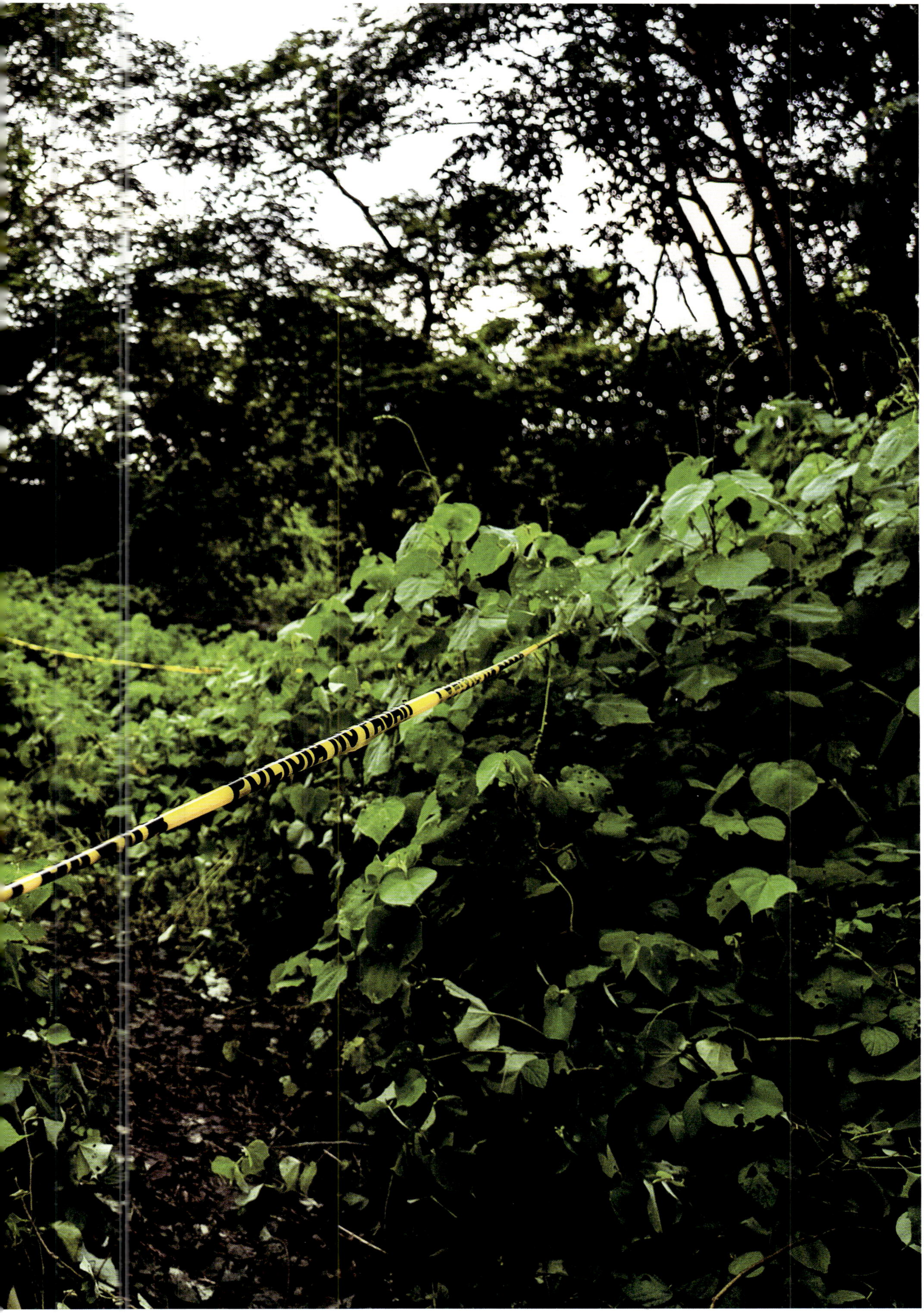

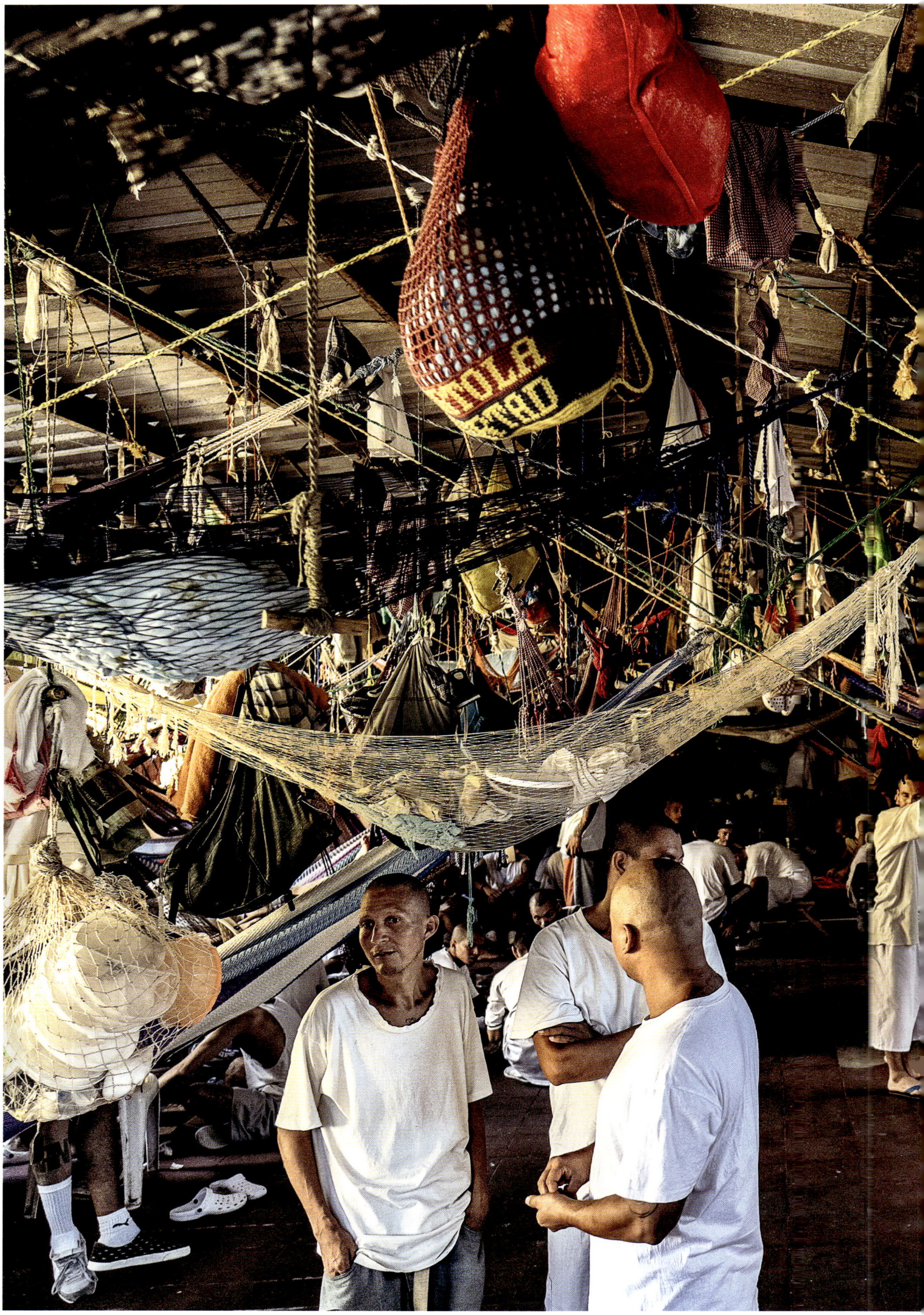

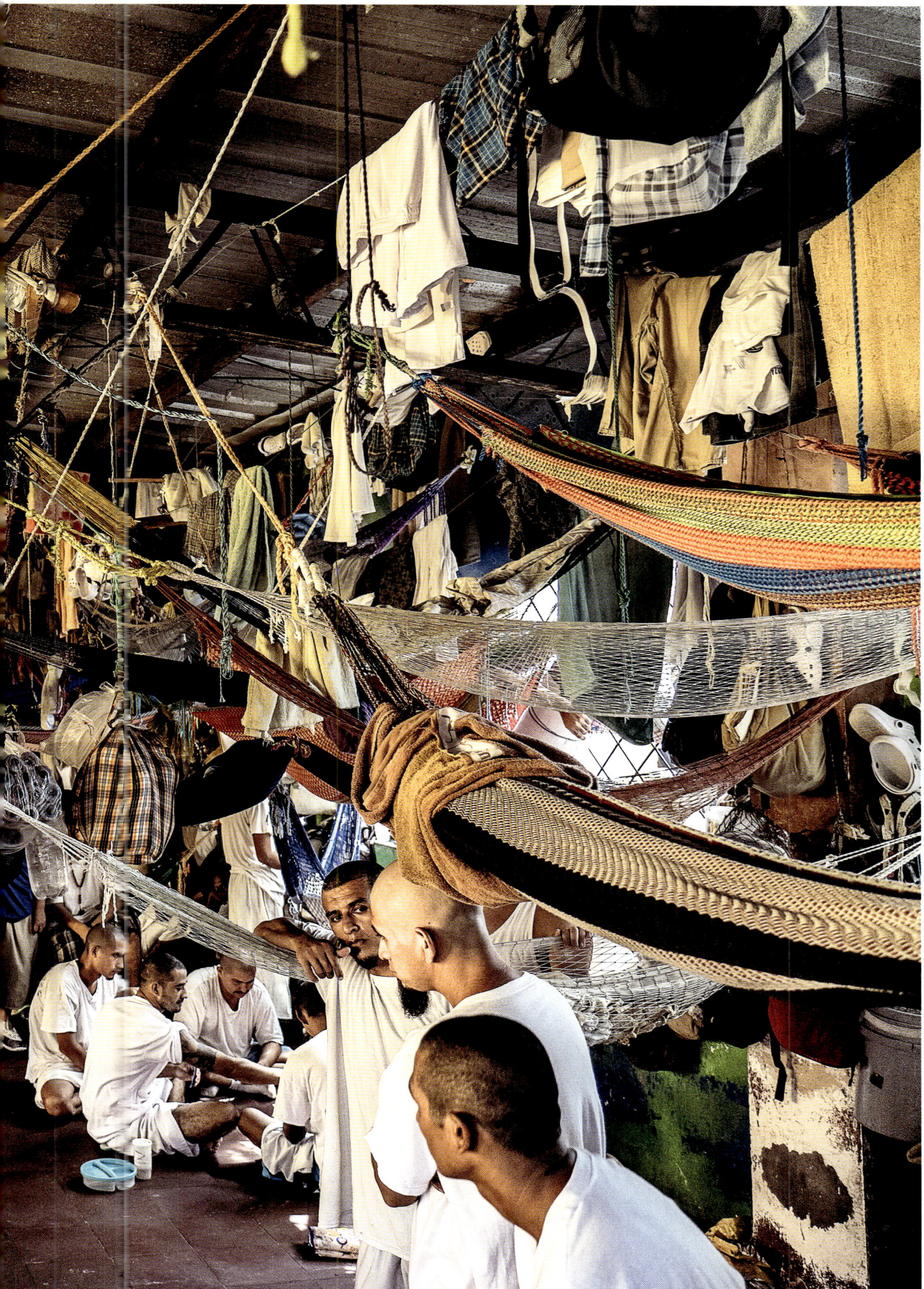

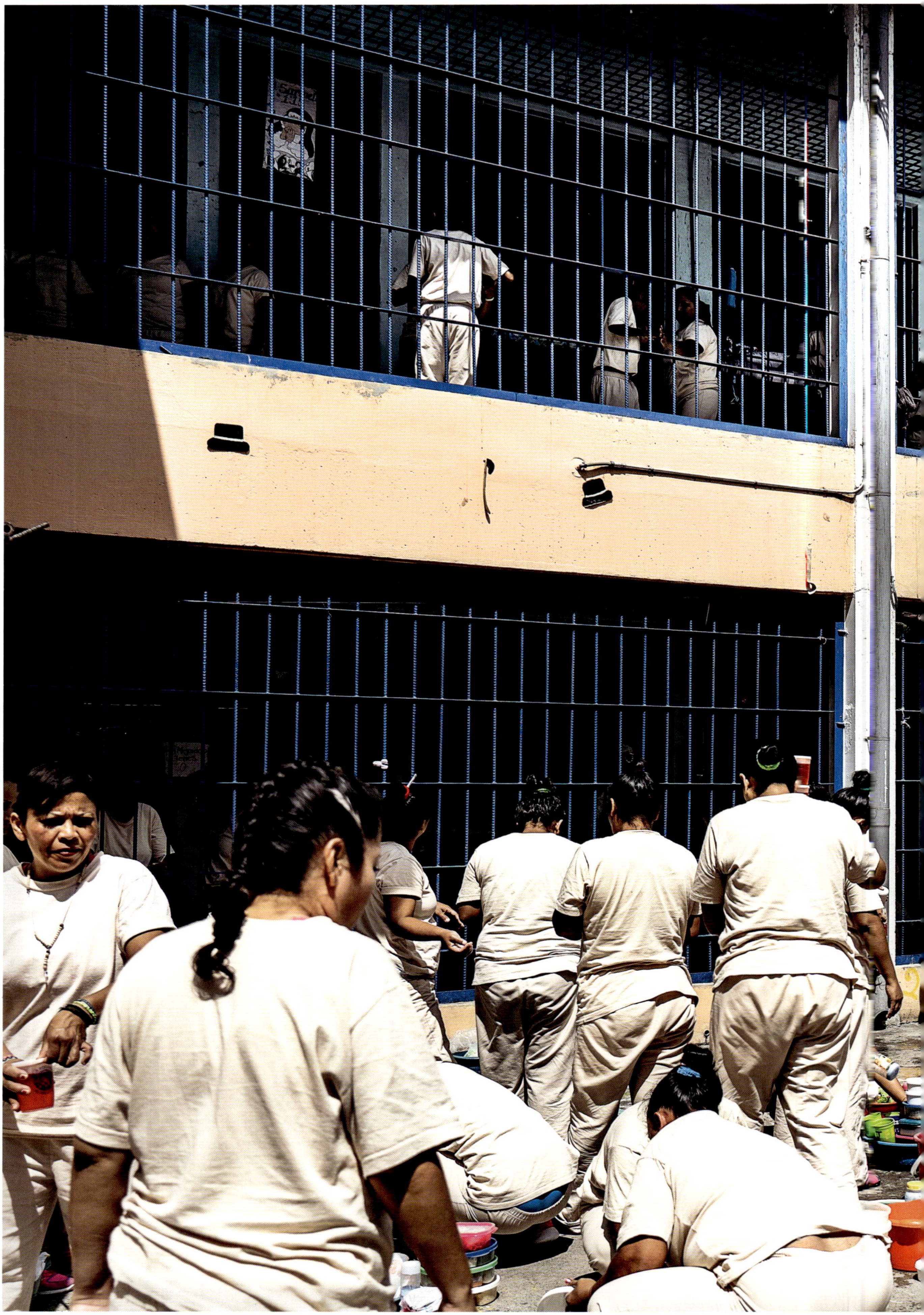

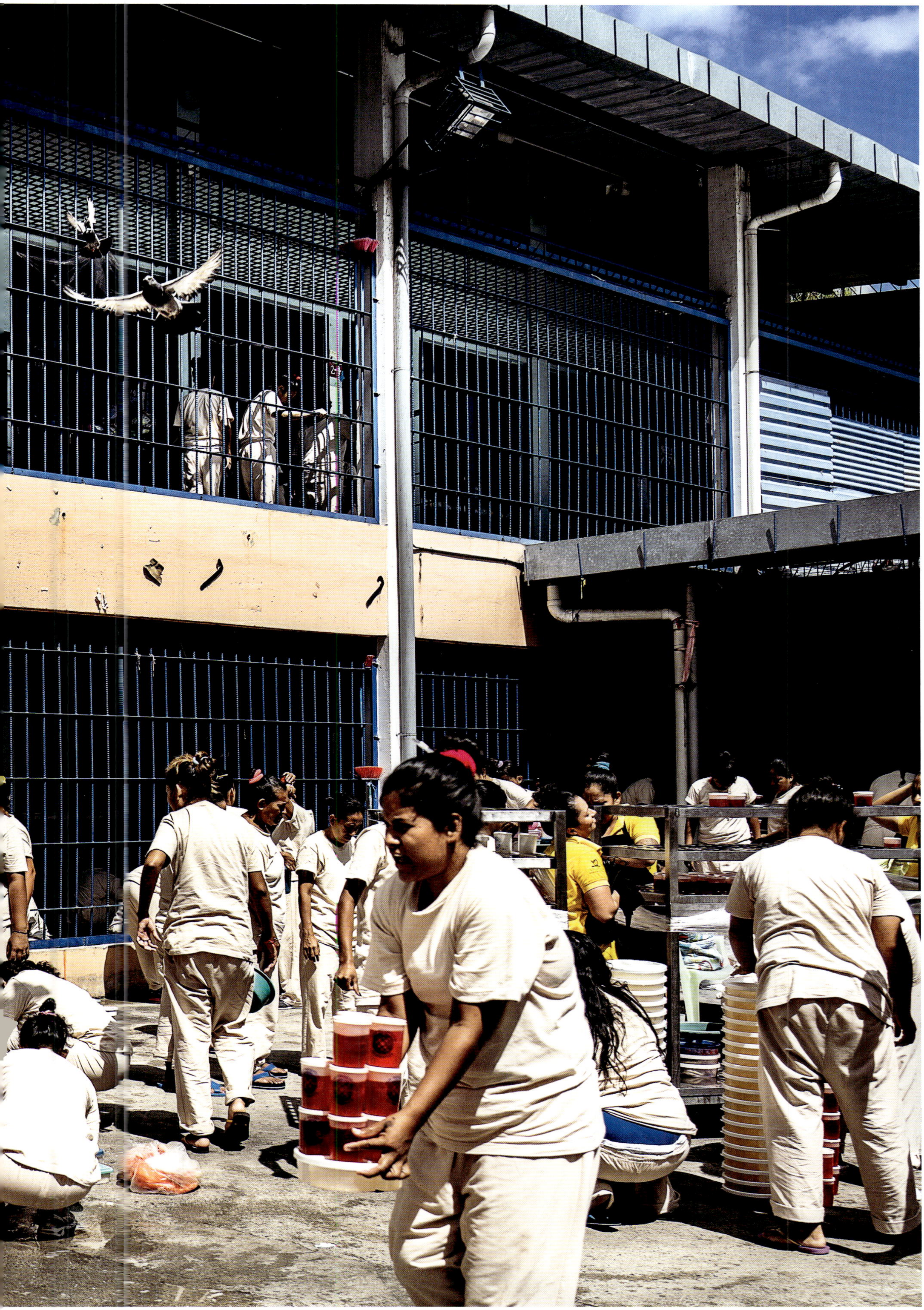

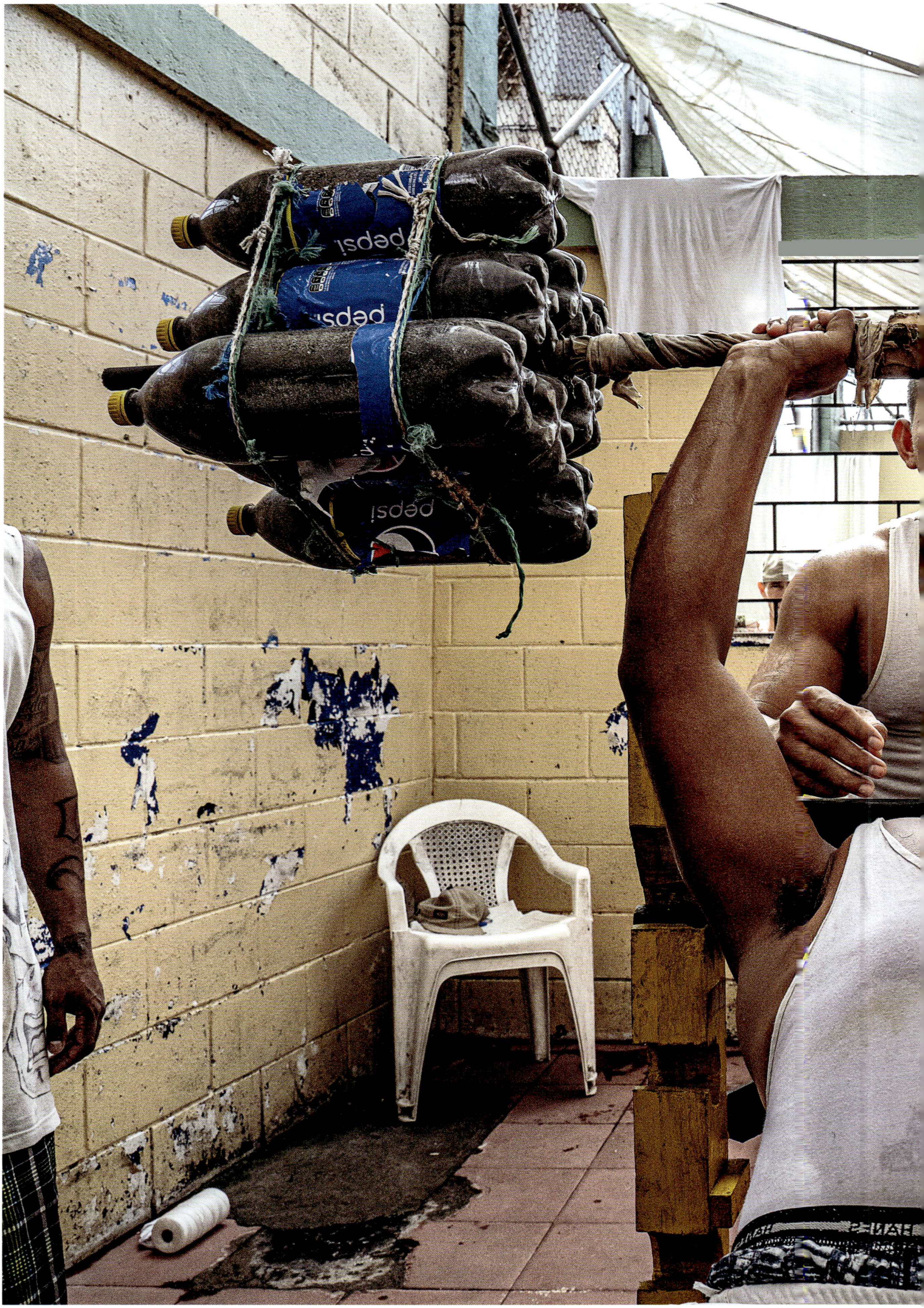
pepsi

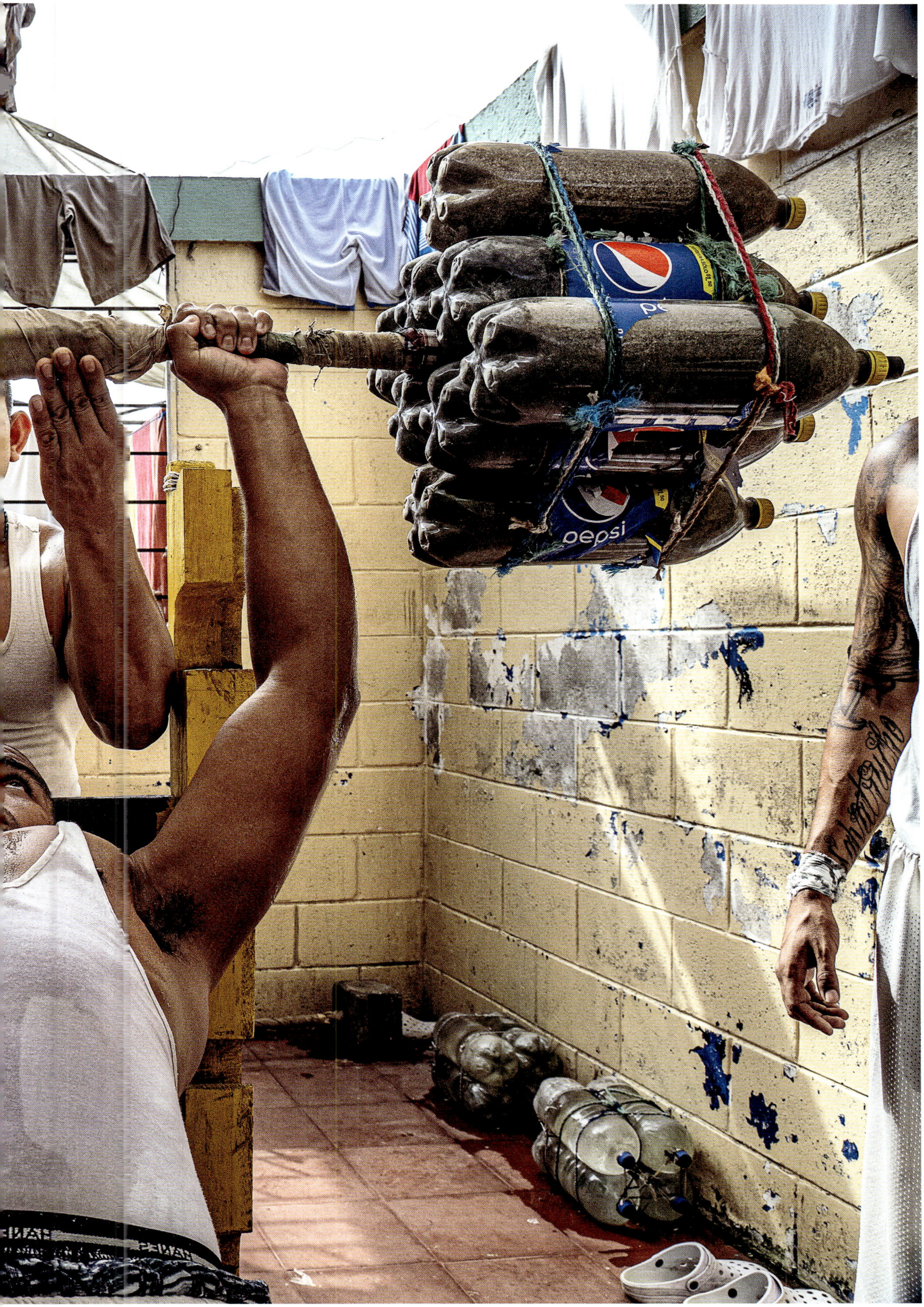
pepsi

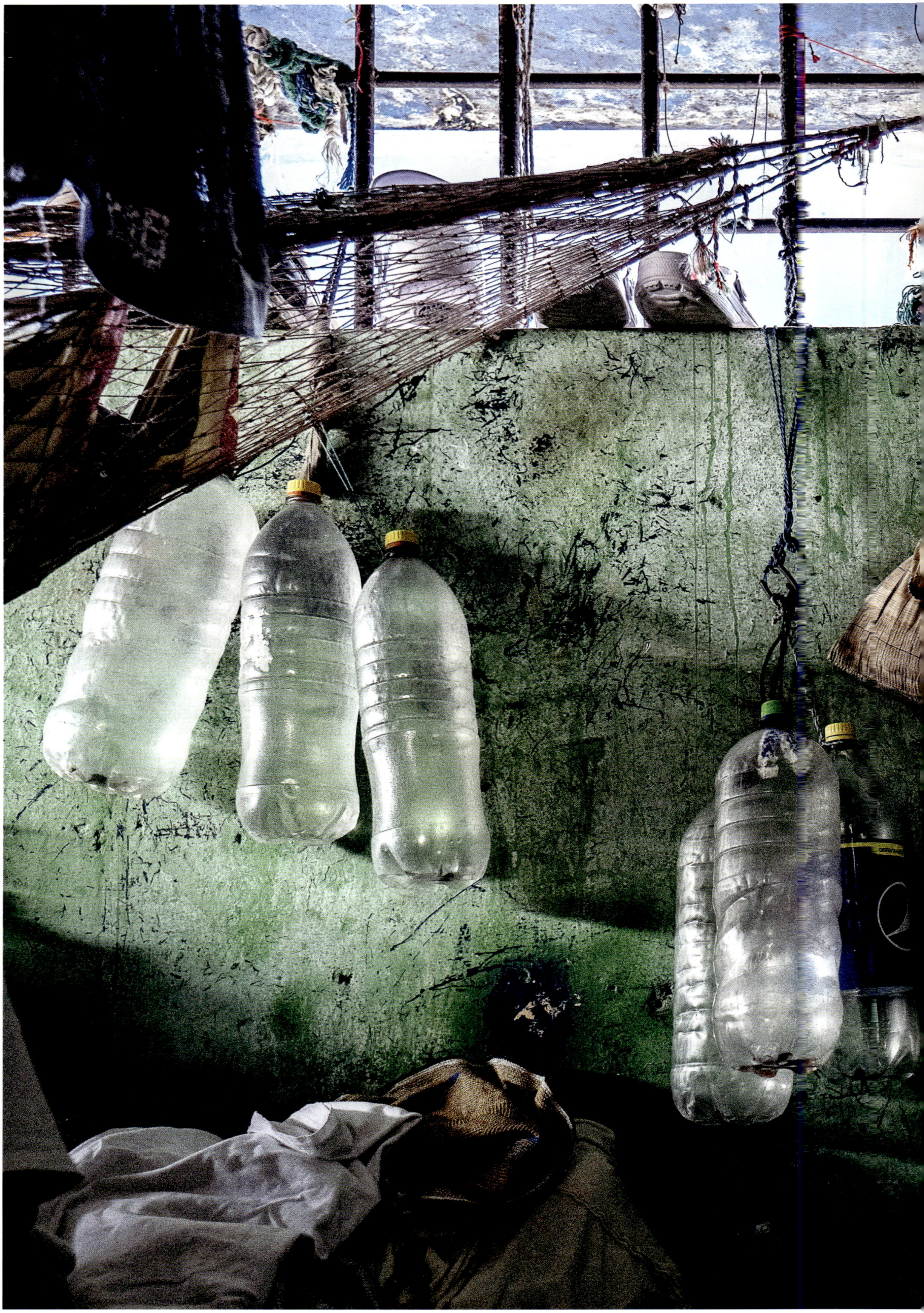

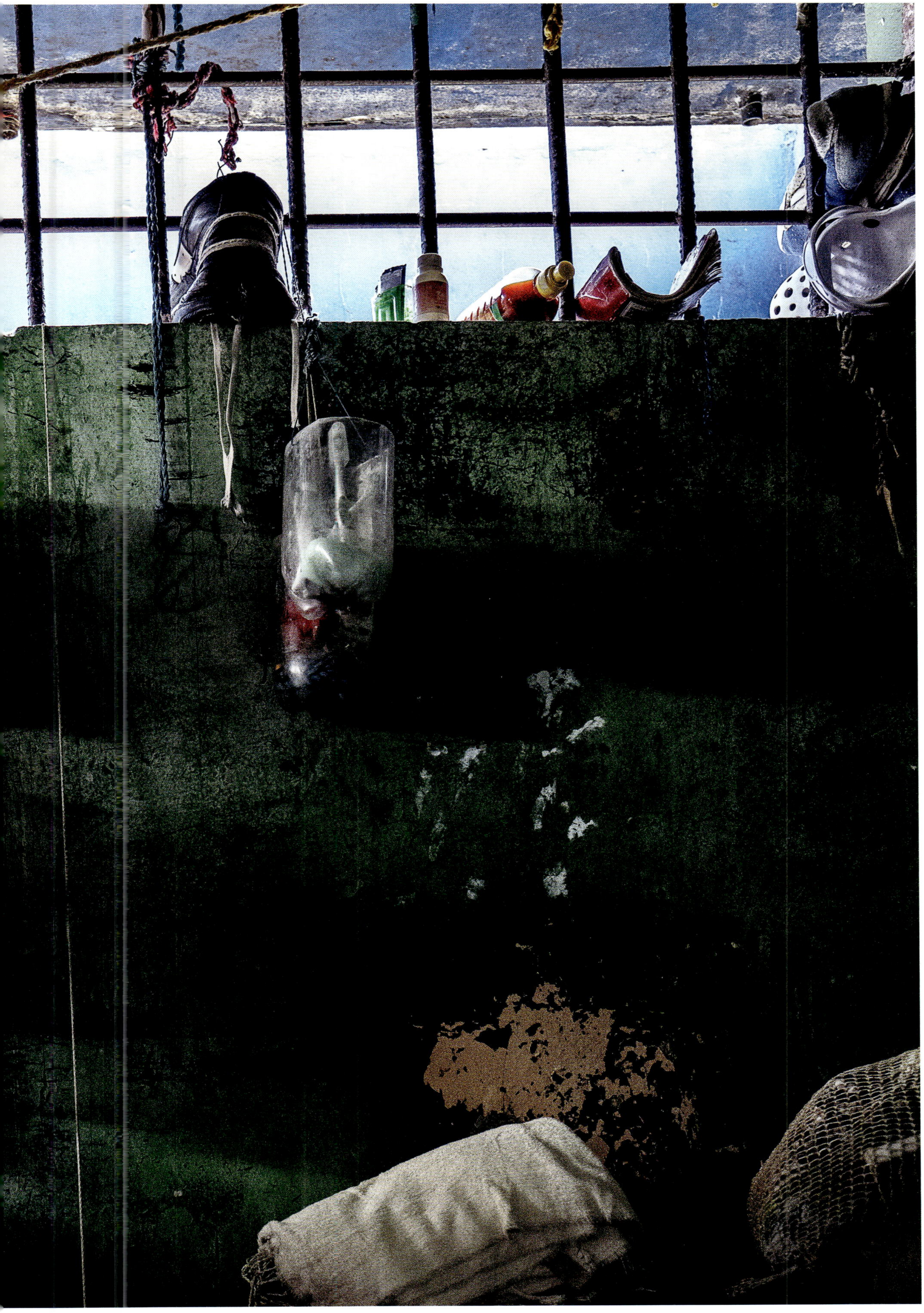

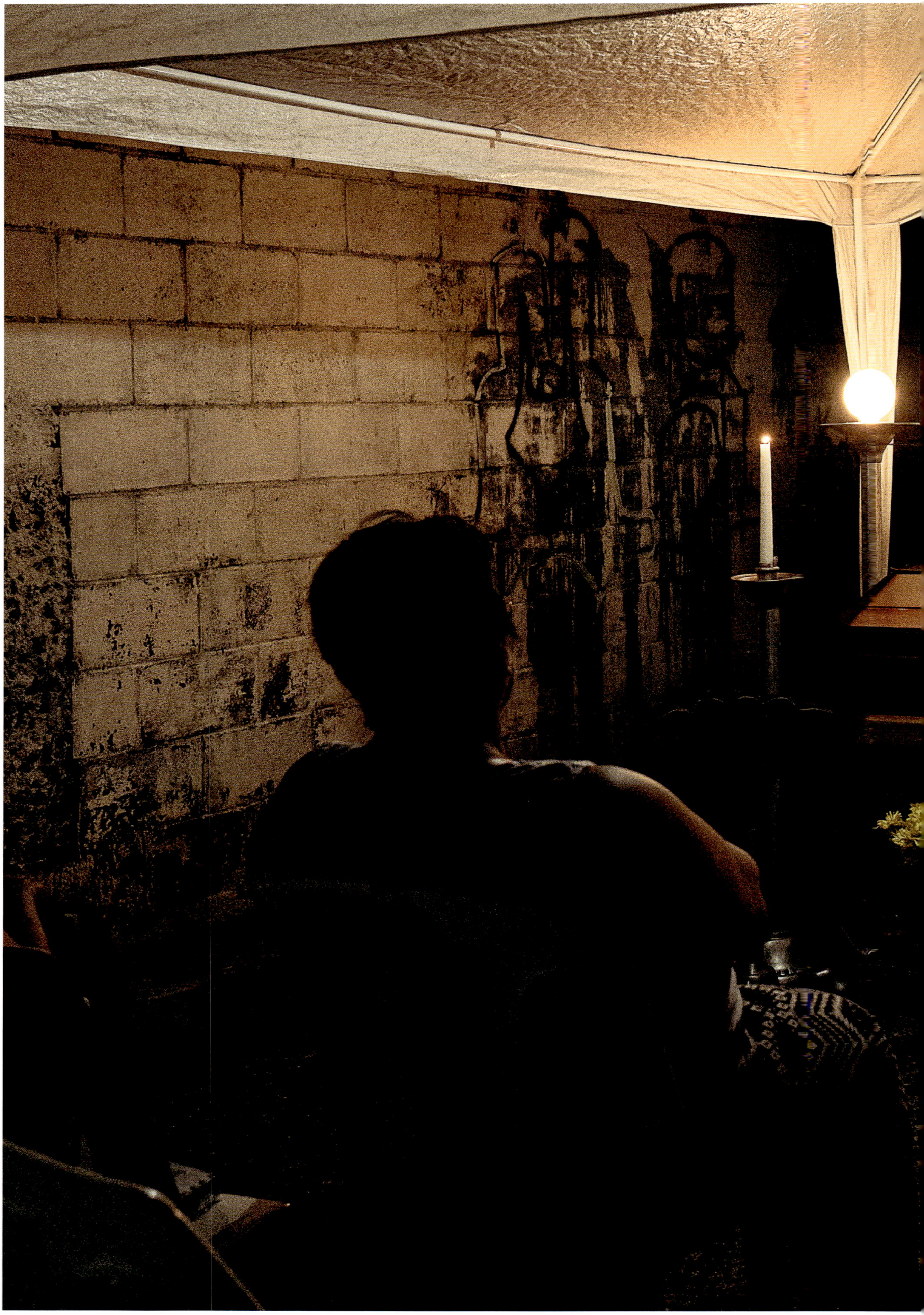

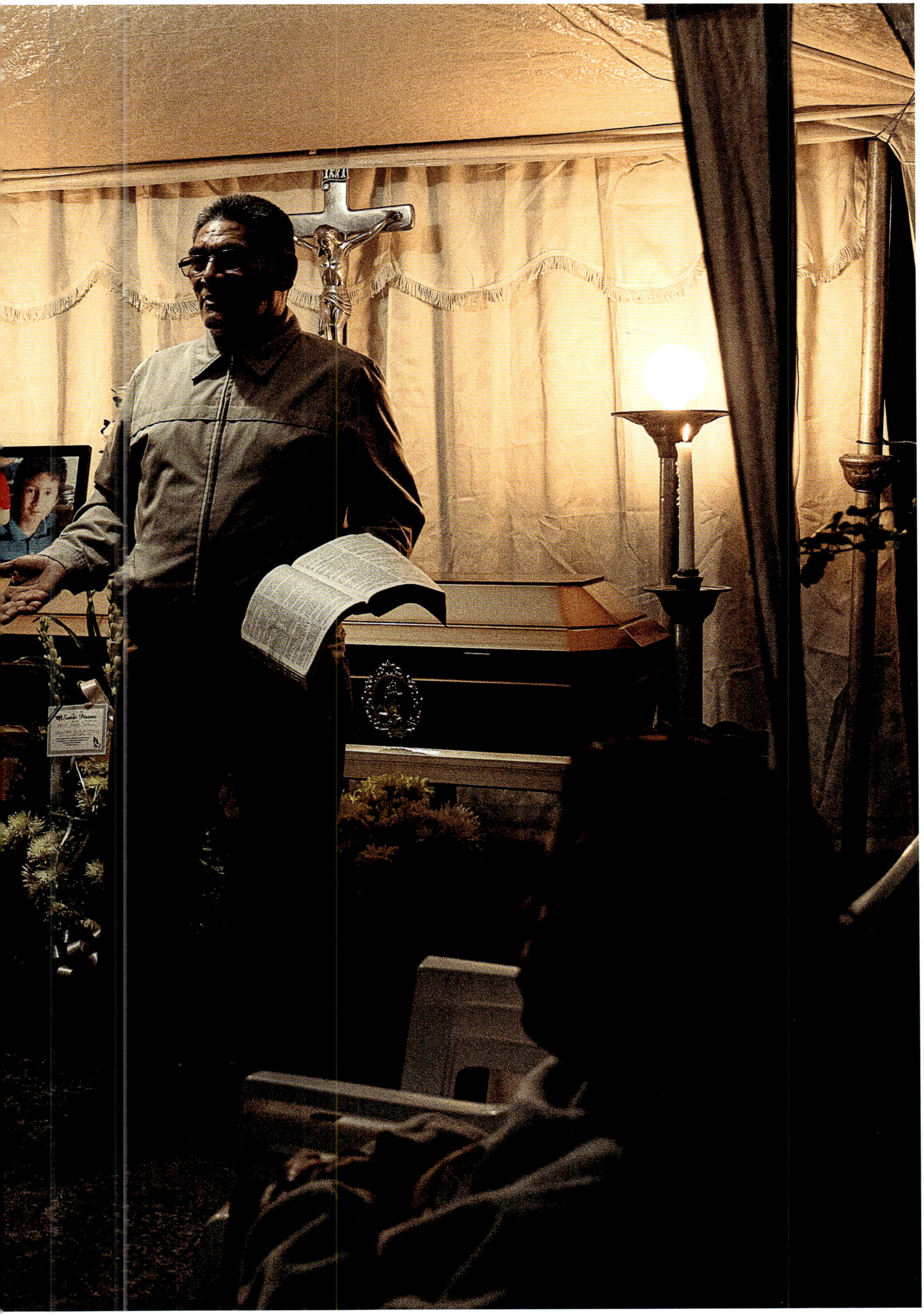

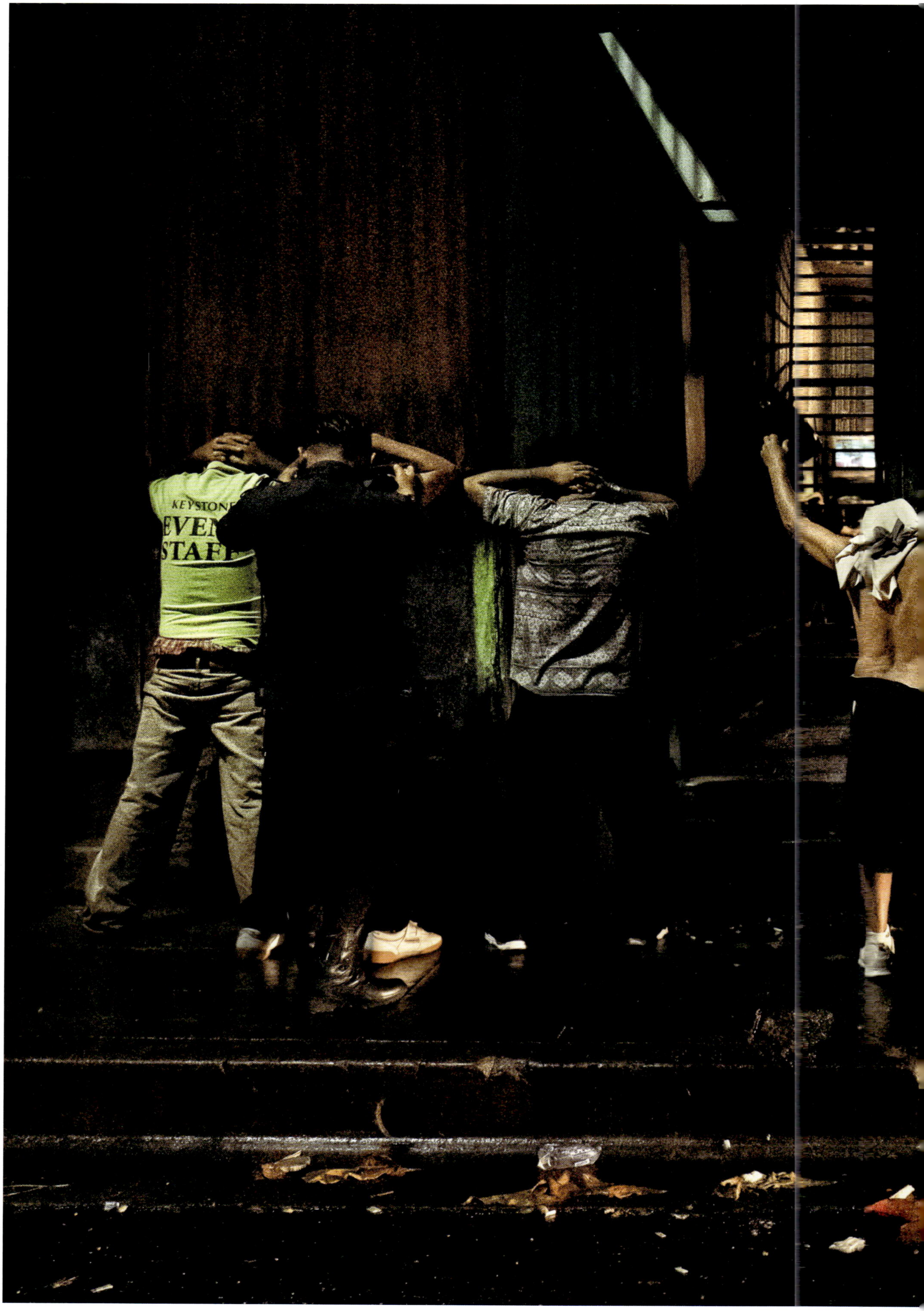
KEYSTONE
EVEN
STAFF

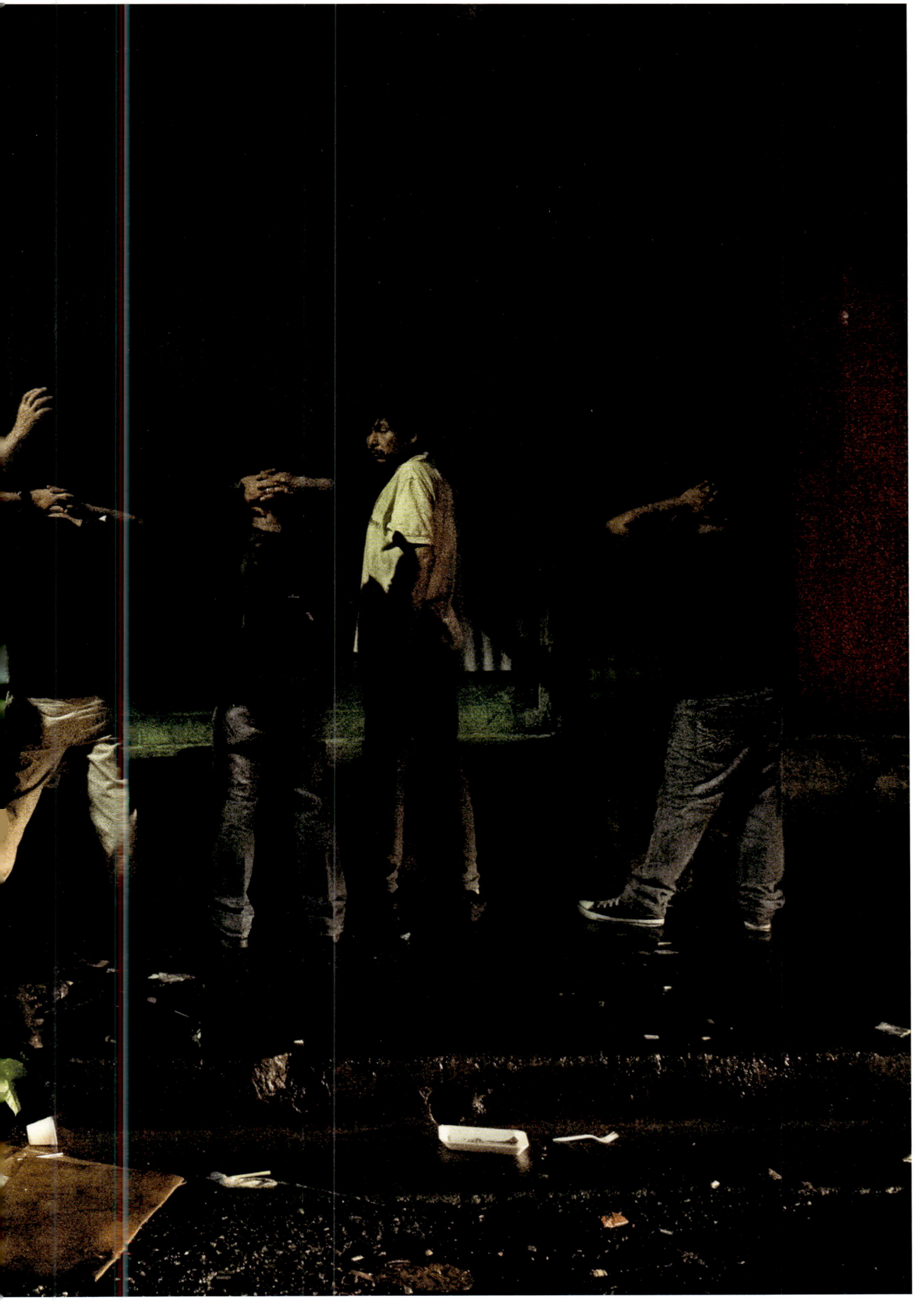

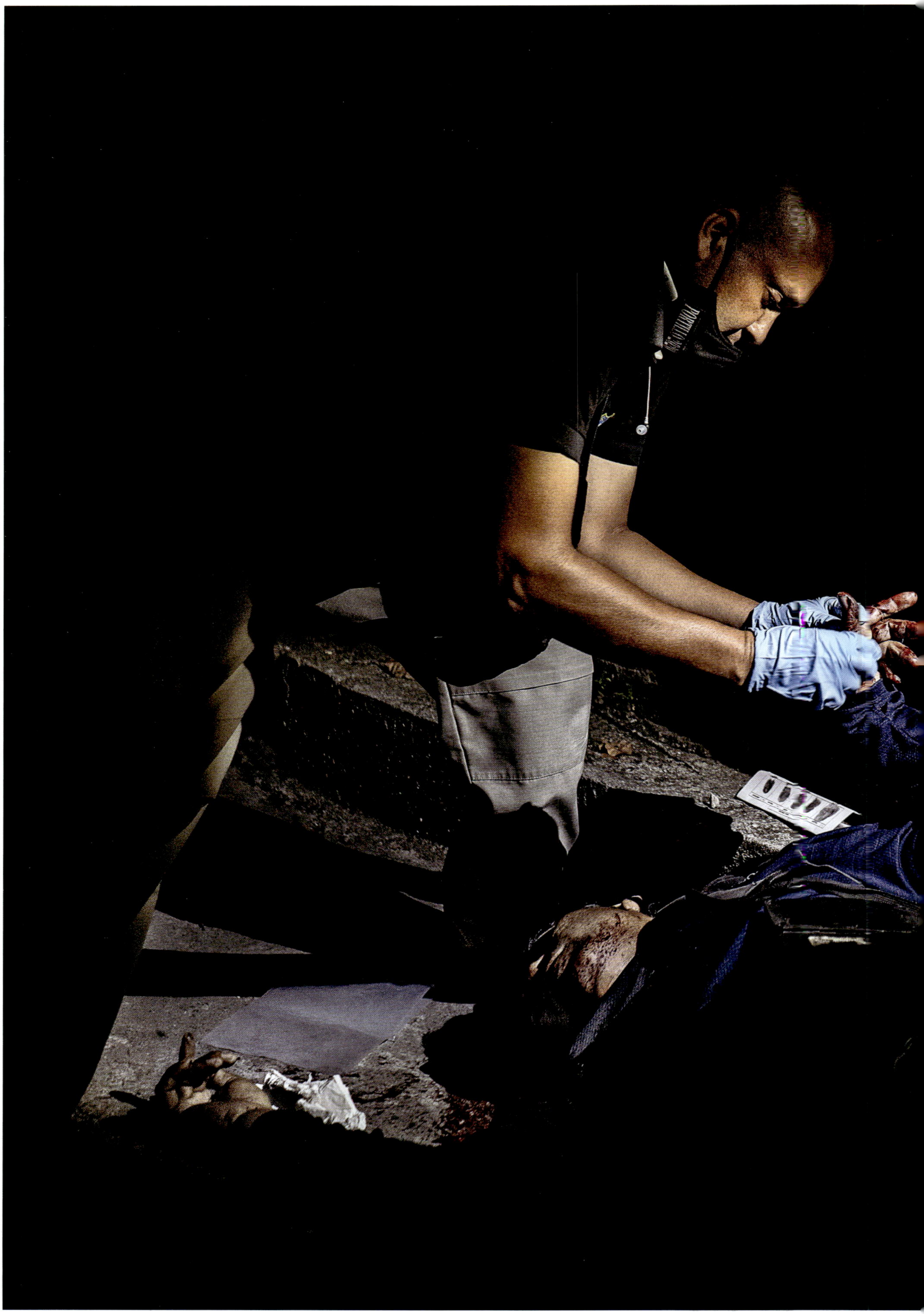

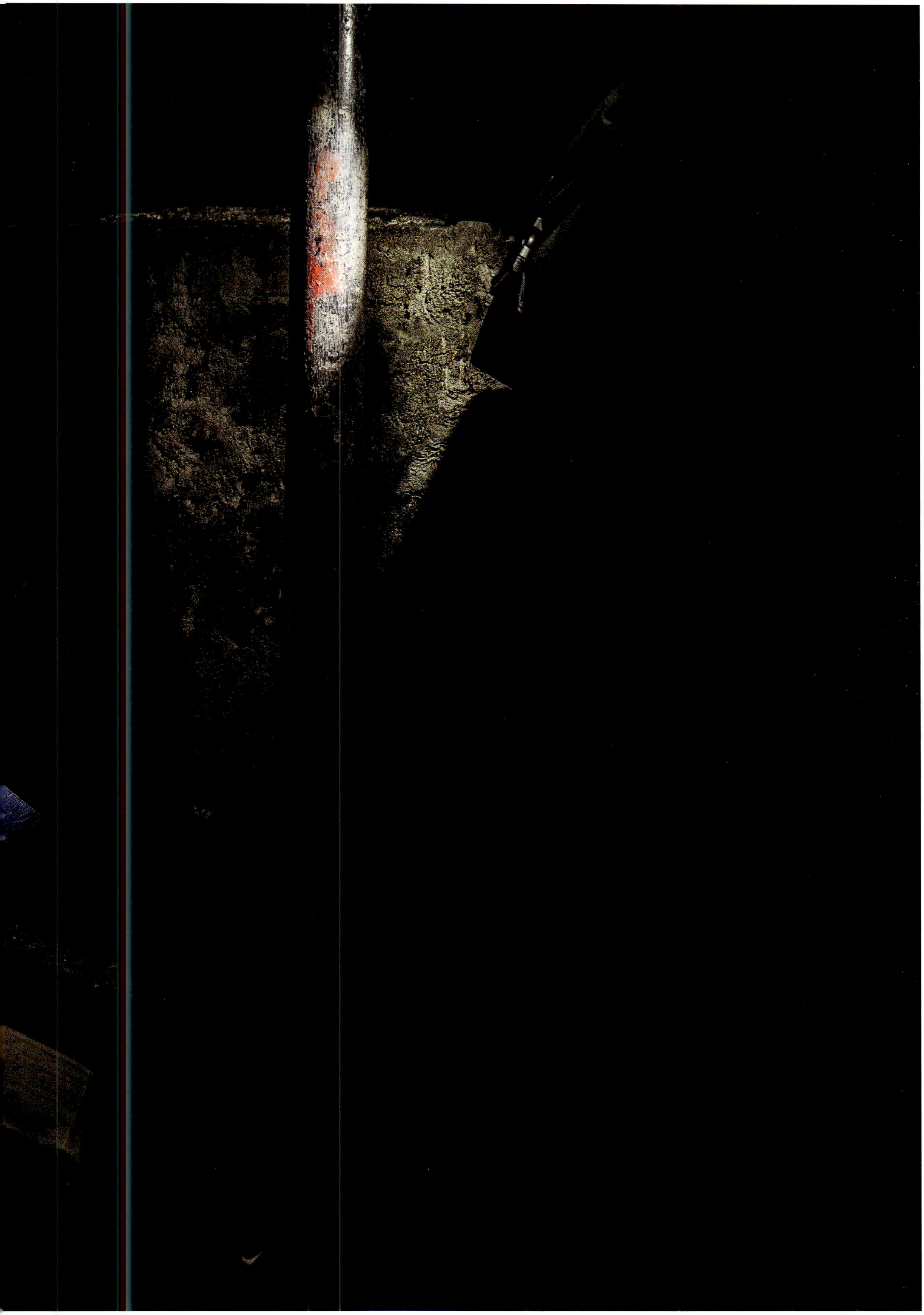

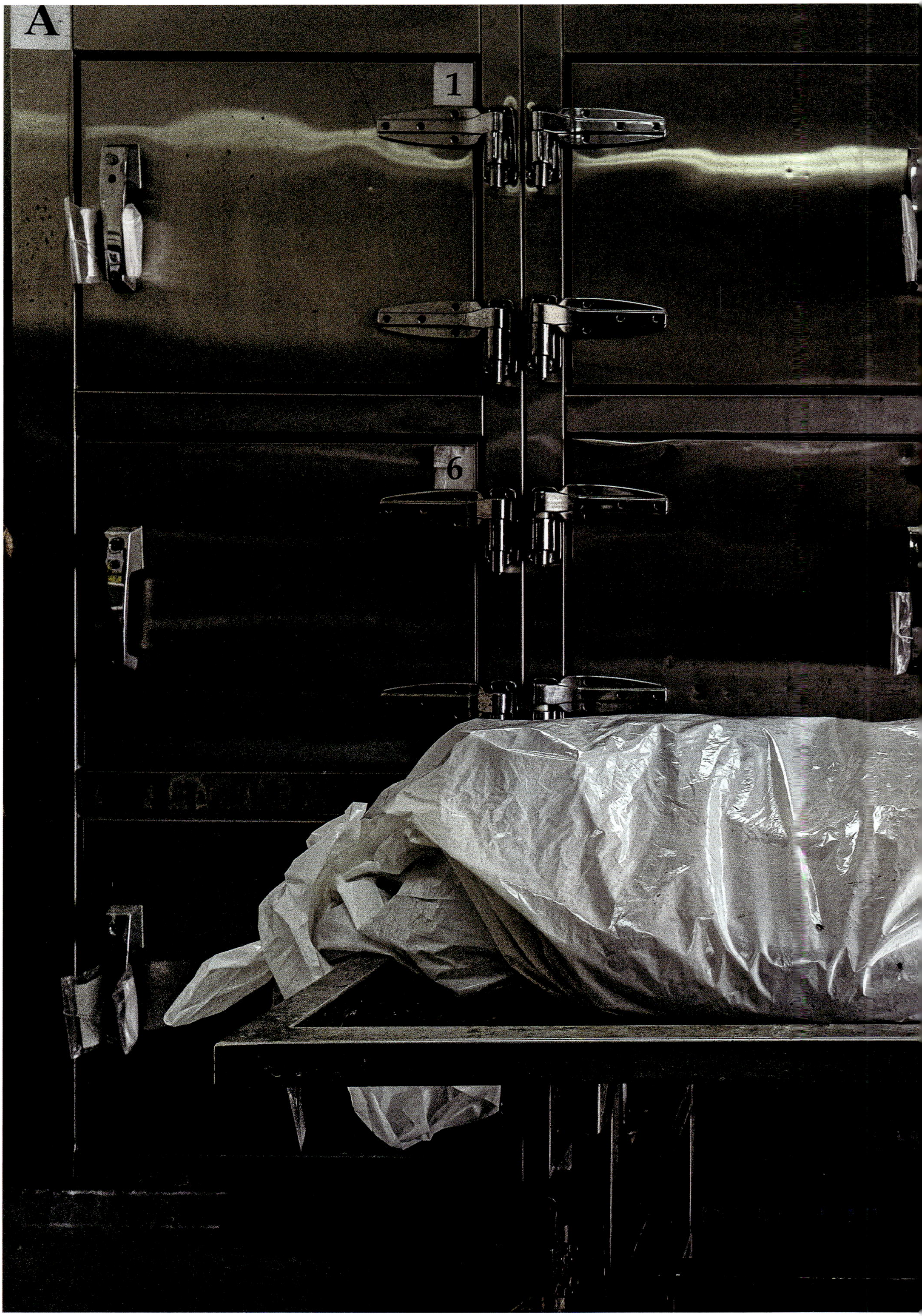
A
1
6

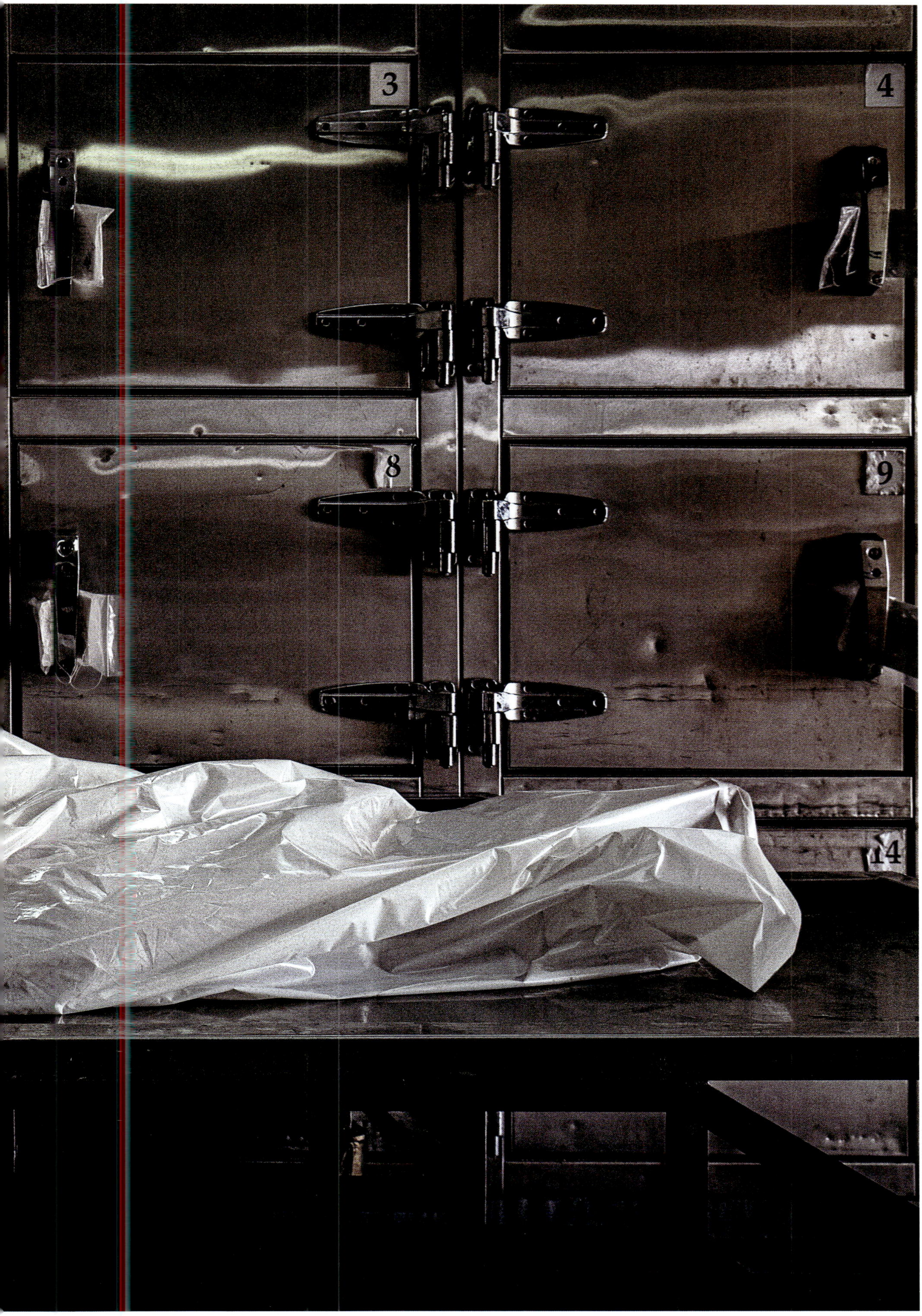
3
4
8
9
14

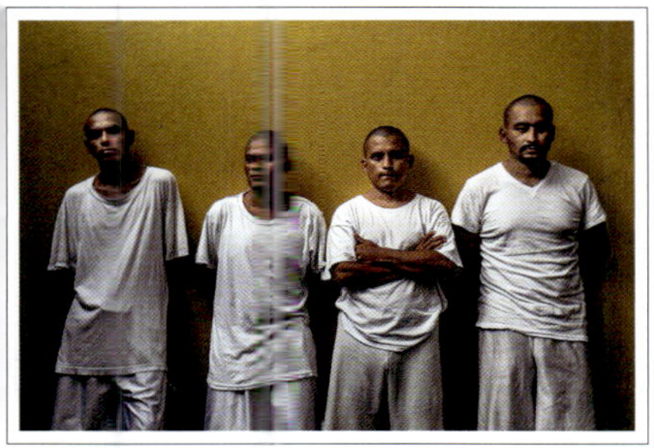

Inmates at the Chalatenango Penal Center—all 1,637 inmates at the Center are members of MS-13.

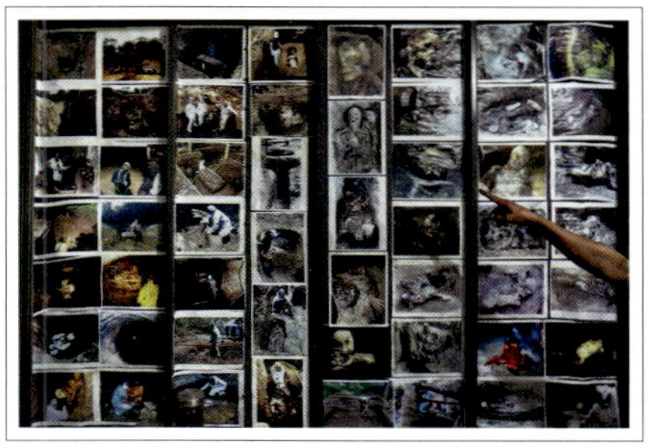

Photographs, mostly taken at clandestine cemeteries, display mutilations or crime scenes on the wall of a forensic criminologist of the Attorney General of the Republic of El Salvador. His methods allow him to preserve evidence through forensic archaeology.

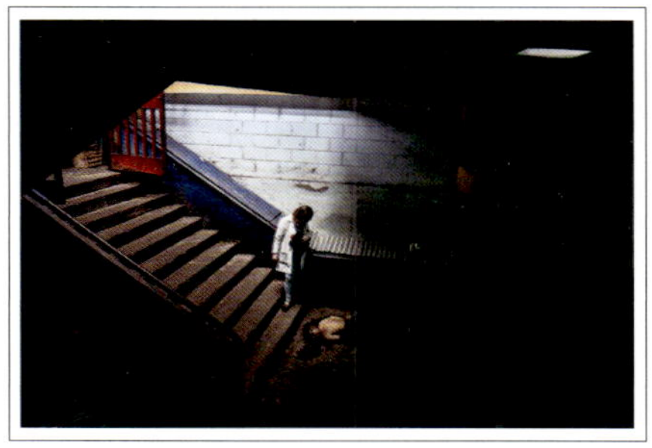

A police officer stands over a body in the San Salvador Central Market, one of the busiest places in the capital of El Salvador. The victim had been handcuffed and shot dead. The National Civil Police (PNC) reported the case occurred around 10:30am.

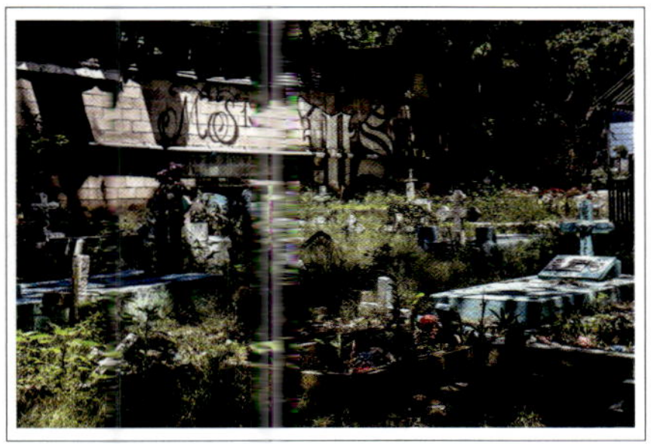

Walls marked with graffiti from MS-13 in Cementerio General de Cuscatancingo, San Salvador.

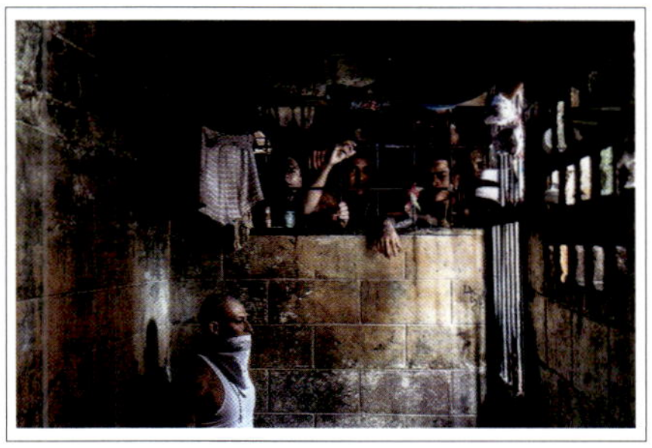

Inmates look out of a cell, while a man wears a bandana to block out the putrid smell in Penal Center of Quezaltepeque.

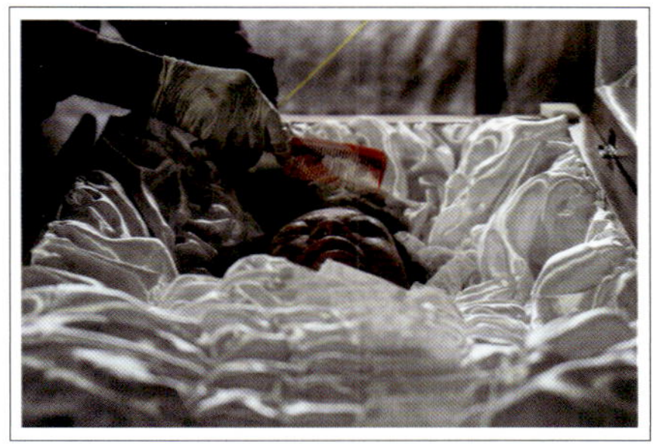

A mortician combs the hair of the body of a homicide victim in preparation for display at the wake in Usulután.

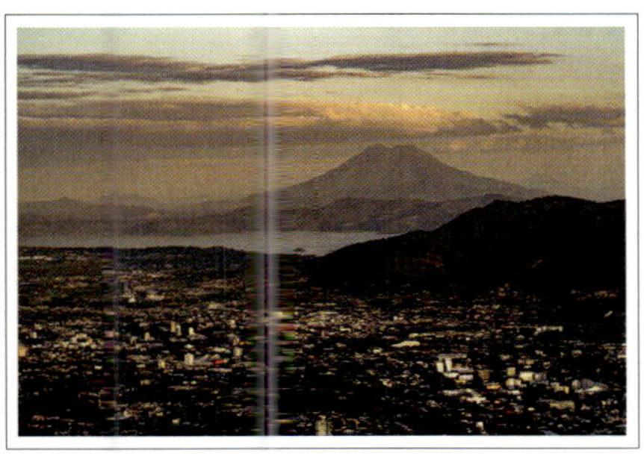

View of San Salvador from Mirador del Boquerón.

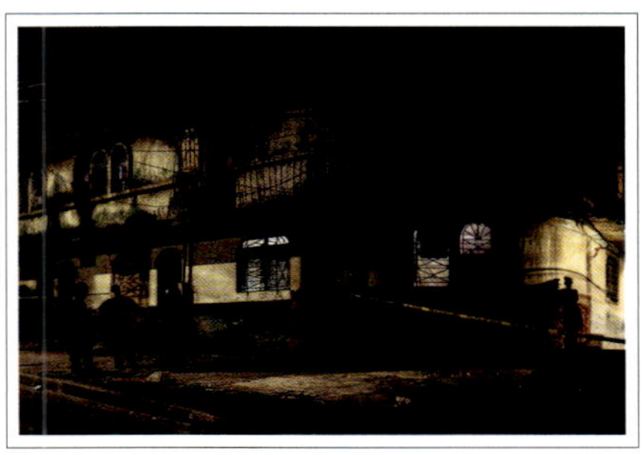

A bystander looks on while police cordon off the area around the body of a murder victim—who was shot eight times—on 38 South Avenue, Terminal de Oriente, Lourdes, San Salvador.

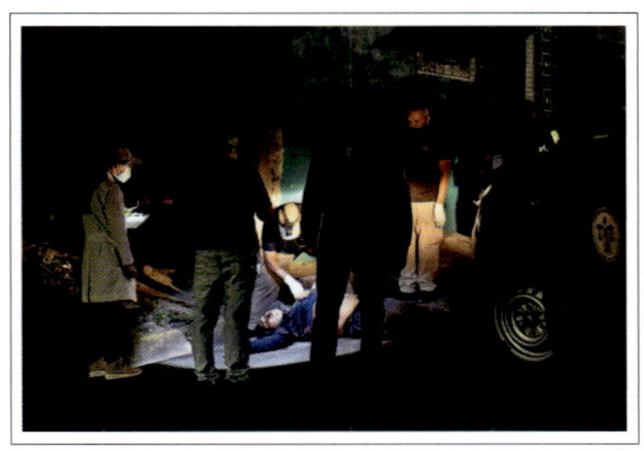

A legal medicine team examines a body in Barrio Lourdes, San Salvador.

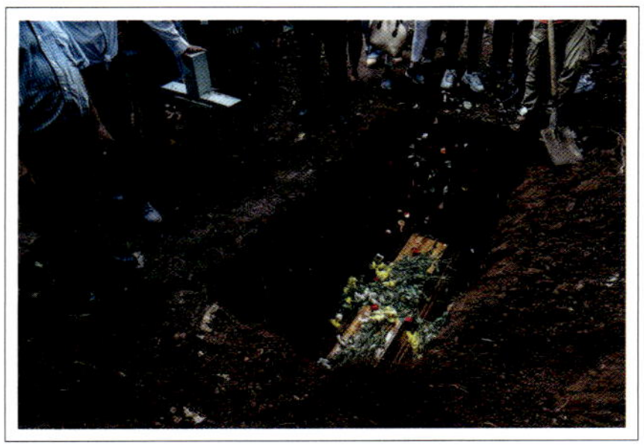

The burial of young alleged gang member, aged 22, in Chapeltique Municipal Cemetery, in San Miguel. He was one of four people killed during a confrontation with agents of special operations police units in a jungle camp.

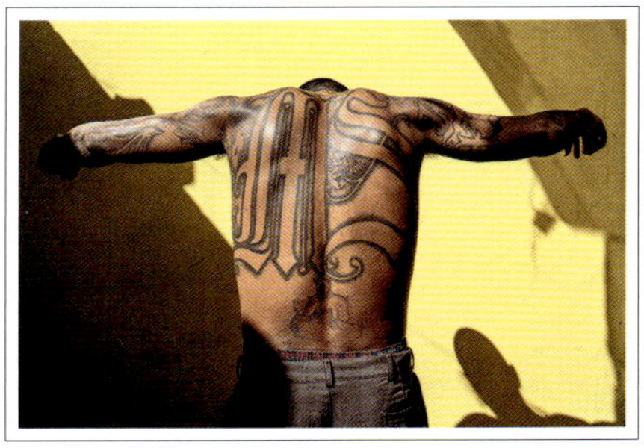

A member of MS-13, aged 27, at the Chalatenango Penal Center.

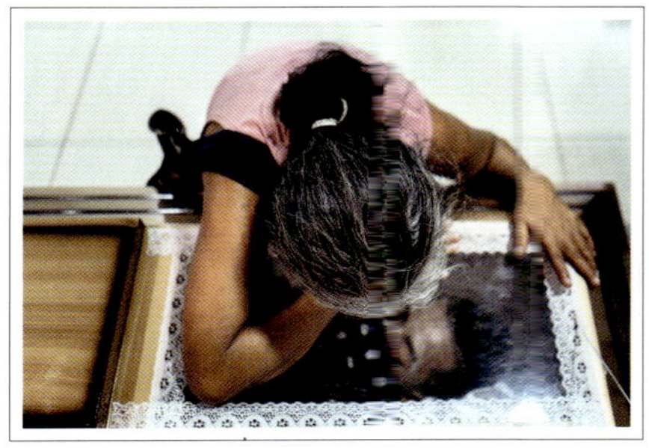

A mother mourns the passing of her son, aged 25, during his wake in San Martín, San Salvador. His face is covered by a bandana due to the brutality of his murder in November, 2018—the third attempt on his life that month.

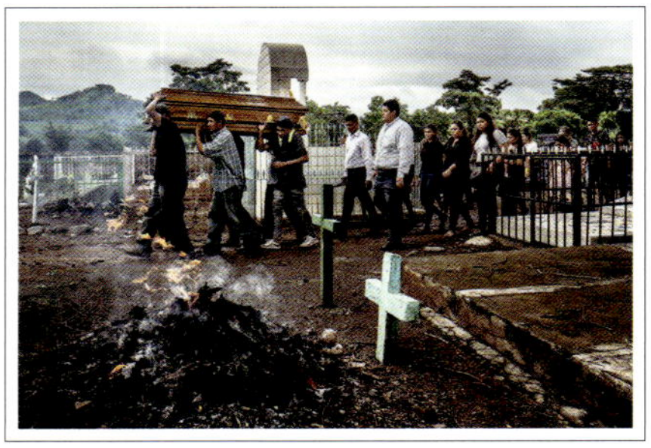

A funeral delegation carries a coffin in Chapeltique Municipal Cemetery in San Miguel.

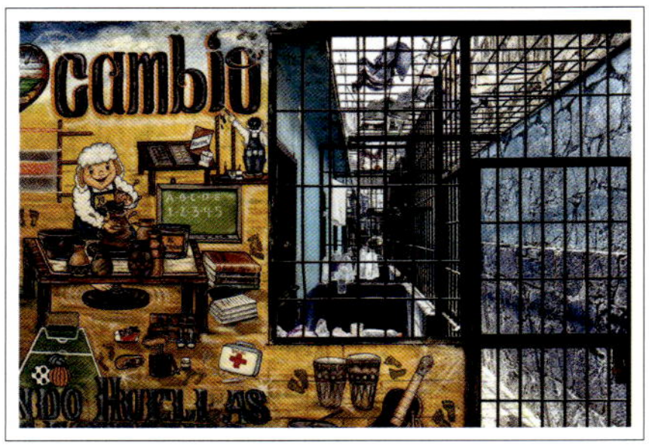

Wall inside one of the high security sectors of the Penal San Francisco Gótera where all inmates are evangelical born-again Christians and nearly 2,000 are gang members. It is the only penal centre where different gangs are incarcerated together—MS-13, La 18, Mao Mao and Mirada Loca.

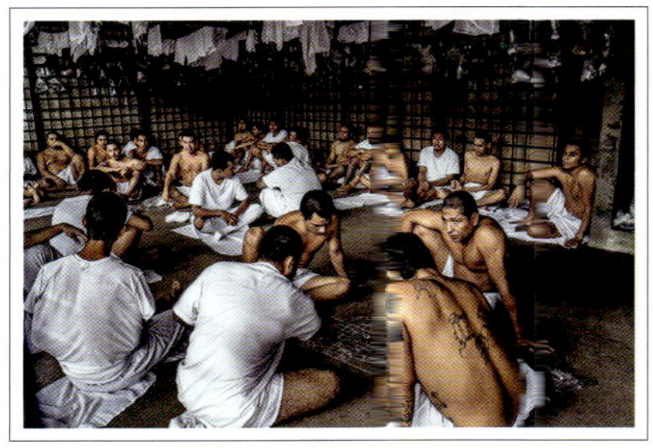

MS-13 gang members play a game in their cell in the Bartolinas Policiales de Lourdes, Colón, San Salvador.

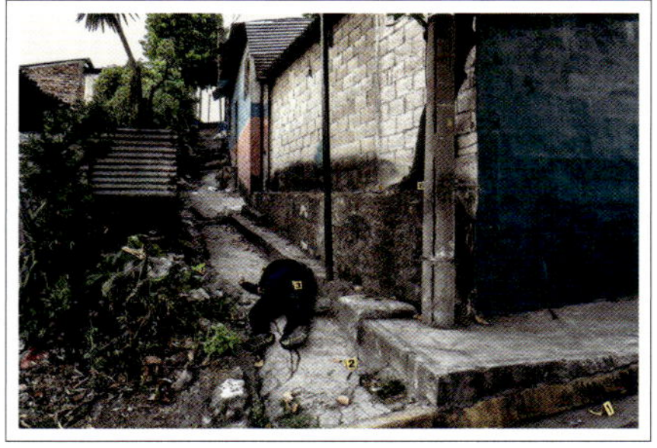

A body found in Lourdes neighbourhood.

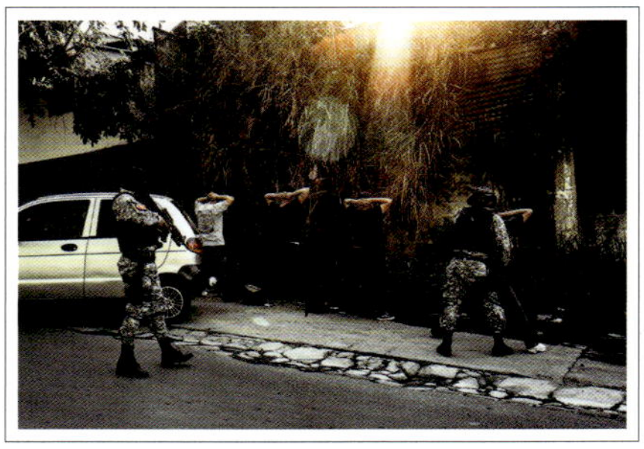

A tactical patrol checks people for weapons and identifying tattoos in the Apopa district.

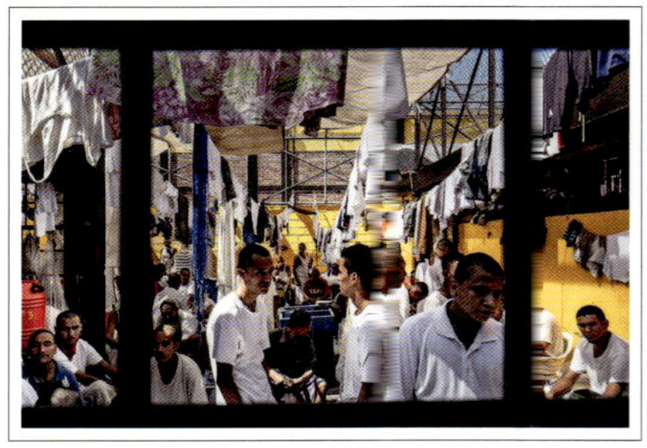

Inmates rest while laundry dries above them in Chalatenango Penal Center.

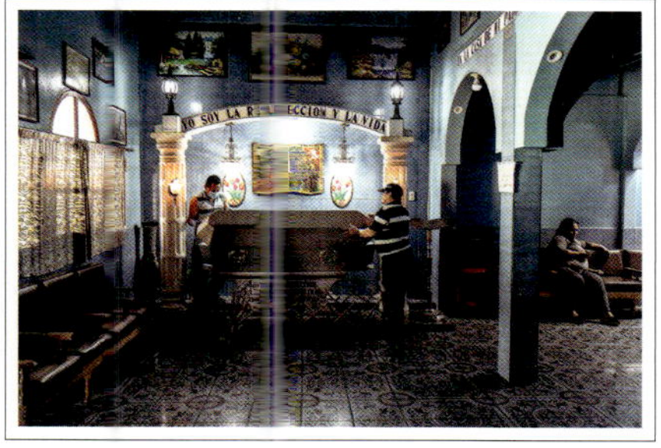

Miguel Ángel (left) and Cesar Barrio (centre), prepare the coffin for the wake of a 37-year-old man who was killed in a motorcycle drive-by shooting in Colonia Santa Cristina, Barrio Santa Anita, San Salvador.

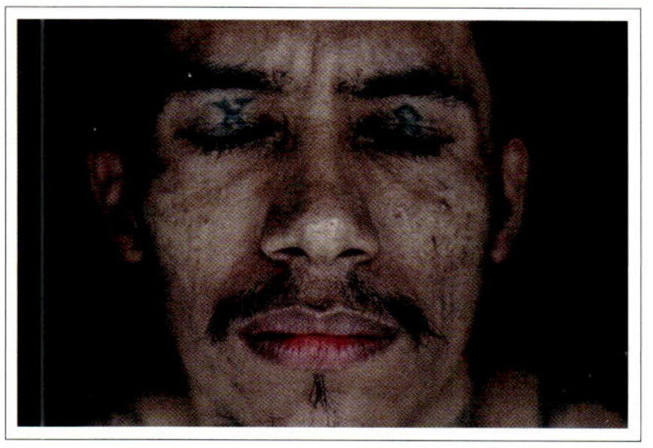

La 18 gang member, aged 35, Bartolinas Policiales de Lourdes, Colón, San Salvador.

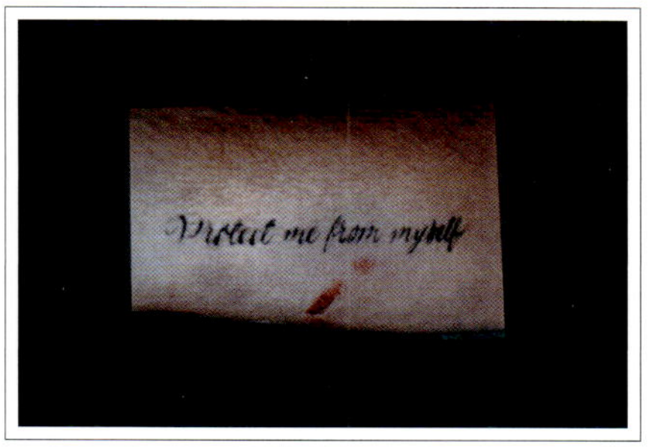

The blood-stained arm of a 28-year-old man who was killed while riding his bicycle—a victim of an alleged gang murder. His tattoo reads 'protect me from myself.' According to law enforcement authorities, he had recently been deported from the United States.

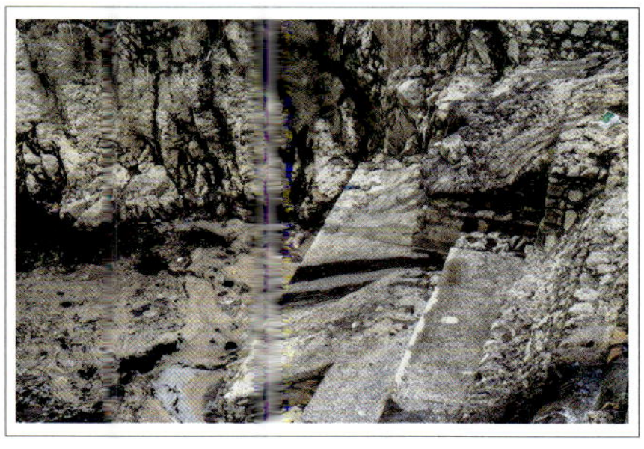

A decomposing body floats in the 'Rio Sucio' (dirty river). The victim had been missing for three days before he was found. Prussia-Venice dam, by Las Mulas Bridge, in the municipality of Ciudad Delgado, San Salvador.

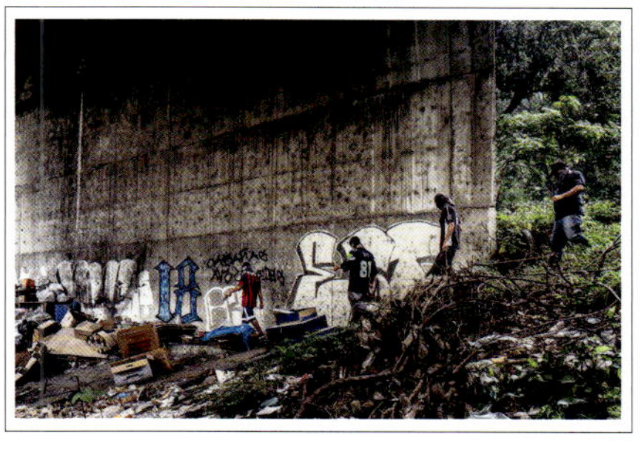

Members of La 18 walk under a graffiti-tagged bridge, marking the gang's territory in San Salvador.

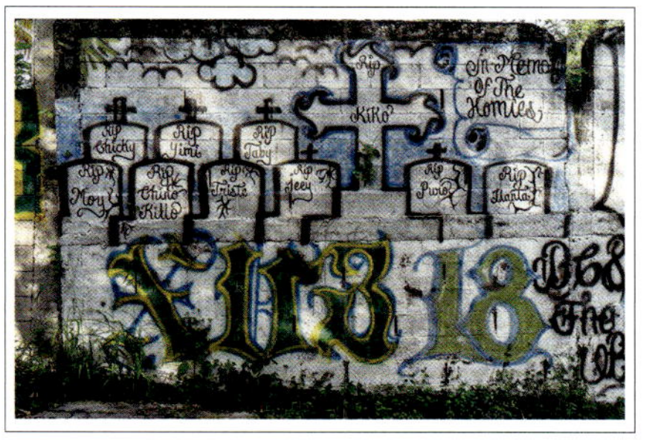

A tribute to the national gang leaders of La 18. In 2016, gang members expelled about 100 families from San Martin municipality in San Salvador—now known as 'ghost town'—for not joining La 18.

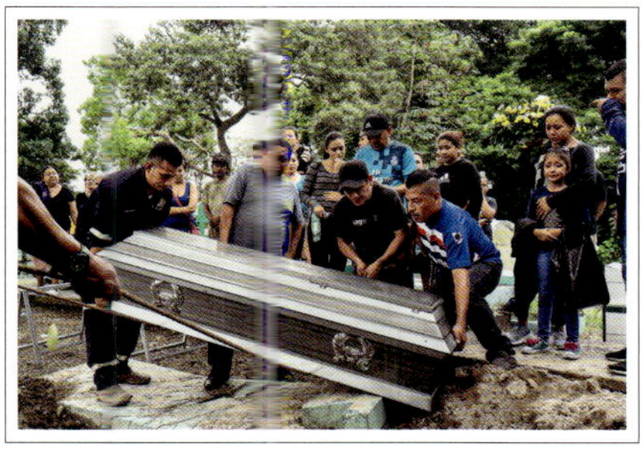

The burial of a 25-year-old man in Ciudad Delgado, San Salvador. His death was one of seventeen murders recorded across the country on the weekend of 20 September 2019.

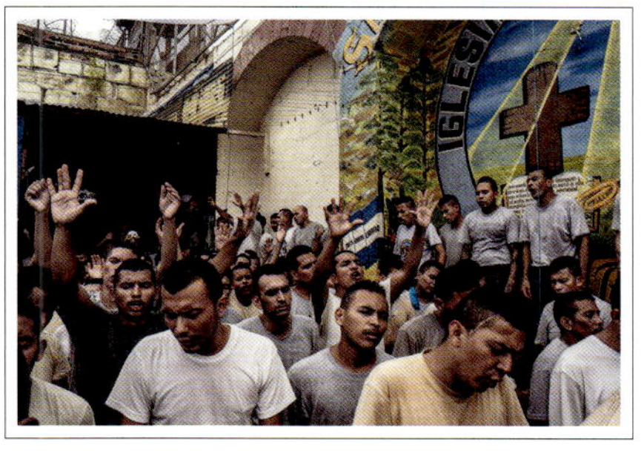

Inmates pray during a sermon at the Penal San Francisco Gótera. The prison encourages a denunciation of gang life and a move toward spirituality, in the form of a Christian-change program.

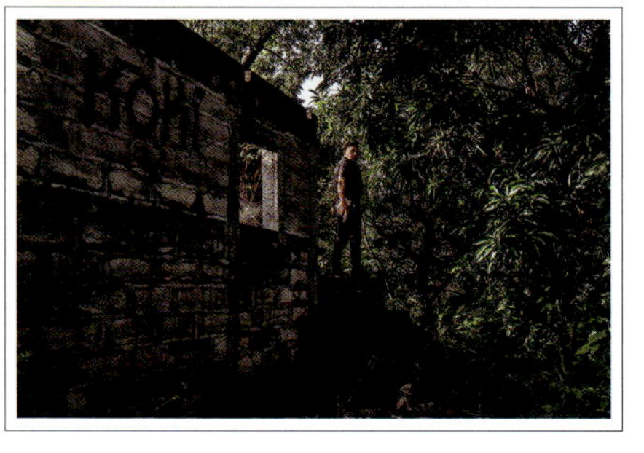

A policeman during a patrol in San Martín, San Salvador. The area is considered a 'hot zone' due to the high presence of Barrio 18. The gang has effective jurisdiction over the area and regularly carries out extortion, armed confrontations, kidnappings, rapes and murders. The PNC has increased its presence but to date has been unable to expel the gang from the area.

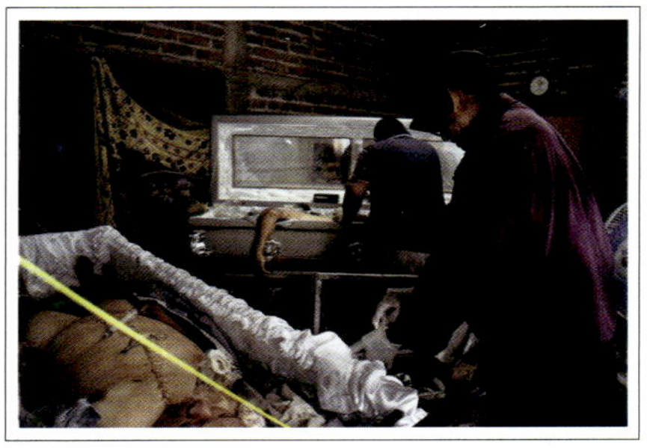

A mortician and his assistant prepare the bodies of a double homicide for the wake in Usulután. Though typically handled in a lab, at the family's request the deceased can be prepared inside the coffins at their homes, as in the case above. According to police reports, mother and daughter, were victims of a double homicide—shot and killed inside their house.

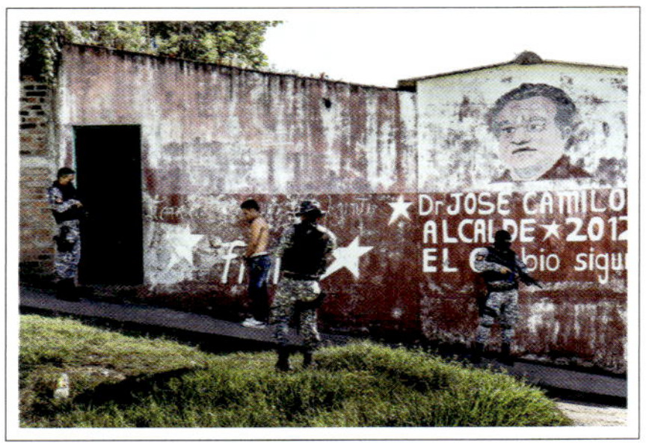

A tactical patrol checks a passerby for weapons and identifying tattoos in Apopa municipality.

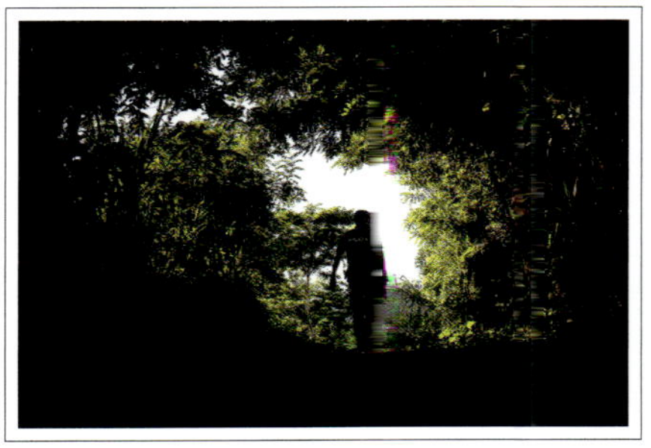

A policeman during a patrol in San Martín, San Salvador.

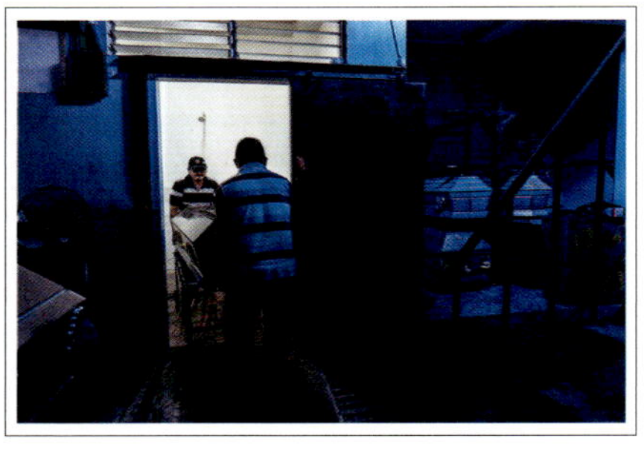

A mortician and his assistant prepare a coffin.

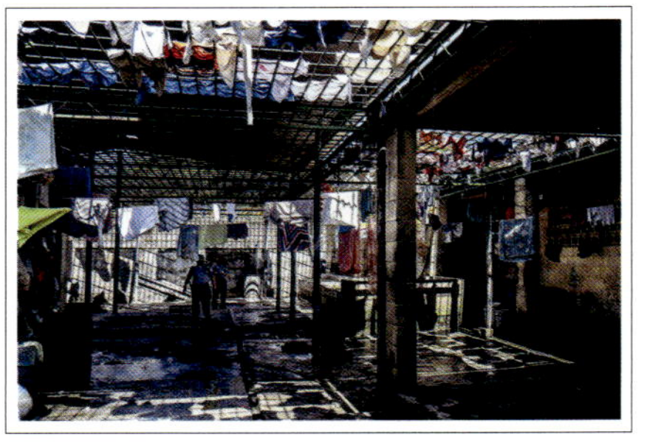

Two guards check the inmates' courtyard in the Penal Center of Quezaltepeque. The Center holds 1,898 inmates—all of whom are La 18 gang members.

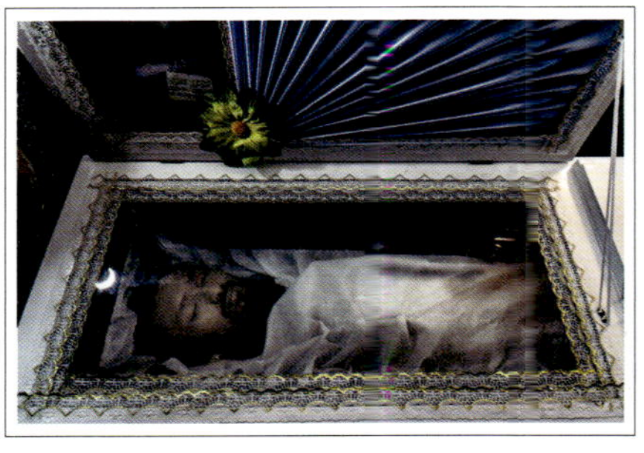

The wake of a 28-year-old man in Aguilares Colonia St. Helena, San Salvador. He lived in the United States from the age of 1[illegible] to 24, when he was deported back toEl Salvador.

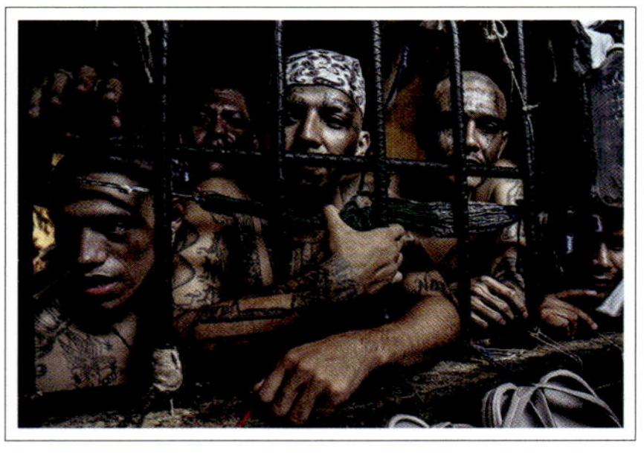

Inmates look out of a cell in the Penal Center of Quezaltepeque.

The government introduced a series of 'extraordinary measures' in 2016 designed to curb gang violence, such as suspending visits, cutting off telecommunications and ending recess time for prisoners. In such an over-crowded prison there are many human rights concerns, not least of all the living conditions being a breeding ground for contagious diseases.

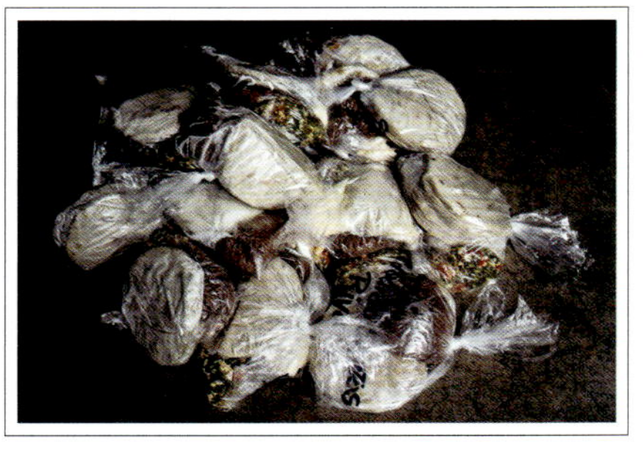

Food parcels consisting of vegetables, rice and lentils piled on the floor for inmates outside their holding cells in Bartolinas Policiales de Lourdes, Colón, San Salvador.

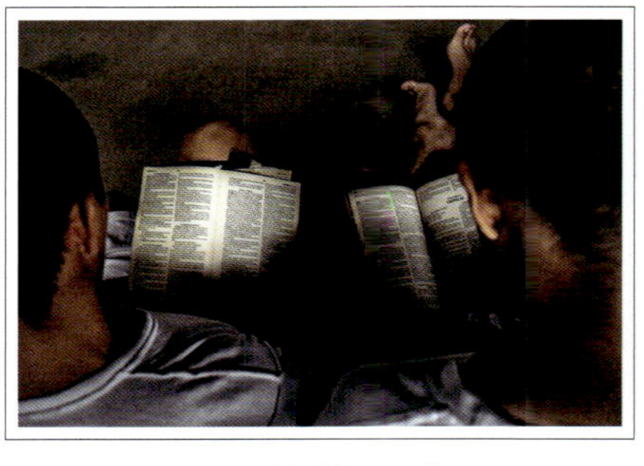

Gang members read bibles in their prison holding cells in Bartolinas Policiales de Lourdes, Colón, San Salvador.

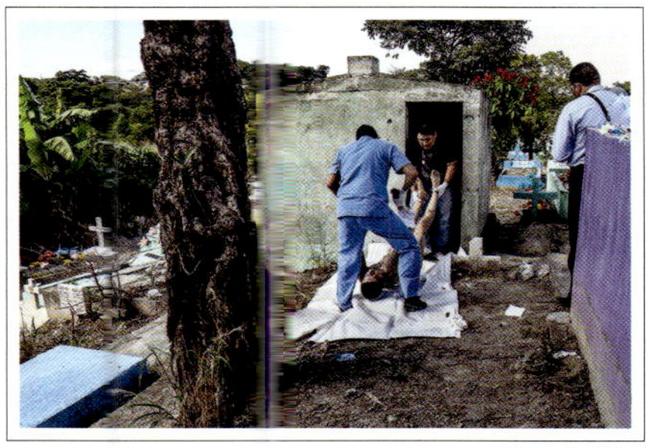

The body of a 23-year-old man is pulled out of a crypt by a legal medicine team in Cemetery of Ciudad Delgado, San Sebastian. Although police sources reported the victim had no gang ties, his body had evidence of torture.

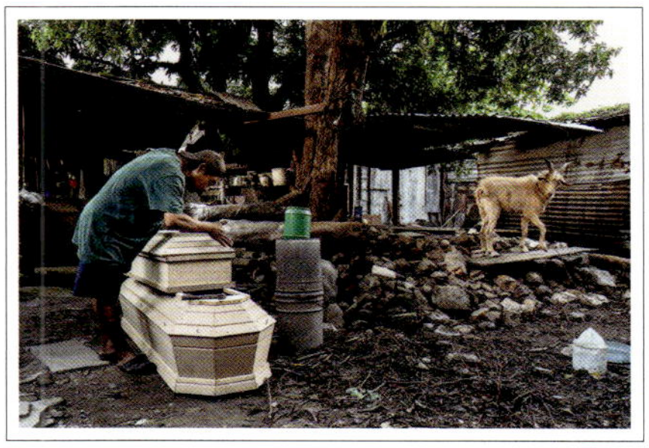

A man prepares coffins at his workshop while his goat looks on in San Salvador.

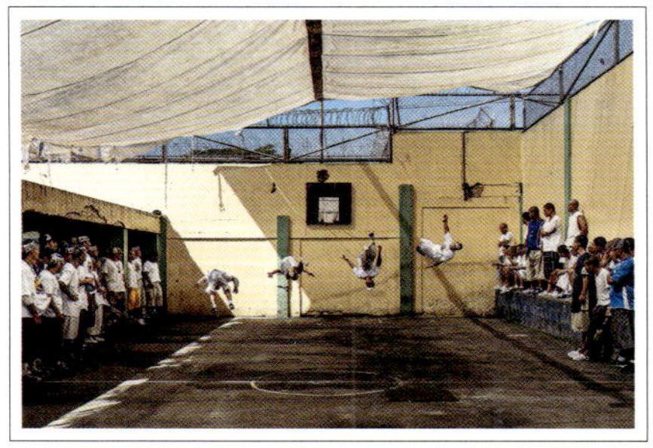

Inmates perform gymnastics at the Chalatenango Penal Center.

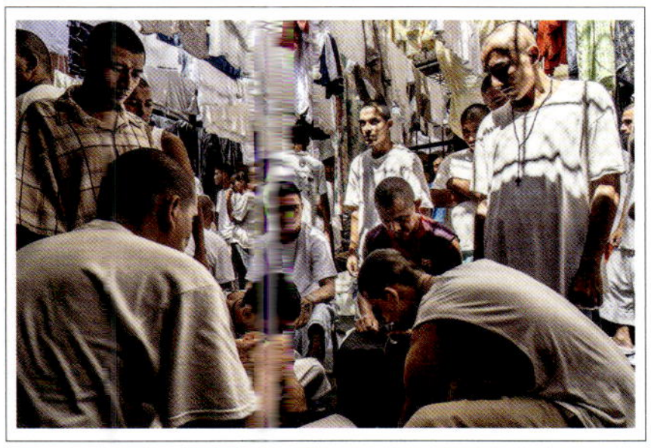

Inmates play cards in Chalatenango Penal Center

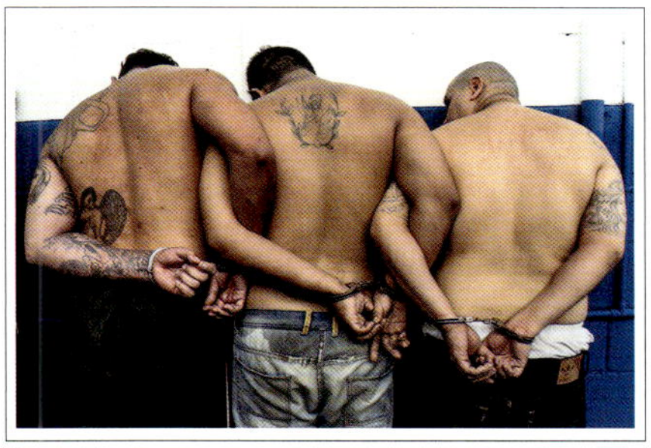

Detained gang members at the Soyapango police unit in San Bartolo, San Salvador.

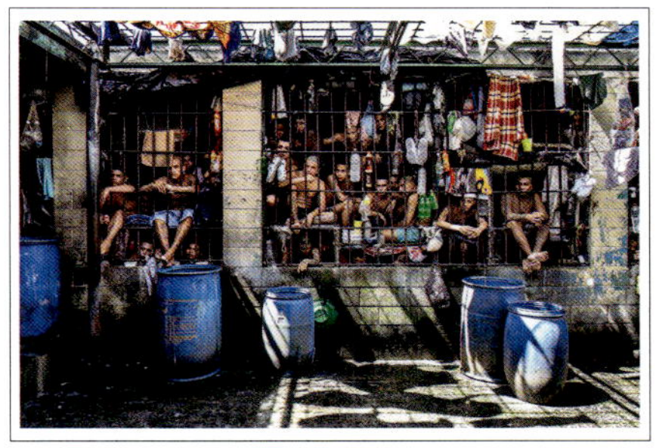

Inmates look out of a cell in a section where 'extraordinary measures' were introduced in the Penal Center of Quezaltepeque.

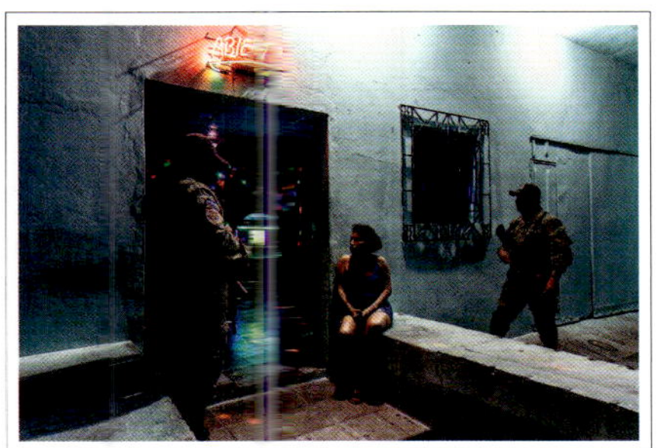

A woman sits outside a bar during a police raid in Lourdes Colón, in the department of La Libertad.

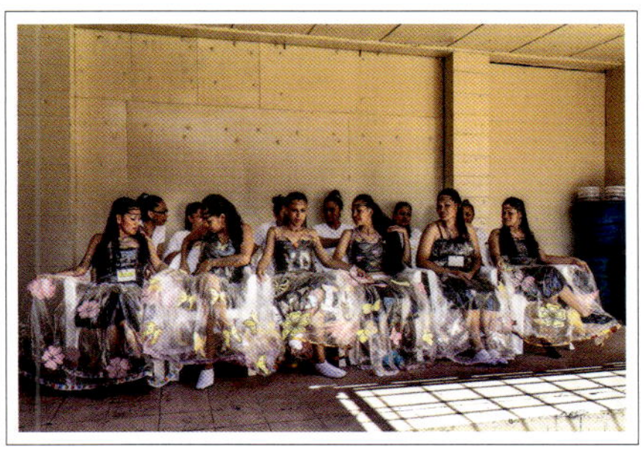

Inmates display their fashion creations as part of the Yo Cambio ('I Change') programme, which attempts to rehabilitate prisoners at the Penal Center of Quezaltepeque.

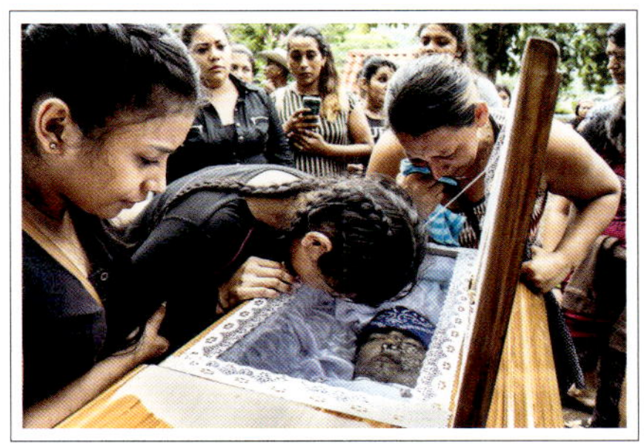

Funeral attendees mourn over the coffin of the deceased at Chapeltique Municipal Cemetery. During the funeral, gang members placed marijuana, a military medal, and a shirt reading 'Cara de Malo' ('Face of Evil') in the grave.

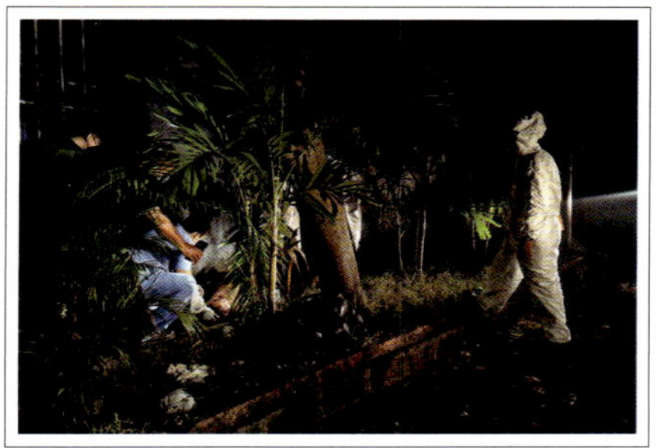

Police officers examine a body on the pavement in the Santa Anita neighbourhood of San Salvador.

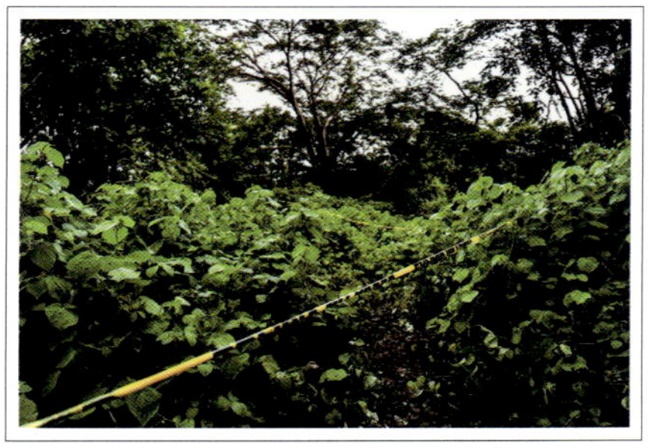

A crime scene where four gang members from the MS-13 and Clica Sailors Locos Salvatruchos (SLS) were killed during a confrontation with police officers of the Jaguares Unit. According to the authorities, between nine and twelve gang members were in the camp with weapons including pistols, rifles and shotguns in the canton Los Ejidos of the municipality of Moncagua in the department of San Miguel.

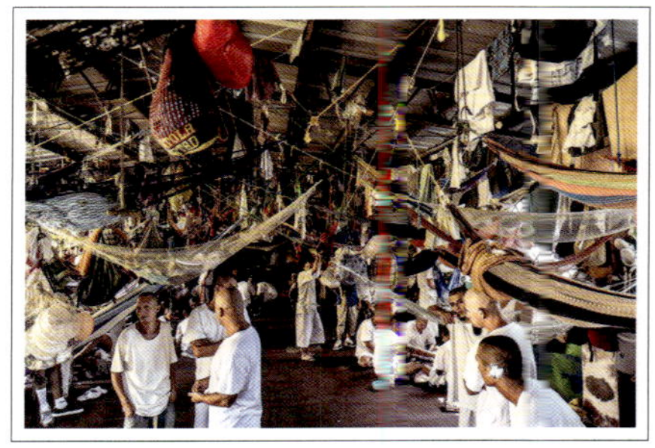

Inside the Chalatenango Penal Center

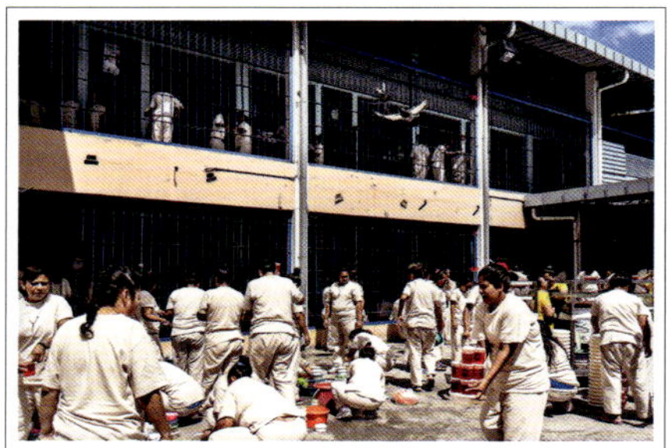

Prisoners prepare lunch at the Ilopango Women's Prison.

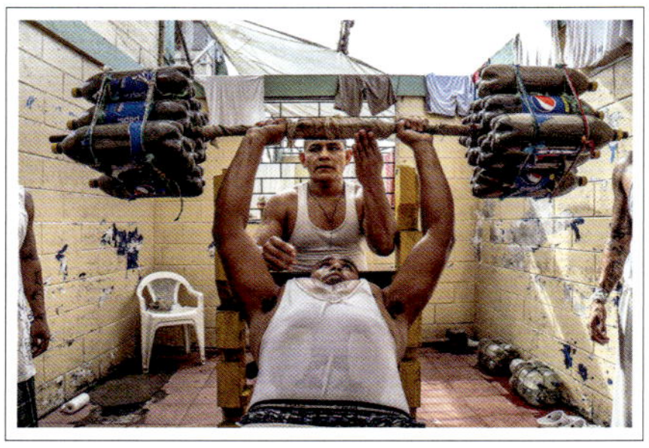

A prisoner lifts a makeshift barbell made of soda bottles and sand at the Chalatenango Penal Center.

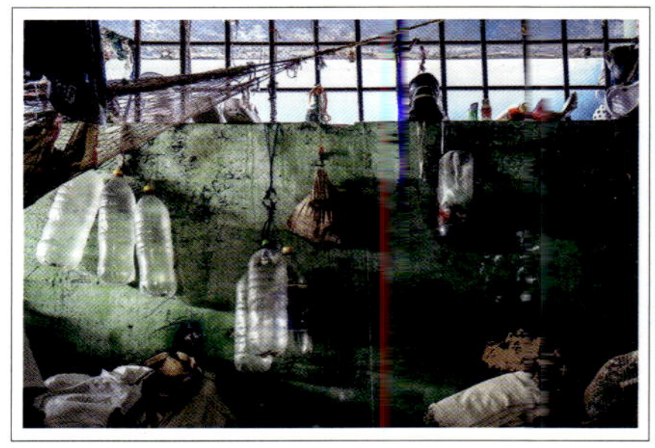

Personal belongings hang on a cell wall in Chalatenango Penal Center.

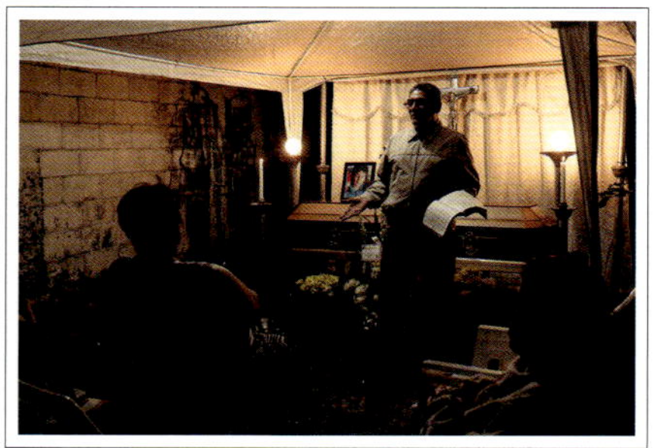

The wake of an 11-year-old boy who was murdered in the Veracruz neighbourhood of San Salvador. According to the Attorney General's Office the boy was playing with friends near the demarcation line between the La 18 and MS-13 gangs when they were kidnapped. His two friends escaped, but he was killed. At his wake, his family said he loved skateboarding, soccer, and the new President Nayib Bukele.

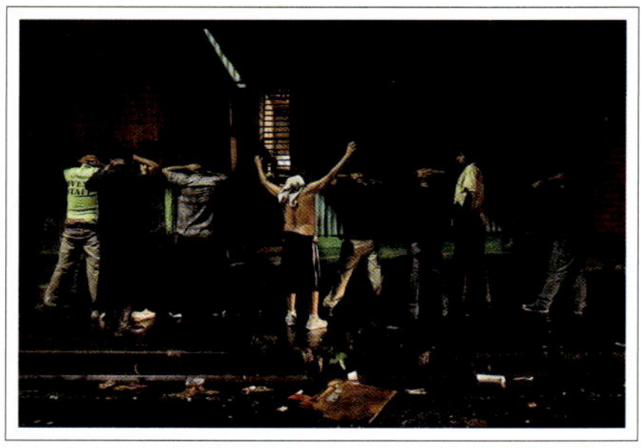

Police check customers of a bar for gang members and gang activity in Calle Concepcion, San Salvador.

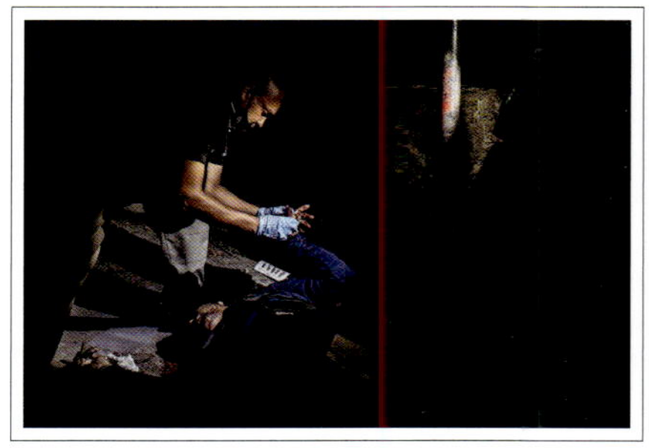

A policeman takes the fingerprints of a murder victim on 38 South Avenue, Terminal de Oriente, Lourdes, San Salvador.

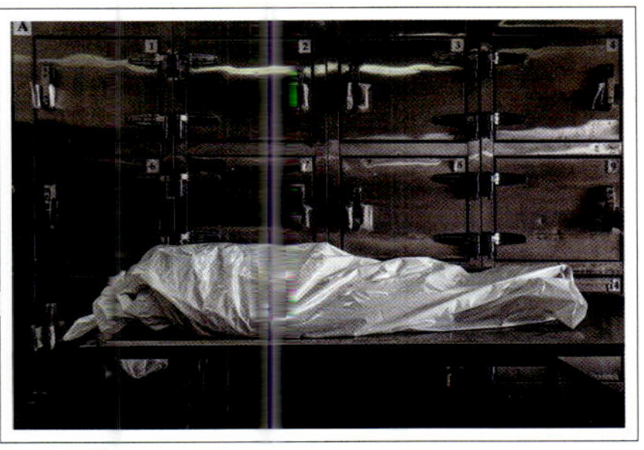

A body in the autopsy room of the Institute of Legal Medicine in San Salvador. The victim was a farmer and former soldier who formed a vigilante group opposing MS-13. Police sources said he was shot thirteen times.

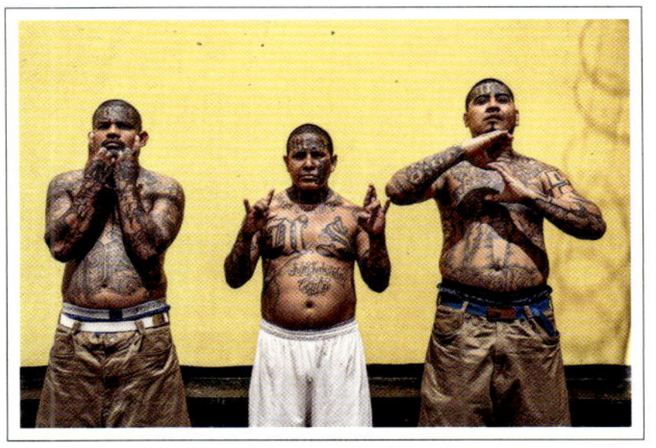

All ages and stated crimes/charges for the portraits taken in prisons were supplied voluntarily by the inmates themselves. This information was not verified with the prison authorities and thus can only be taken at face value.

Three inmates—all MS-13 gang members—flash their gang signs at Chalatenango Penal Center.

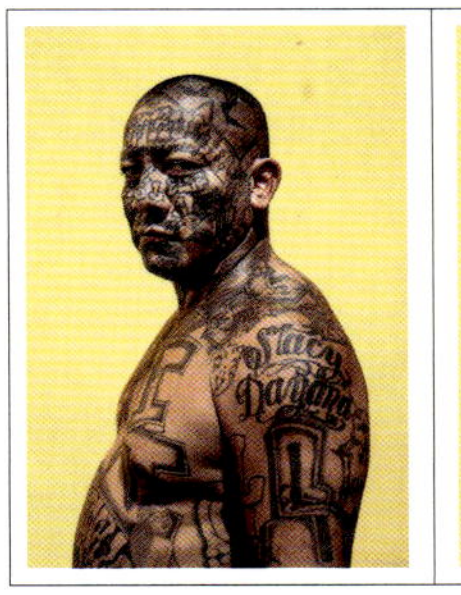

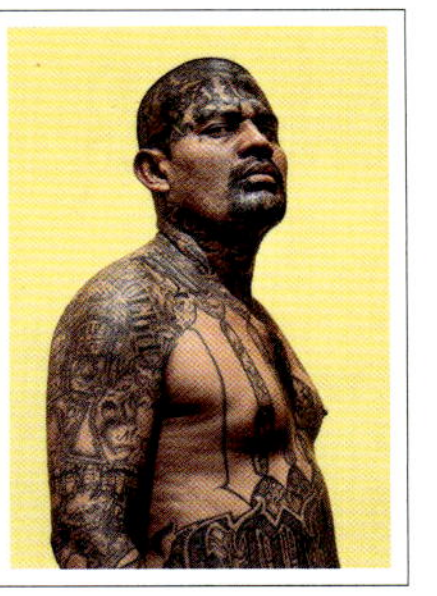

MS-13 gang member, aged 43, at the Chalatenango Penal Center.

MS-13 gang member, aged 37, at the Chalatenango Penal Center.

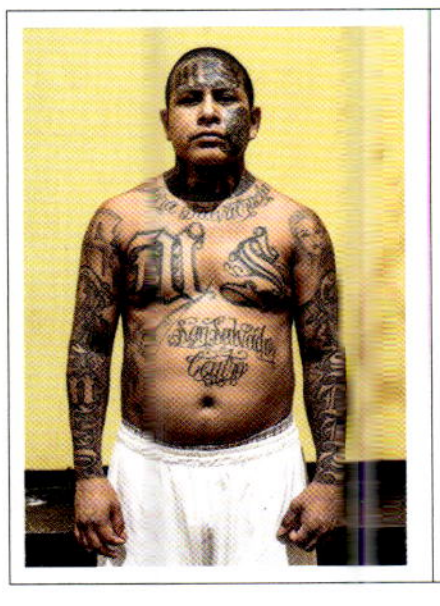

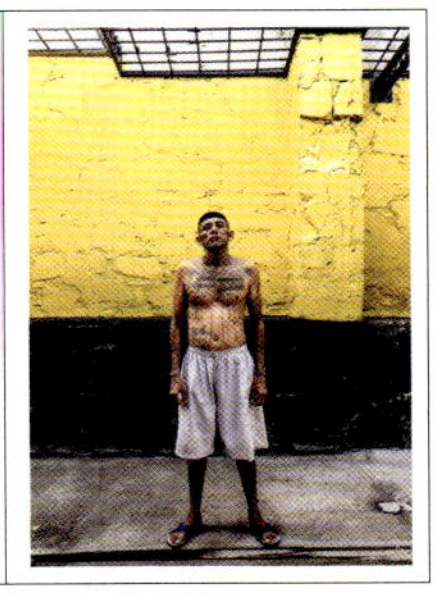

MS-13 gang member, aged 27, at the Chalatenango Penal Center.

Inmate, aged 35, at the Penal San Francisco Gótera.

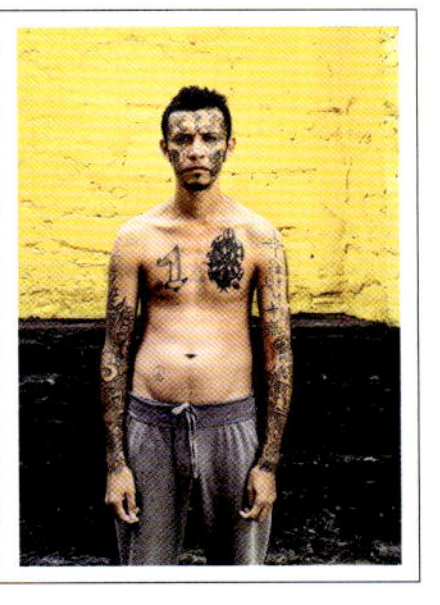

Inmate, aged 30, at the Penal San Francisco Gótera.

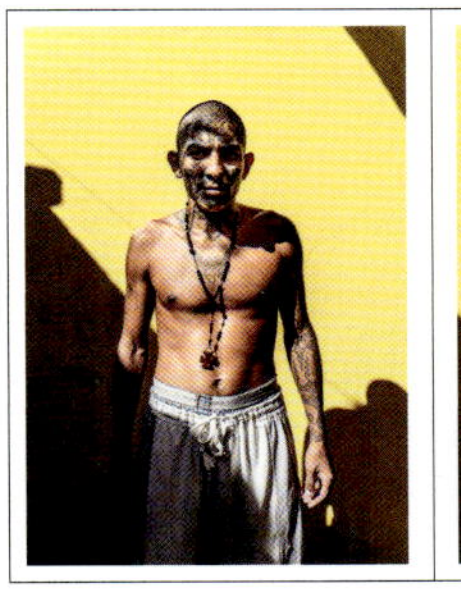

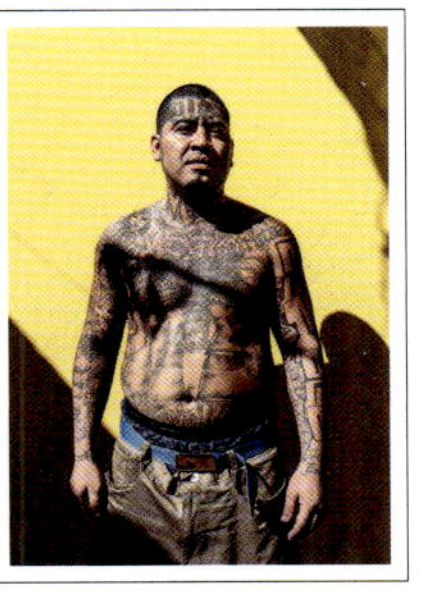

MS-13 gang member, aged 29, at the Chalatenango Penal Center.

MS-13 gang member, aged 28, at the Chalatenango Penal Center.

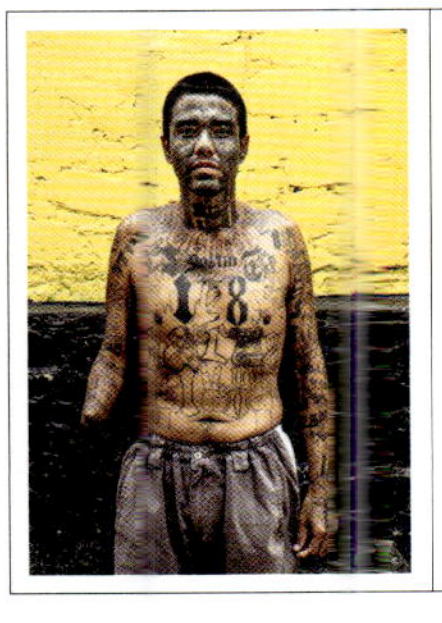

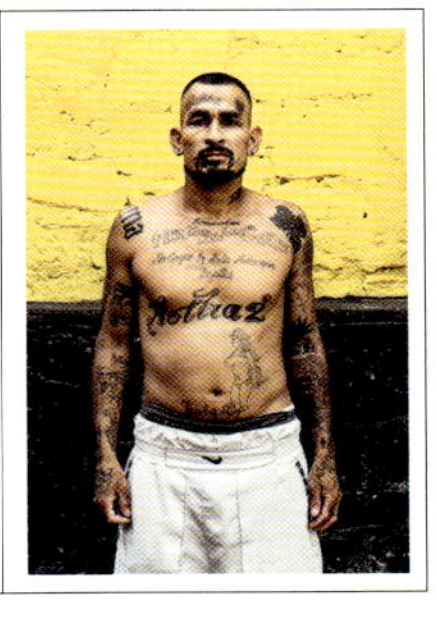

Inmate, aged 38, at the Penal San Francisco Gótera.

Inmate, aged 35, at the Penal San Francisco Gótera

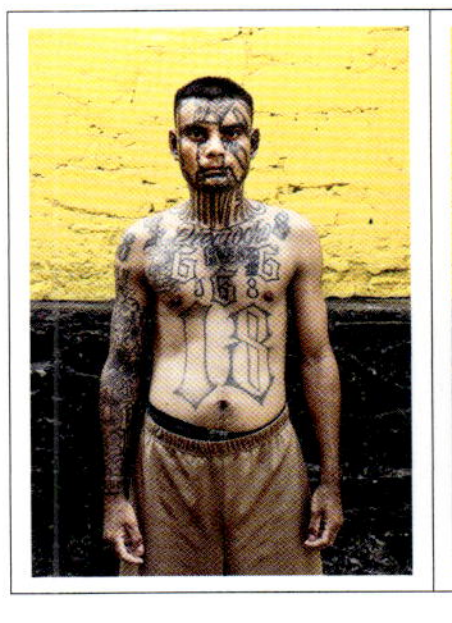

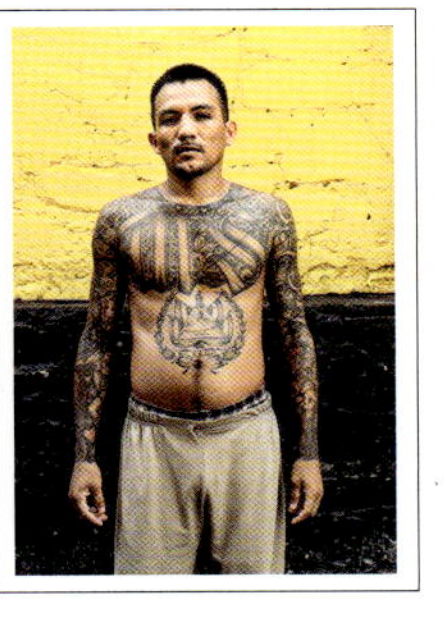

Inmate, aged 23, at the Penal San Francisco Gótera.

Inmate, aged 27, at the Penal San Francisco Gótera.

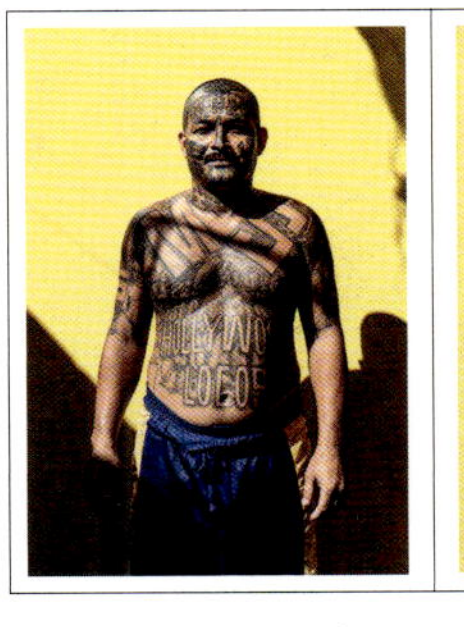

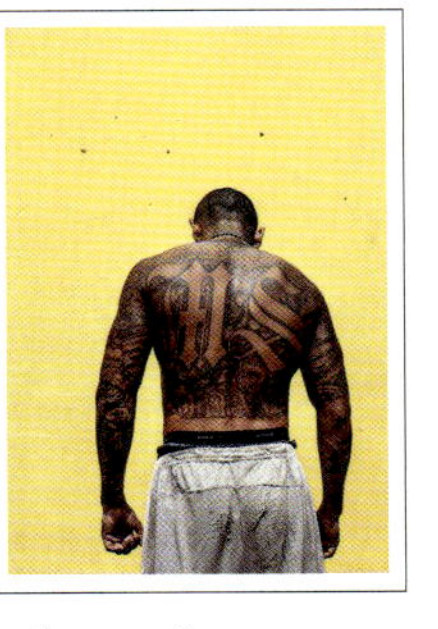

MS-13 gang member, aged 38, at the Chalatenango Penal Center.

MS-13 gang member and aspiring bodybuilder, aged 30, displays the 'MS' tattoo on his back at the Chalatenango Penal Center.

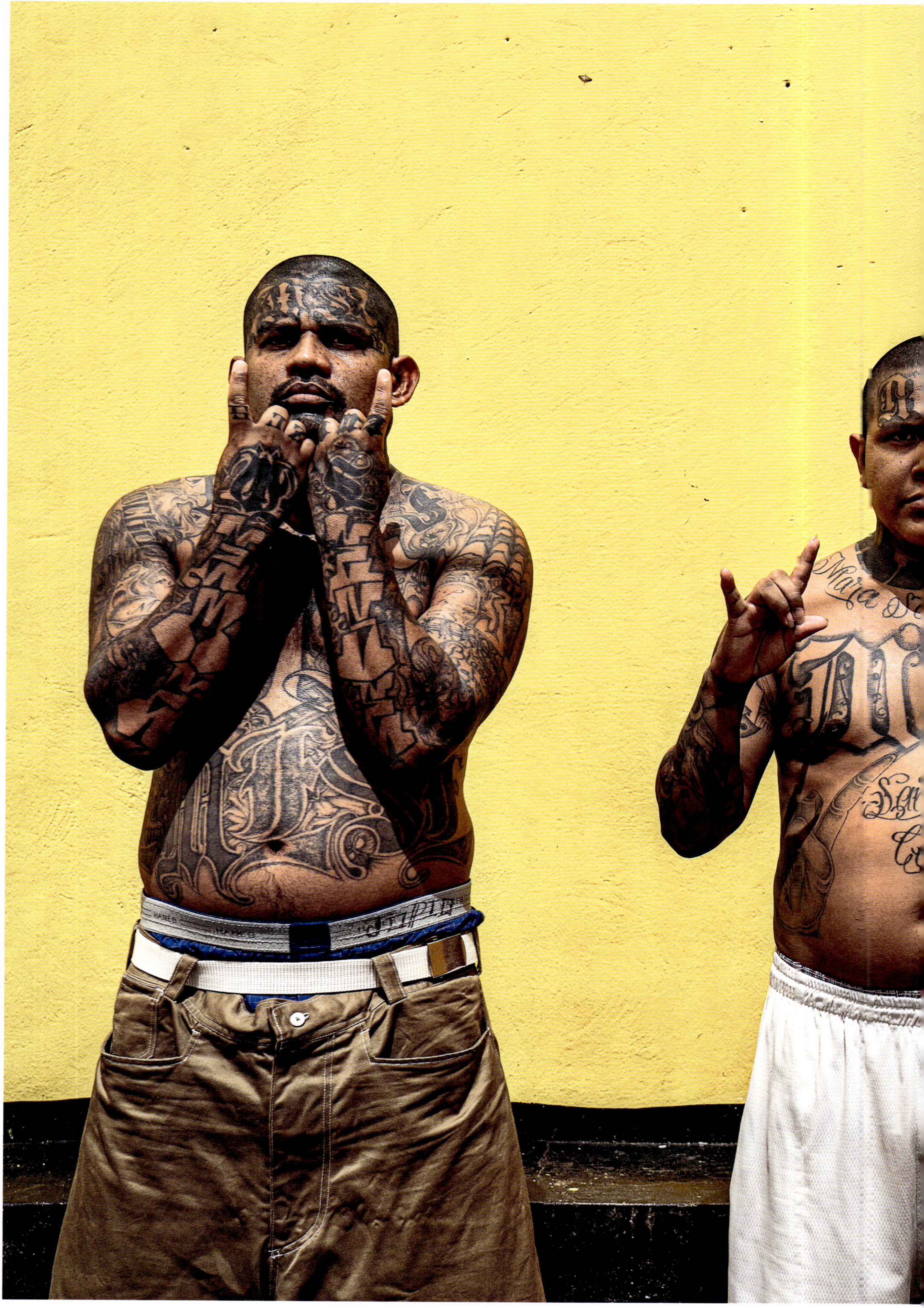

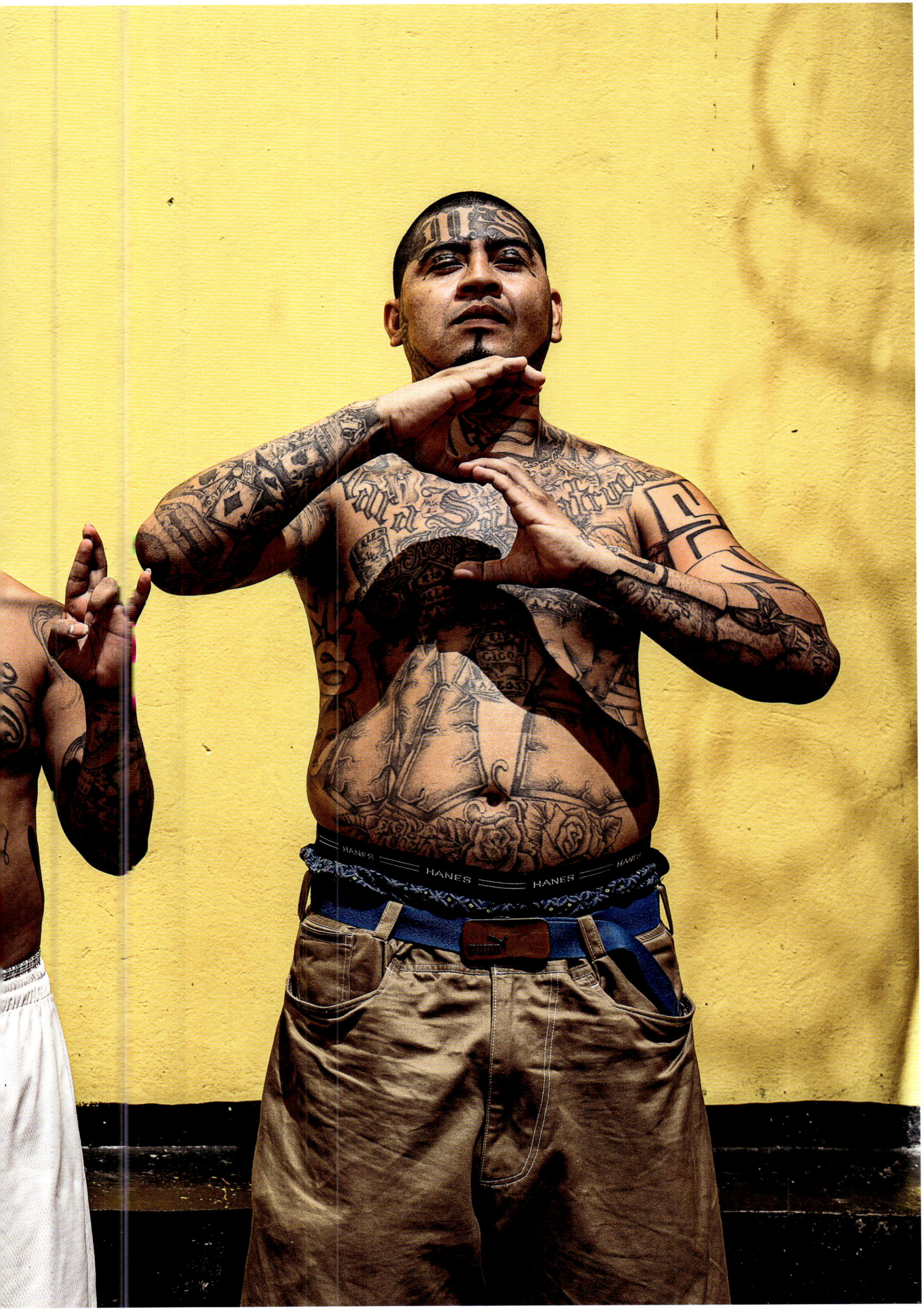
HANES

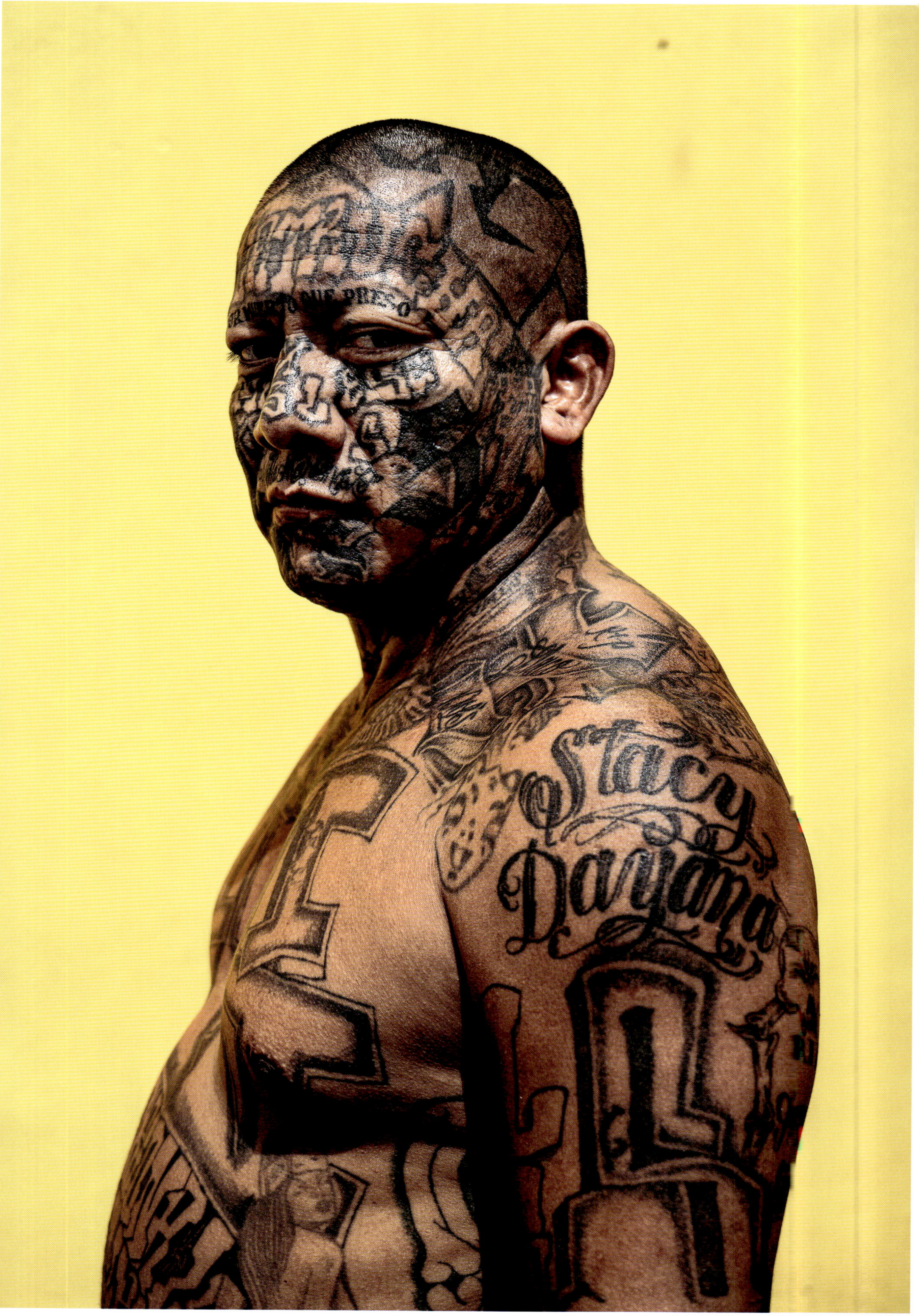
Stacy
Dayana

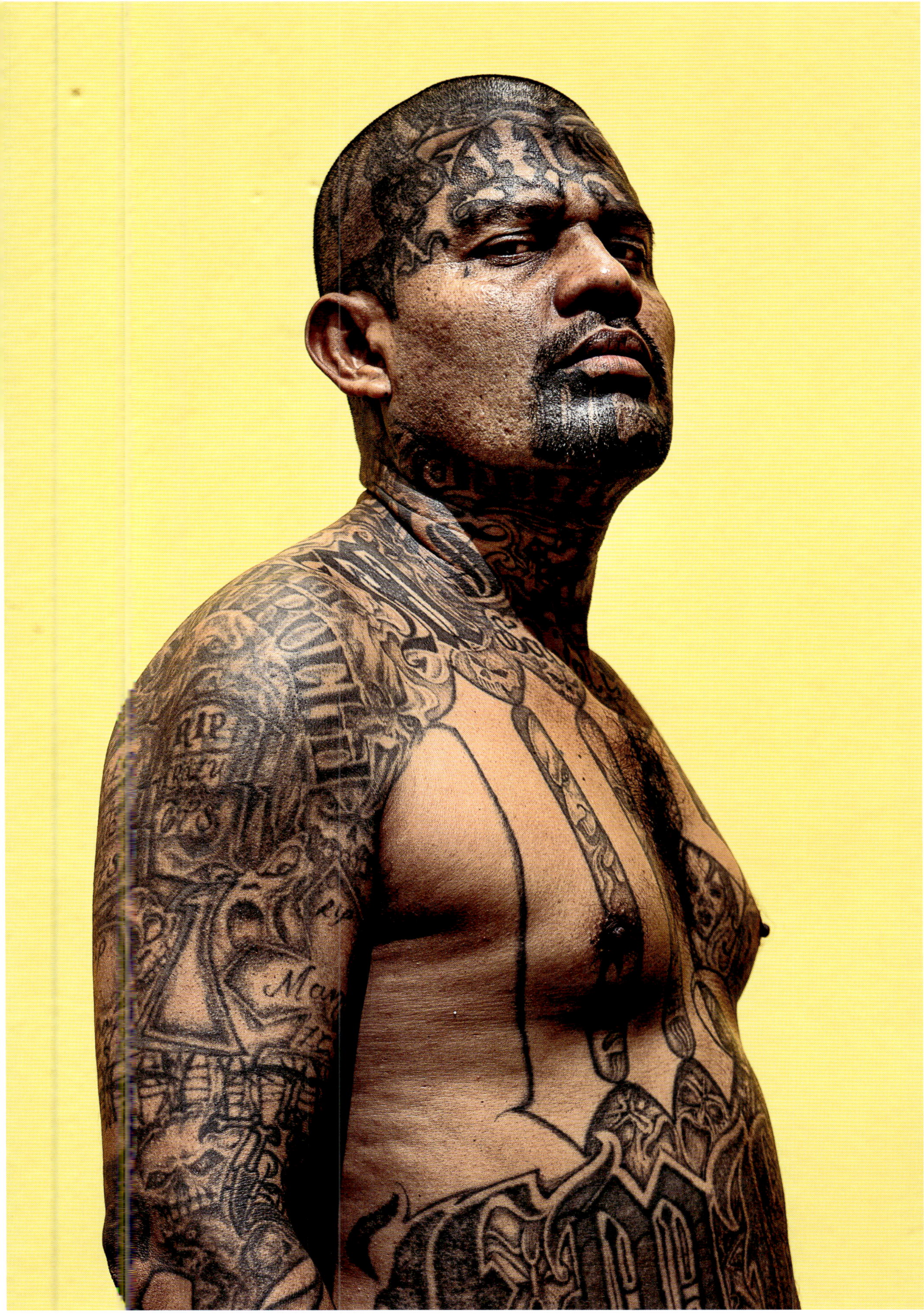

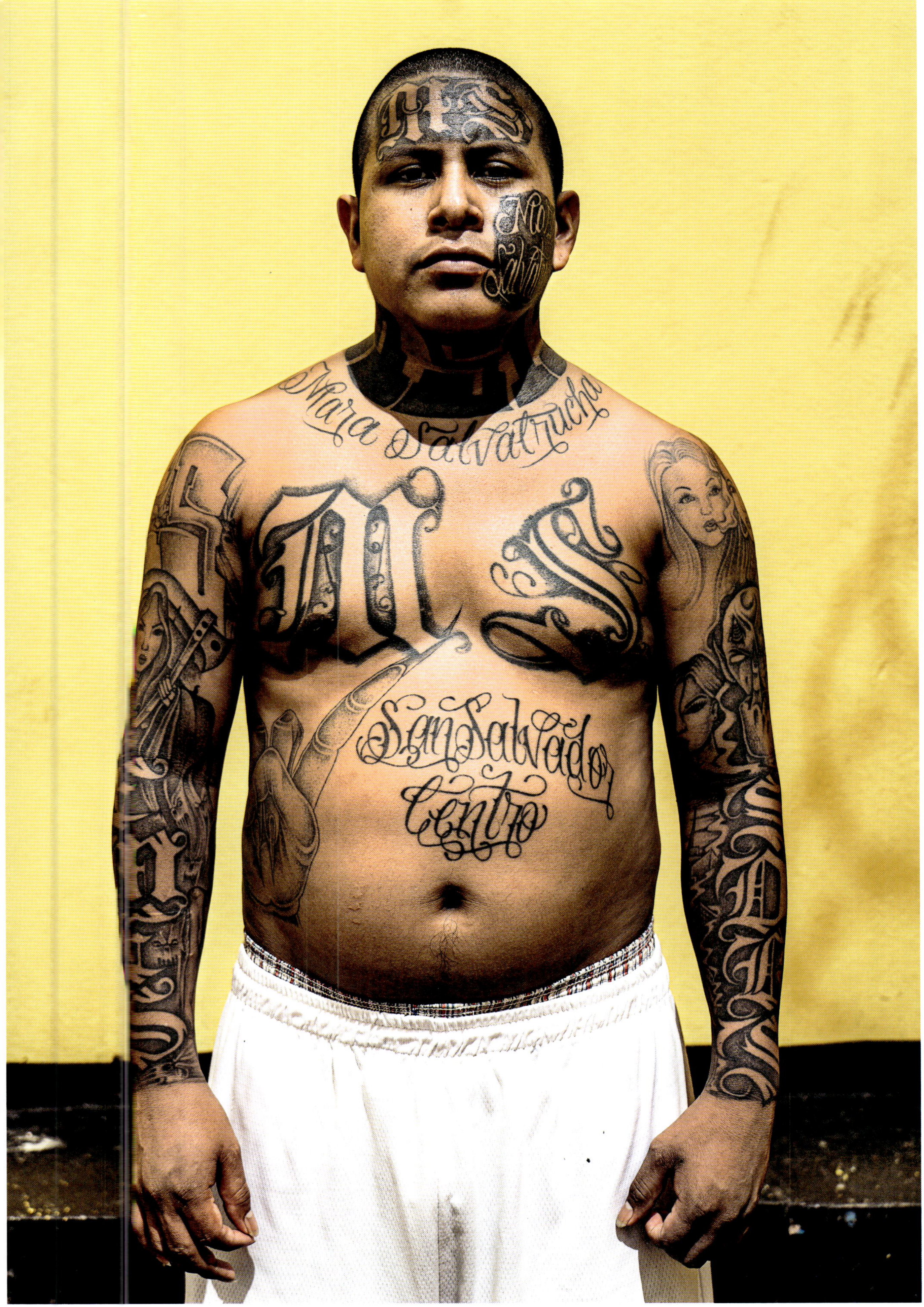
Mara Salvatrucha
MS
San Salvador
Centro

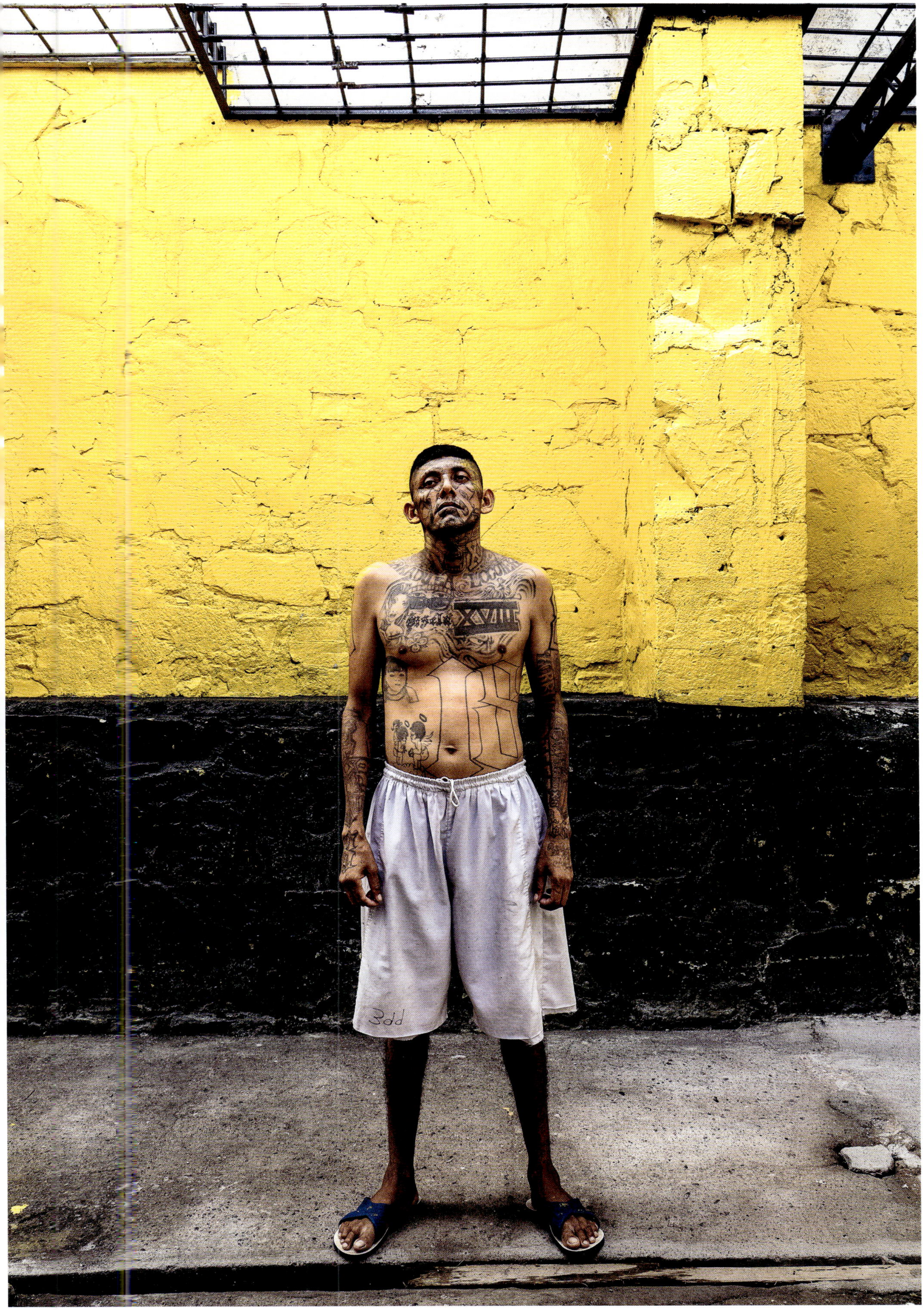

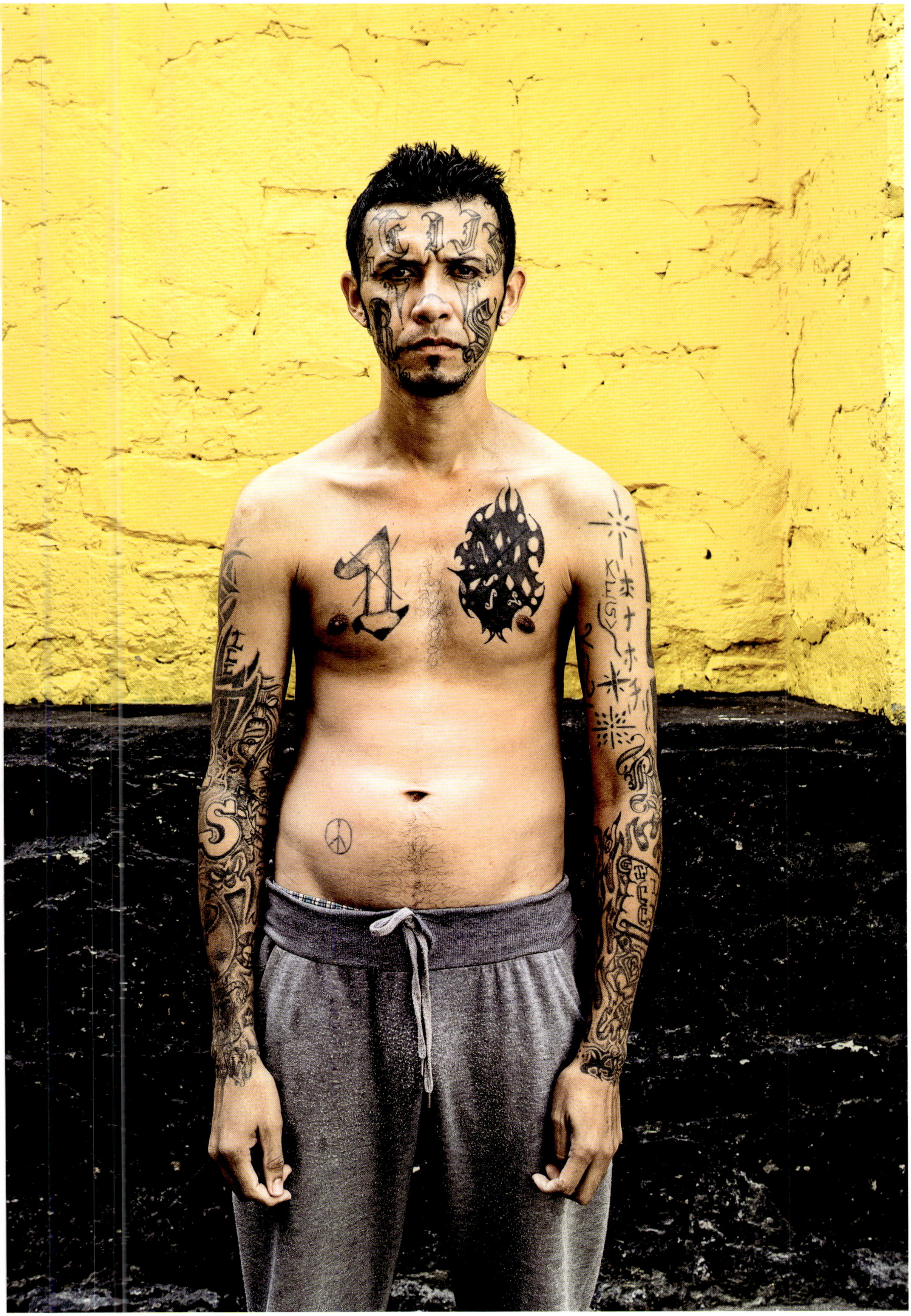

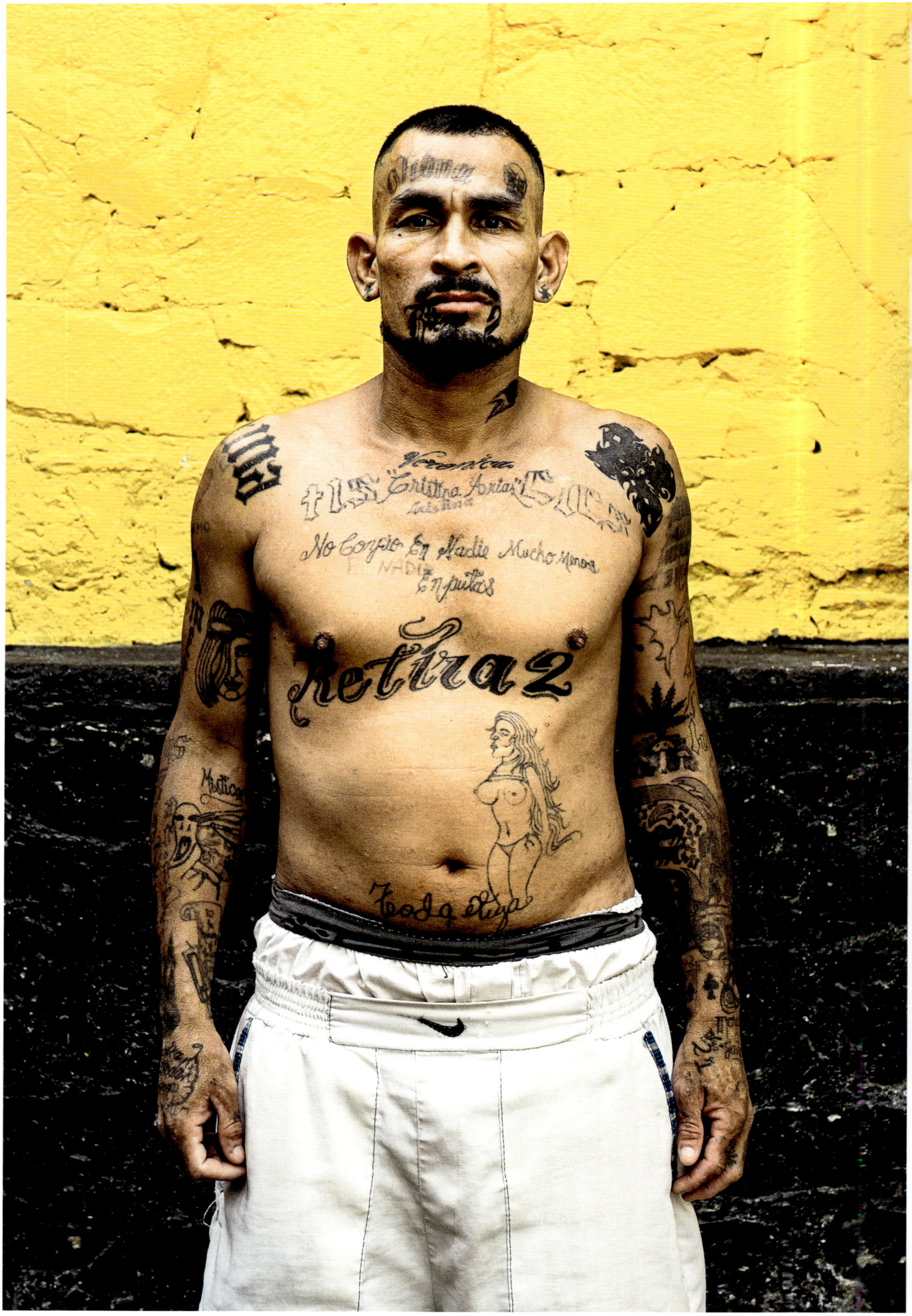
Retira2

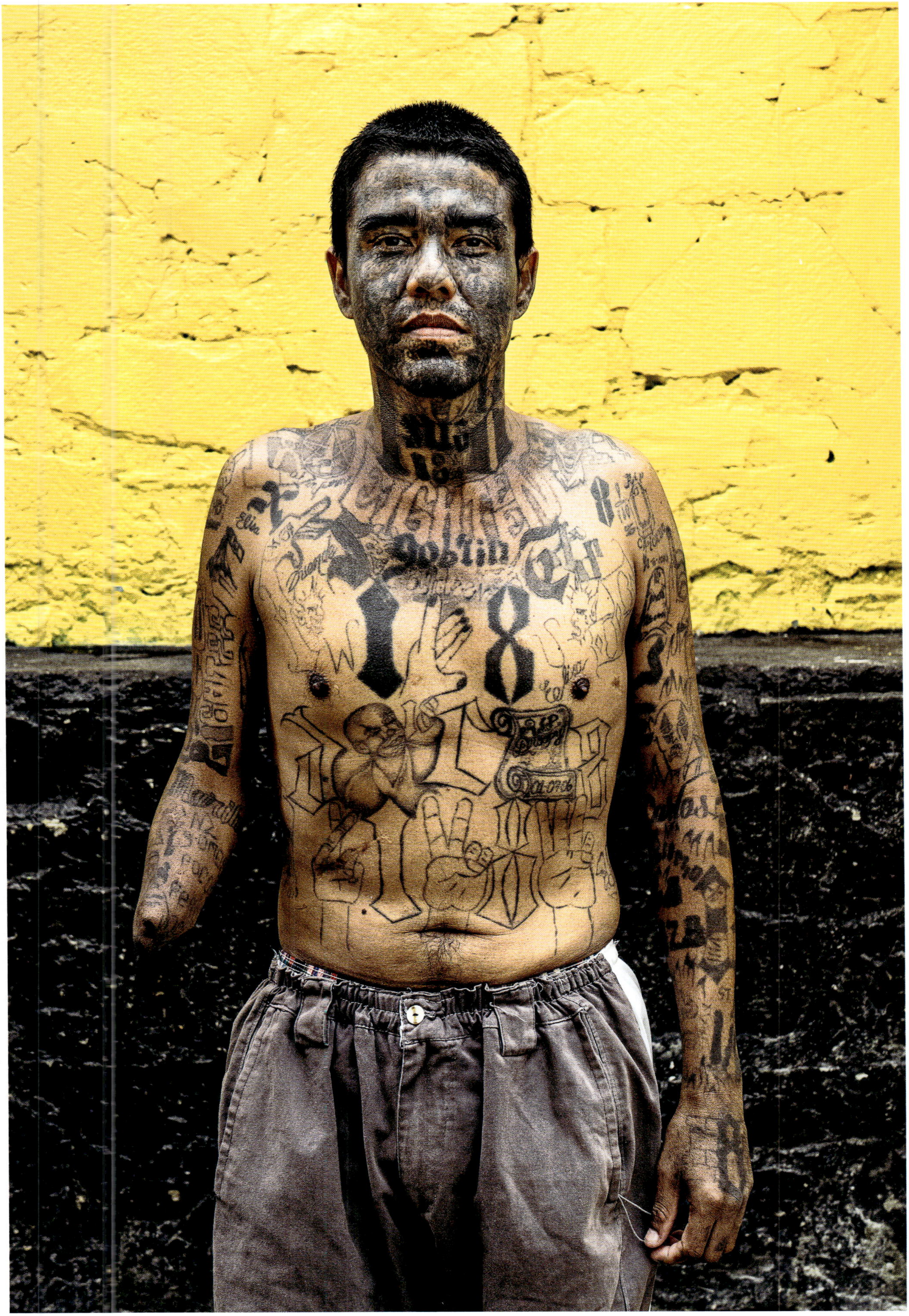
18

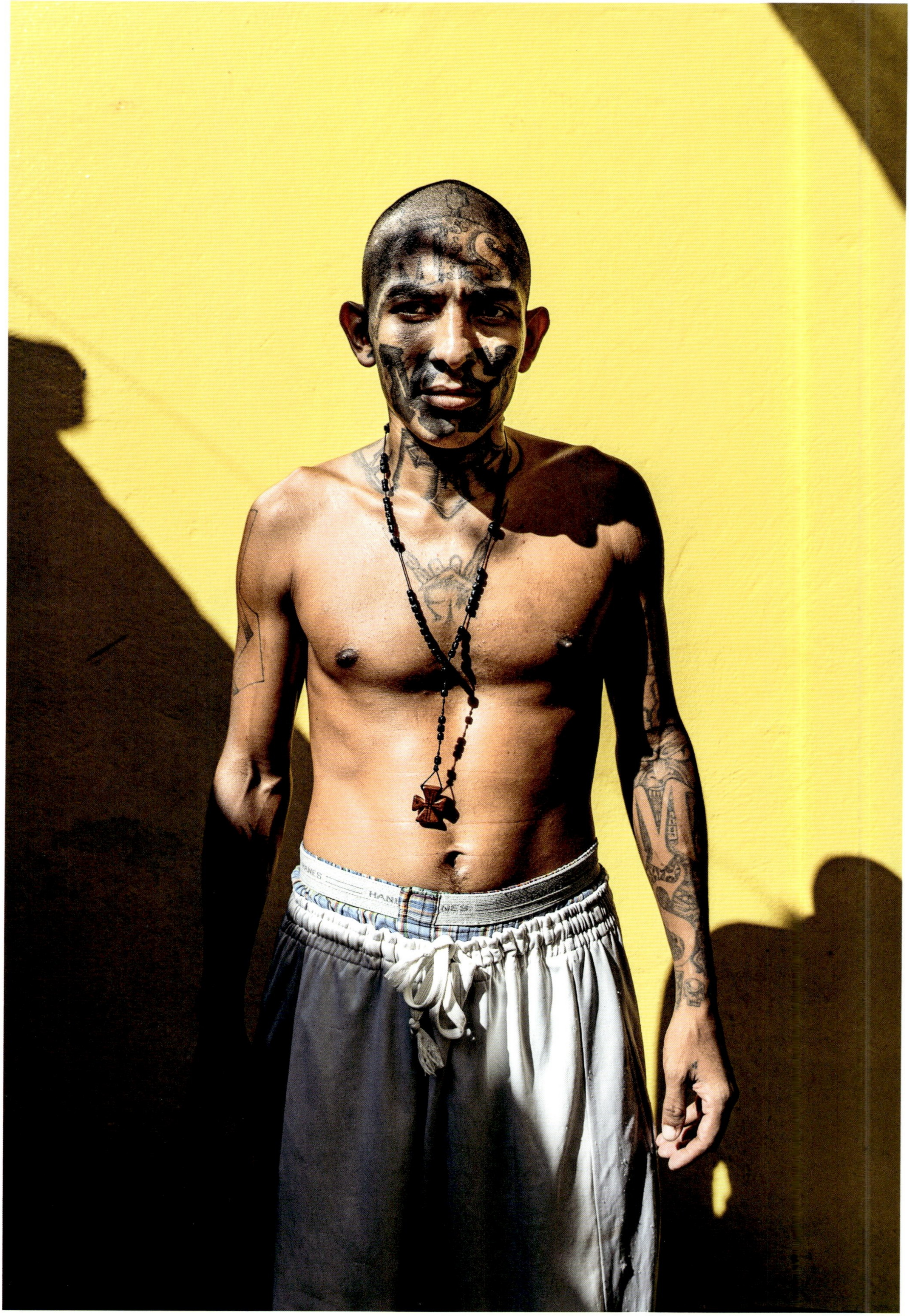

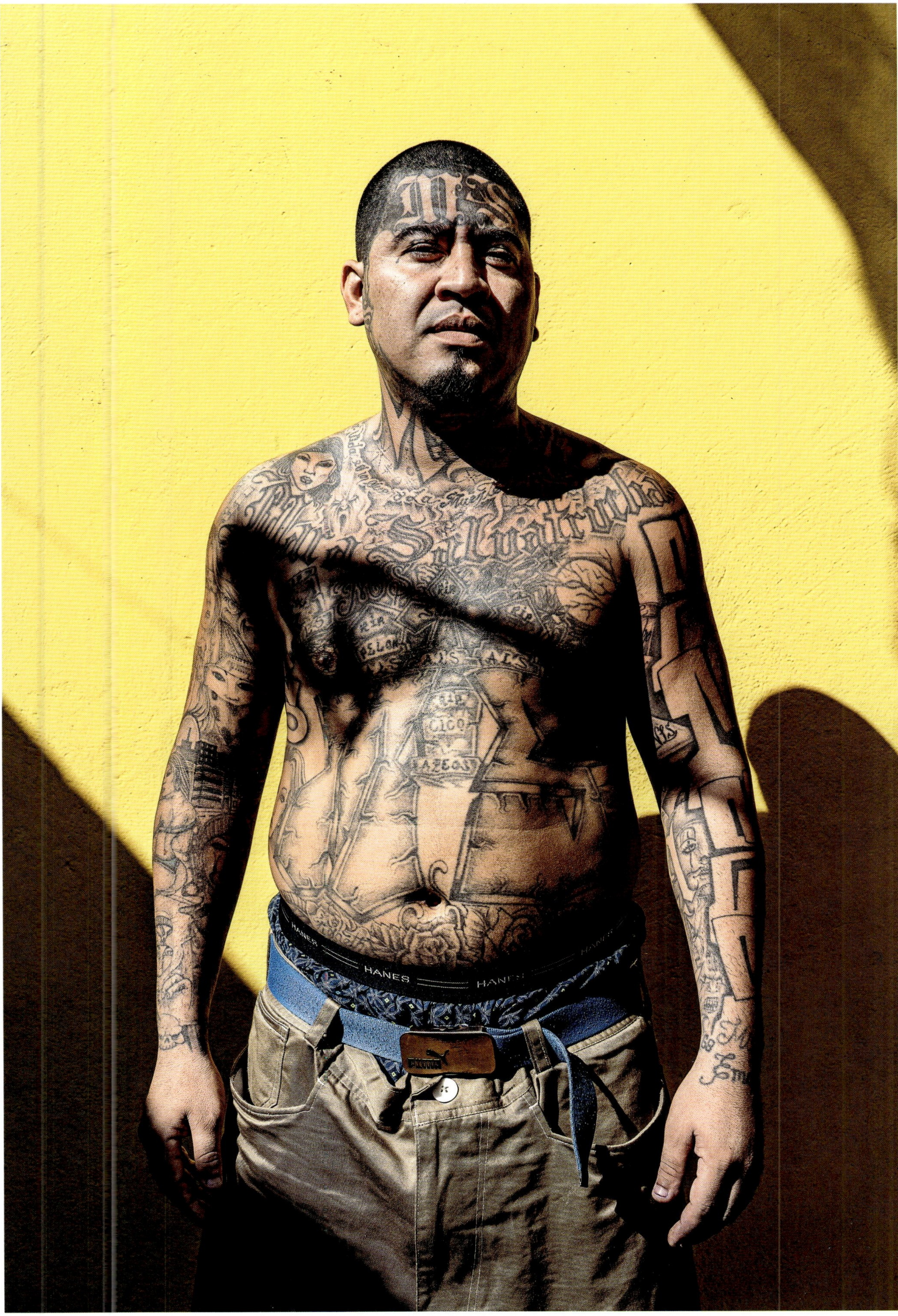
HANES
HANES
HANES
HANES

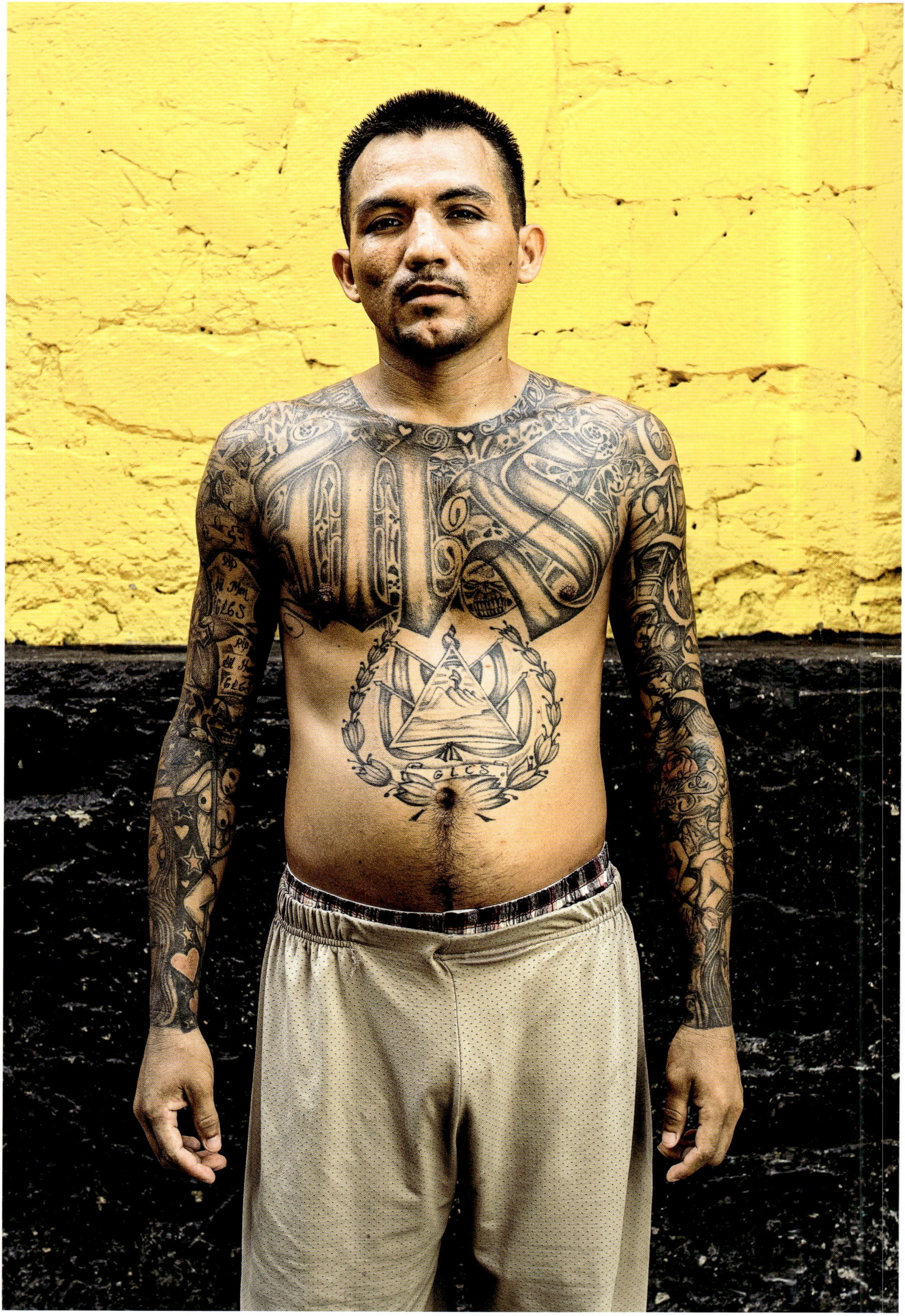
GLCS

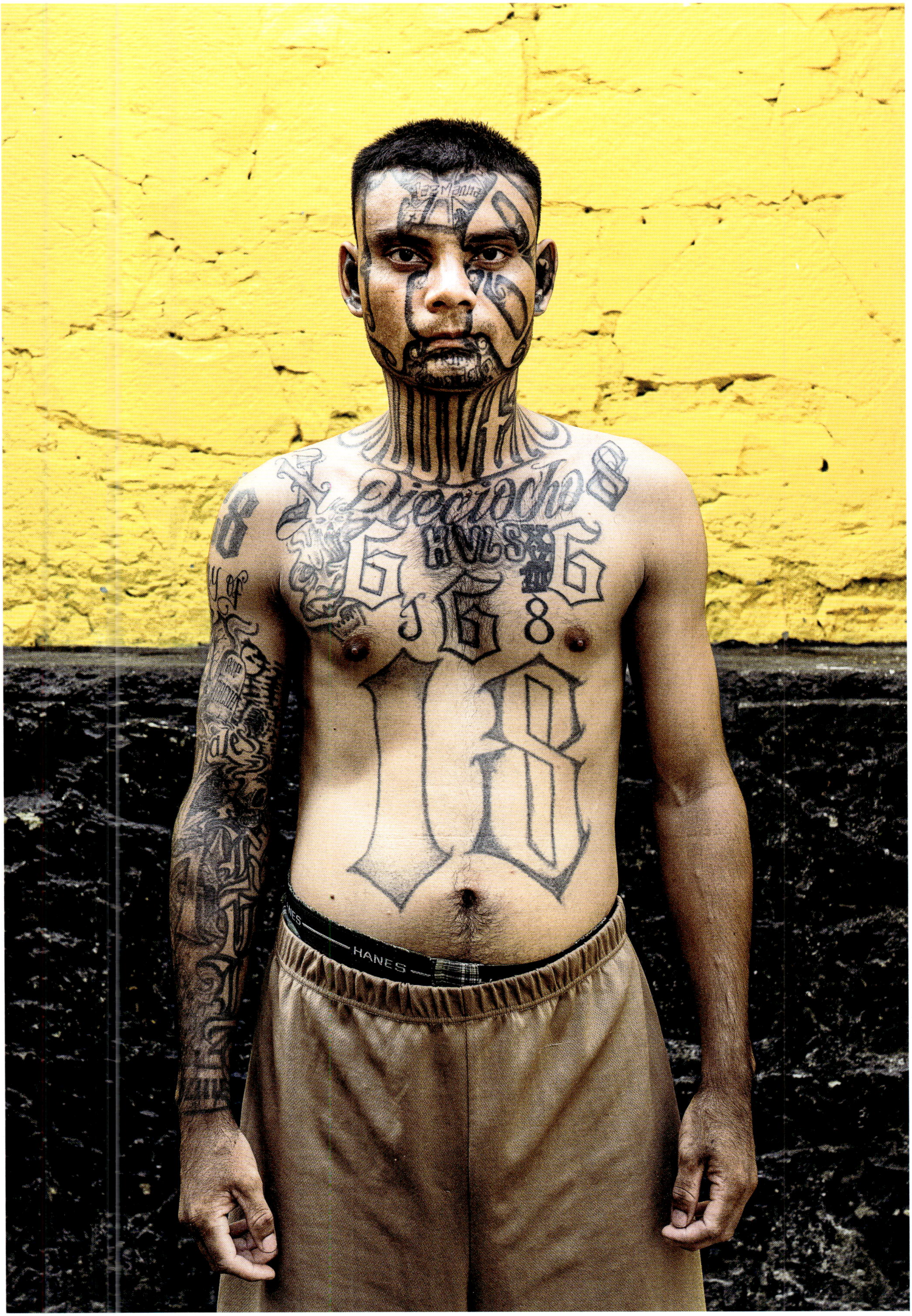
Dieciocho
18
HANES

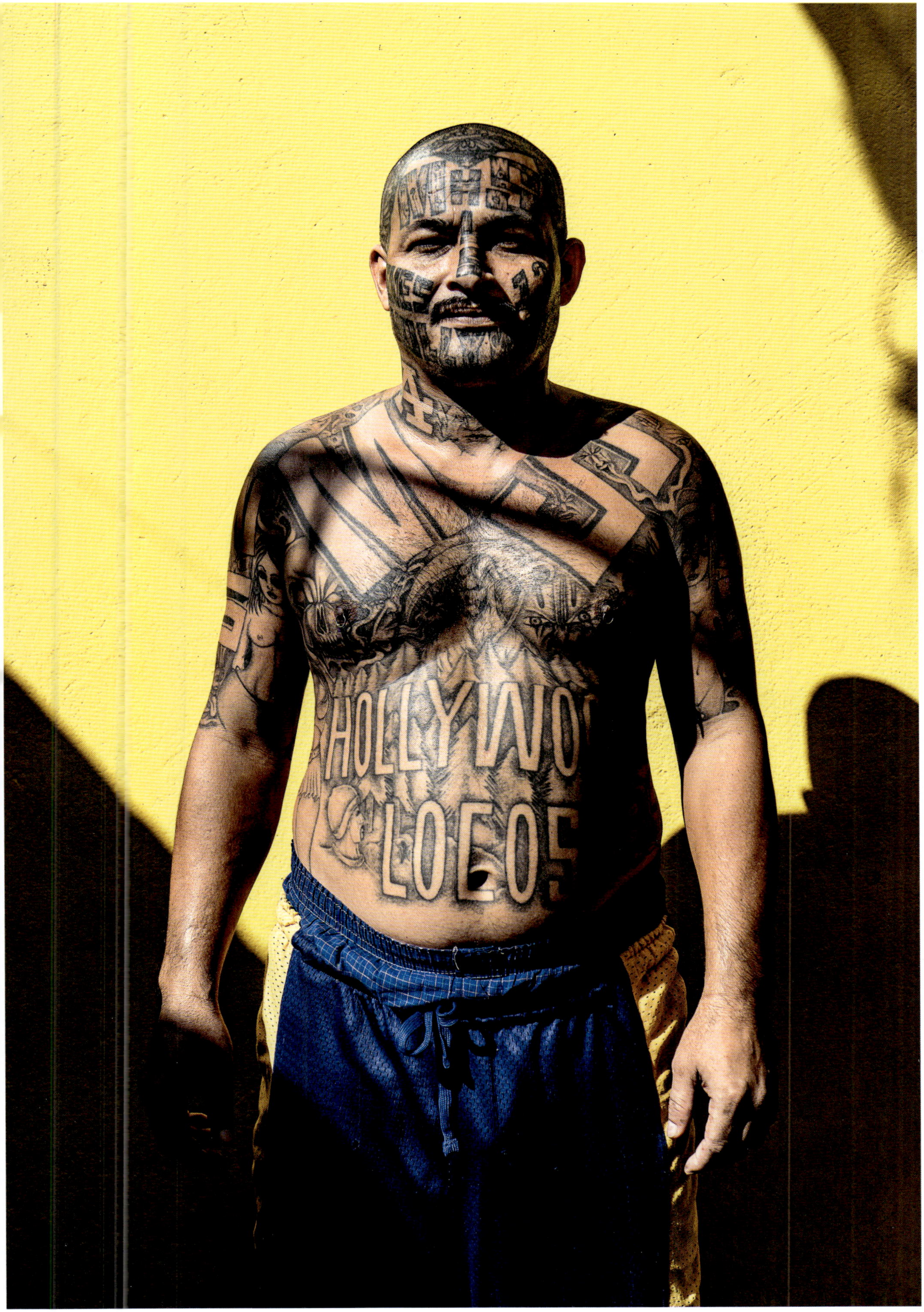
HOLLYWO
LOCOS

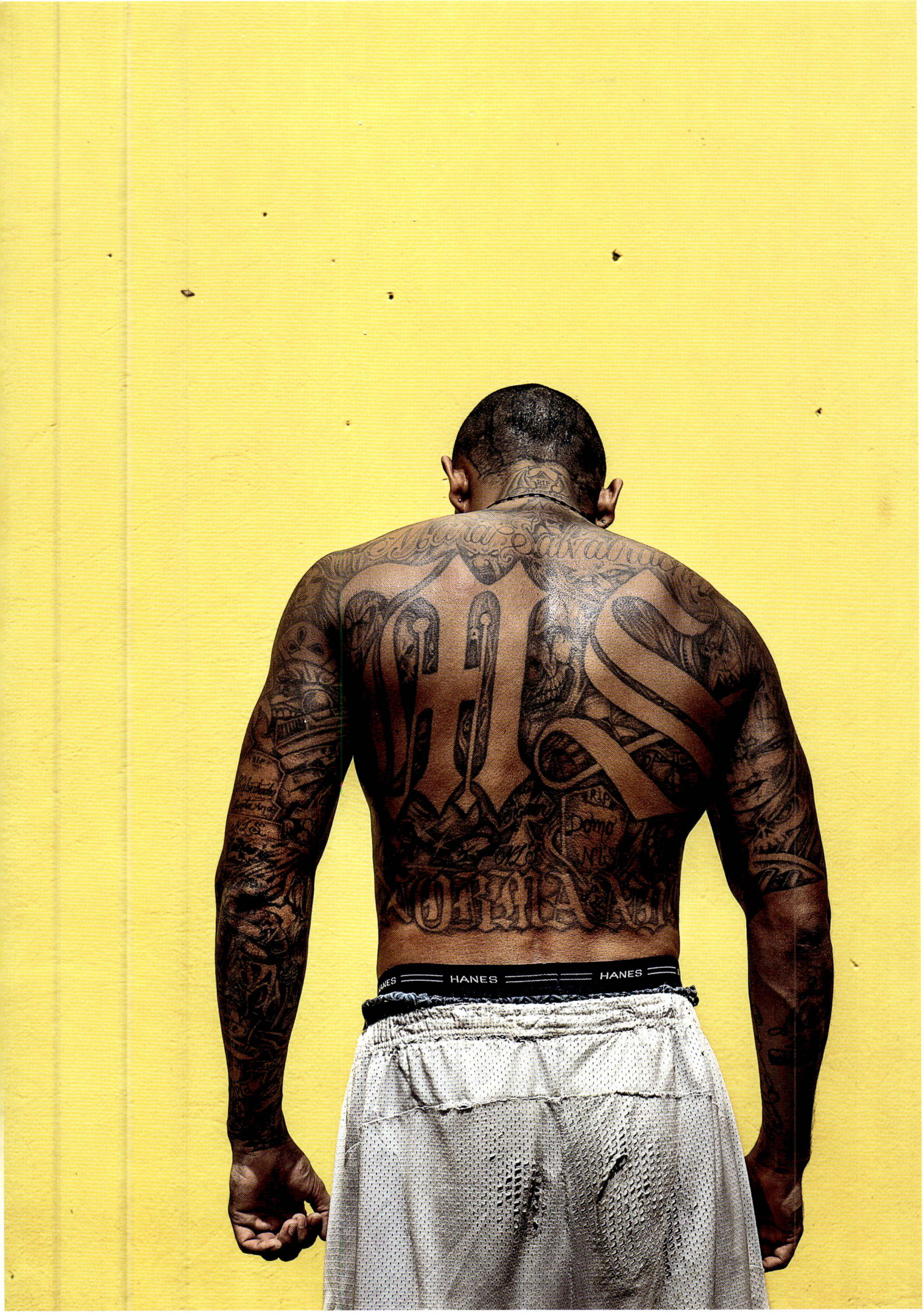
HANES
HANES

I would like to thank the following people—
all of whom helped make this book possible:

Mikael Eliasson
Salvador Sagastizado
Vanessa Buschschlüter

I would also like to thank all the Salvadoran people who welcomed me into their homes, families and communities to share their stories. I am truly grateful for their courage, help and support in this work.

Names of some individuals have been purposely omitted to protect the person and their families.

Sin Salida
First published in 2021 by
GOST Books, London

info@gostbooks.com
gostbooks.com

All images were made 2018–2020

Edited and designed by GOST:
Katie Clifford, Gemma Gerhard, Justine Hucker, Allon Kaye, Eleanor Macnair, Claudia Paladini, Ana Rocha

Works Sourced—InSight Crime and Center for Latin American & Latino Studies (CLALS) at American University. *MS13 in the Americas*

Printed in Italy by EBS

British Library cataloguing-in-publication data. A catalogue record of this book is available from the British Library.

ISBN: 978-1-910401-63-7